EXPERT WITNESSING

EXPLAINING AND UNDERSTANDING SCIENCE

EDITED BY

CARL MEYER

CRC Press

Boca Raton   London   New York   Washington, D.C.

Library of Congress Cataloging-in-Publication Data

Catalog record is available from the Library of Congress.

This book contains information obtained from authentic and highly regarded sources. Reprinted material is quoted with permission, and sources are indicated. A wide variety of references are listed. Reasonable efforts have been made to publish reliable data and information, but the author and the publisher cannot assume responsibility for the validity of all materials or for the consequences of their use.

PREFACE

The communication problems between science and the courts are notorious. They are widely deplored and sometimes exploited. The U.S. Supreme Court has twice tightened the law of evidence to control the flow of information, but, amazingly, little has been done to analyze the nature of the problem and reduce the barriers.

This volume results from the first-hand experience of the authors that the cultural and interdisciplinary communication barriers between science and law can be greatly reduced to everybody's advantage if the parties understand each other and respect each other's needs and positions.

Since this volume deals with an intercultural field, and the contributors belong to professions that are governed by different methodologies and conventions, the content of the volume, and the appearance of the individual chapters reflect some lack of cohesion and some interdisciplinary links. We hope that this, by itself, stimulates others to step forward to fill some of the gaps.

This book is for scientists, engineers physicians, judges. litigators and those who work in contact with the courts.

Chapter 1 provides an overview of the setting in which the interaction takes place, and the nature of the problem. Chapter 2 explains why litigators prefer jury trials to bench trials when scientific issues are involved. Chapter 3 explains fundamental difference between science and law. Chapter 4 explains the cultural barriers between scientists and physicians that can adversely affect their cooperation in the proof of causation in toxic injury cases. Chapter 5 explains the present transition in the law of evidence. Chapter 6 describes how the use of Experts in the civil law countries of Continental Europe contrasts with the U.S. common law system. Chapter 7 describes how scientists approach scientific problems and interdisciplinary communications, and explains the phenomenon of "junk science." Chapter 8 provides a description of the nuts and bolts that scientists need to put together to communicate effectively at trial. Chapter 9 describes how complex scientific information needs be presented to be useful to the trier of fact. Chapter 10 describes how a forensic expert analyzes and presents large toxic releases to jurors. Chapter 11 explains hidden traps in dealing with epidemiological data. Chapter 12 describes how logical errors in medical diagnosis can be exposed. Chapter 13 describes the translation of scientific issues into common sense language. Chapter 14 contains a description of the communication problems between scientists and lawyers that occur during patent litigation.

The text is preceded by short biographies of the book contributors, and is followed by an author and subject index.

The motivation for this book is derived from a symposium entitled Explaining Science to Judges and Jurors, that was held during the September 1997 annual meeting of the American Chemical Society in Las Vegas, Nevada. This book would not have been possible without the sponsorship of the Division of Chemistry and the Law of the American Chemical Society. The authors wish to thank this Division, and especially the then chair, Dr. Alice O. Robertson, Michael Kaminski, the Divisional Program Chair, and Shirley Radding, one of the founders of the Division, for their continued encouragement and help. Furthermore, the symposium and the present book would not have been possible without the many valuable suggestions and leadership provided by Patricia Ayd, who also served as chair for the panel discussion that stimulated personal contacts among the contributors and provided material for the book's contributors.

We are especially grateful for the stimulating contribution and boost which the Hon. David Hagen provided by his active participation in the panel discussion at the symposium in the midst of presiding over a difficult trial.

Finally, the editor wishes to thank each of the contributors for their encouragement and cooperation.

Carl Meyer

BIOGRAPHIES

PATRICIA M. AYD is an attorney practicing in Denver, Colorado. She has twenty years of experience in all phases of litigation practice. This includes insurance defense, products liability, personal injury, workman's compensation, employment discrimination claims and commercial litigation matters. As a result of her representation of numerous insureds, insurance companies and adjusting companies, Ms. Ayd has substantial litigation experience in the defense of third party liability cases, premises liability cases and cases relating to payment of first party insurance benefits. Ms. Ayd's practice presently emphasizes defense of insurance carriers in first party benefits and bad faith and third party bad faith matters. In her auto related practice, Ms. Ayd has continually dealt with issues of interpretation of the Colorado No-Fault statute, negligent entrustment and negligent supervision and hiring. She provides coverage opinions and has been retained as expert witness in these matters. Ms. Ayd has extensive appellate practice experience with emphasis on a variety of insurance matters. Ms. Ayd's commercial litigation has included defense of business entities against claims of discrimination, wrongful discharge, EEO claims, including Title VII claims and civil rights violations, as well as litigation of contract and wage disputes for a variety of business clients. She has become increasingly involved in activities dealing with alternative dispute resolution, serving as an arbitrator in numerous cases. She has received extensive mediation training and has become increasingly involved in mediation as an alternative to litigation. Address: Patricia Ayd, P.C., Denver, CO 80205.

RICHARD A. BJUR, J.D., Ph.D., is a Professor of Pharmacology at the University of Nevada School of Medicine, Director of the Office of Technology Liaison at the University of Nevada, Reno, Assistant General Counsel for the University and Community College System of Nevada, and is a member of the teaching faculty at the National Judicial College. Dr. Bjur earned his B.A. degree in chemistry at Lewis and Clark College in Portland, Oregon, and his Ph.D. degree in pharmacology at the University of Colorado. He completed postgraduate training in pharmacology at the National Institute for Medical Research in London and at New York University Medical Center. After joining the faculty at the University of Nevada School of Medicine, Dr. Bjur received his J.D. degree from the Nevada School of Law. He is a member of the State Bar of Nevada and is a registered patent attorney. In addition to teaching at the medical school, Dr. Bjur teaches medical/legal issues, intellectual property and scientific evidence at both the University of Nevada, Reno and The National Judicial College. Address: Mail Stop 318, University of Nevada School of Medicine, Reno, NV 89557, Telephone: 702-784-4116, Email: bjur@med.unr.edu

ROBERT A. BOHRER is a Professor of Law at the California Western School of Law in San Diego, CA. He practiced with the Chicago law firm of Bell, Boyd & Lloyd before deciding to return to academia. Taking a leave of absence from his firm to enter the Harvard Law School LL.M. program, his focus quickly shifted from commercial real estate transactions to medieval English legal history and the comparative law of Japan. The change from law practice to law school was an exciting one and Professor Bohrer soon decided to make it permanent. He has written about such varied topics as the constitutionality of I.Q. testing in the public schools, Congressional control of affirmative action, the risks of toxic substances, and, most recently, biotechnology law. Professor Bohrer is Director of the Biotechnology InCyte program at the University of California, San Diego's Center for Molecular Genetics. Professor Bohrer is the only law professor appointed to the Board of the United States Patent and Trademark Office. He teaches Biotechnology Law, Environmental Health and Safety Regulation, Administrative Law, and Torts. A native of Chicago, Professor Bohrer received his B.A. from Haverford College and his J.D. from the University of Illinois, where he was on the Law Review and served as an Instructor of Business Law in the College of Commerce. Address: California Western School of Law, 225 Cedar St., San Diego, CA 92101-3090

LINDA S. ERDREICH, Ph.D., is a Principal Scientist at Bailey Research Associates in New York, where she works in research and consulting in the health sciences. She is an adjunct associate professor in the Department of Environmental and Community Medicine, Robert Wood Johnson Medical School, University of Medicine and Dentistry of New Jersey. Dr. Erdreich received an M.S. in Biostatistics and Epidemiology and a Ph.D. in Epidemiology from the University of Oklahoma. Dr. Erdreich has worked in chronic disease research for 20 years, and has extensive experience in health risk assessment, beginning at the U.S. Environmental Protection Agency (EPA); this experience included developing exposure limits for specific chemicals in support of regulations, site specific assessments, and development of risk assessment methods for non-carcinogens that are used as a basis for Federal standards under the Clean Air Act and the Safe Drinking Water Act. Dr. Erdreich worked on several of the agency's Risk Assessment Guidelines, and served on the agency's Risk Assessment Forum. Dr. Erdreich is active in the standard-setting process for radio frequency fields, as a member of the Standards Committee of the Institute for Electric and Electronic Engineers (IEEE). She is an elected member of the American College of Epidemiology, and Committee on Man and Radiation (COMAR) of the IEEE's *Engineering in Medicine and Biology Society,*. Address: Bailey Research Associates, Inc., 292 Madison Ave., Suite 200, New York, NY 10017. Email: l.erdreich@att.net

ANN LENNARSON GREER, is a professor of sociology at the University of Wisconsin, Milwaukee. Professor Greer has conducted extensive theoretical and field research on the diffusion of new medical knowledge and technology from its source to the clinical community, and how clinicians reach consensus. She has been able to show why medical practitioners tend to distrust academic and federally sponsored medical research, why they continue to rely on local experience and local opinion leaders, and why it is unpredictable whether, and in what form, the local medical communities will adopt new medical methodology and technology. One of her discoveries has been that, contrary to traditional view, the opinion leaders in the local clinical community are not the same people as the innovation promoters, and that the local status of the innovation promoters may initially be low. Her findings are important for anyone dealing with any type of interdisciplinary or inter-cultural information transfer. Address: Department of Sociology, University of Wisconsin-Milwaukee P.O. Box 413, Milwaukee, WI 53201, (414) 229-6944; fax: (414) 229-5332, e-mail: agreer@csd.uwm.edu

MICHAEL D. KAMINSKI is a partner in the patent law firm of Foley & Lardner. University of Michigan (B.S.Ch.E., magna cum laude, 1982; B.S., Chemistry; A.B., Communications, with high honors, 1982); University of Michigan Law School (J.D., cum laude, 1986). Admitted to bar, 1987, Illinois; 1988, District of Columbia; Kappa Tau Alpha; Alpha Chi Sigma. Member, 1985-1986 and Executive Editor, 1986-1987, Michigan Yearbook of International Legal Studies. Co-Author: "Intellectual Property Law in Illinois," Cambridge Institute, 1988; "Federal Circuit Practice, 1989-1990: A Look at Significant Decisions Affecting Patent Practices," Selected Legal Papers, Vol. VIII, Nos. 1 and 2 (1990); "Federal Circuit Practice, 1990-1991: A Look at Significant Decisions Affecting Patent Practice," Selected Legal Papers, Vol. IX, No. 1 (1991); "Necessarily Non-Obvious? – Dillon and Pleuddemann," Selected Legal Papers, Vol. IX, No. 1 (1991); "Double Patenting: One Way, Two Way, Whose Delay," Patent Prosecution and Litigation, National Invention Center (1992); "Section 112, Paragraph Six: What Ends Are Justified by the Means?" Intellectual Property Law, 1992, State Bar of Texas Professional Development Program; " The Significant Federal Circuit Cases Interpreting Section 112," 41 Am. U. Law Rev. 621 (1992); "Extending Patent Term Under General Foods," National Invention Center, 1993; "Double Patenting: One Way, Two Way; Whose Delay, " 1 U. Balt. Int. Prop. L.J. 180 (1993); "The Legal Significance of Trade Show Activity Under United States Patent Law," 76 J.P.T.O.S. 445 (1994); "A Year in Review; The Federal Circuit's Patent Decisions in 1993," 43 Am. U. Law Rev. 1450 (1994); "Conducting U.S. Patent Prosecution With a View Toward Potential Litigation," 74 Patent World 36 (1995); "Being Prepared for U.S. Litigation Can Make All the Difference," 75 Patent World 32 (1995); "New Boundaries and Burdens for a Patentee Attempting to Claim Certain Lost Profits Infringement Damages," 76 Patent World 17 (1995). Editorial Boards: IP World, 1997- present, Patent World, 1995; AIPLA Quarterly Journal, 1994 - present, Michigan Law School, 1986. Adjunct Instructor, John Marshall Law School, 1988. Legal Writing Instructor, Illinois Institute of

Continuing Legal Education, 1989. Adjunct Professor of Patent Law, Washington College of Law, American University, 1991. Adjunct professor of patent law, George Mason University, 1997-present. Member: Federal Circuit and American Bar Associations; The District of Columbia Bar; Bar Association of the District of Columbia; American Chemical Society; American Intellectual Property Law Association. Practice Areas: Patent Law; Patent Litigation. Address: Foley & Lardner, 3000 K Street, N.W., Washington, DC 20007

CLAUS-PETER MARTENS studied law at the University of Bochum, where he was a research assistant and junior lecturer at the Chair of Public Law and European Law. Following an LL.M. Degree in International and European Community Law at the University of Cambridge, where he was a Hanns Seidel Foundation Scholar, he was awarded a doctorate in jurisprudence by the University of Bochum for his thesis entitled "Die wesentliche Änderung im Sinne des § 15 BImSchG" ("Fundamental Alterations As Defined by Air Pollution Control Act"), published in 1993. Dr. Martens was admitted to the Frankfurt Bar in 1991 and subsequently joined the Frankfurt office of the law firm Pünder, Volhard, Weber & Axster. In 1995 he moved to the firm's Berlin office and became a partner in 1996. From the outset, he has been involved in environmental law, public planning and construction law. In particular, his chief area of practice encompasses anti-pollution law, waste law, public utilities and urban development law, along with environmental liability and eco-auditing. He specializes in negotiations with public authorities, applications for permits for industrial plants, planning procedures, and the management and supervision of installations. He also litigates in these areas. Dr. Martens is co-author of "Environmental Liabilities and Regulation in Europe" (1993), "European Environmental Markets" (1995), a commentary on the new "Federal Waste Management Act" and co-editor of "German Environmental Law for Practitioners" (1996), which appears in both German and English. He has also published several articles in legal journals. Recent papers have concentrated on the environmental impact of electromagnetic fields and of major telecommunications network installations, environmental liability, eco-auditing, water and waste law and building law. Address: Pünder, Vollhard, Weber & Axter, 19787 Berlin, Germany. His firm also maintains offices in Moscow, Tokyo, and China.

CARL B. MEYER, Ph.D. in Chemistry at the University of Zürich, J.D., California Western School of Law, is a partner in the law firm of Kapsa & Meyer in San Diego, California and Las Vegas, Nevada, concentrating on civil and administrative litigation, arbitration and mediation. Prior to 1986 he was a professor of chemistry at the University of Washington and a principal investigator at the Lawrence Berkeley National Lab at UC Berkeley. He acted as a consultant to the chemical and the forest products industry, and served as director of industrial research for an international trade association. He has authored or co-authored more than 100 peer-reviewed technical research articles, four technical books and four law review articles; has taught high school, undergraduates and chemistry graduate students and has supervised Ph.D. candidates and postdoctoral fellows. He is a fellow of the American Institute of Chemists and has served the U.S. EPA as an IPA, the U.S. Consumer Product Safety Commission as a part time employee, and has served as vice-chair of a ASTM standardization subcommittee. He has served as an expert witness for industry, consumers and governmental agencies in North America and Europe in litigations in federal, state and international courts. Address: Kapsa and Meyer, 2701 Second Avenue, San Diego, CA 92103, and 325 So Third Street, #3, Las Vegas, Nevada 89101, e-mail cbmeyer@msn.com

ROBERT D. MORRISON, Ph.D., received his B.S. in Geology from the University of Redlands, a M.S. in Environmental Studies from Cal State Fullerton, and a M.S. from the University of Southern California in Environmental Engineering. He received his Ph.D. in Soil Physics from the University of Wisconsin at Madison. Dr. Morrison has over 25 years of working experience as an environmental consultant. Dr. Morrison specializes in the forensic review and interpretation of scientific data used in support of litigation involving soil and groundwater contamination. Dr. Morrison has published extensively and has lectured throughout the world on issues related to soil and groundwater contamination. Dr. Morrison has provided confidential and expert witness testimony in cases concerning allegations in the billions of dollars. Dr. Morrison has served on numerous ASTM committees and on the U.S. EPA Advisory Board. Address: R. Morrison and Associates, Inc., 201 East Grand Avenue, Suite 2B, Escondido, California 92025, (619) 480-1 178, e-mail :Rmand@aol.com.

SUSAN R. POULTER, Ph.D., J.D., is a Professor of Law at the University of Utah College of Law, and has a B.S. in chemistry and a Ph.D. in organic chemistry, both from the University of California at Berkeley. She received her law degree from the University of Utah College of Law in 1983, and practiced environmental law for seven years at the firm of Parsons, Behle & Latimer, and as Assistant General Counsel of IRECO Incorporated. She returned to the College of Law as a faculty member in 1990, where she teaches environmental law, intellectual property and toxic torts; she has published articles on scientific evidence and has spoken to judges and practicing lawyers on scientific evidence in toxic tort cases. Address: University of Utah College of Law, Salt Lake City, UT 84112

JAMES T. RICHARDSON, J.D., Ph.D., is Professor of Sociology and Judicial Studies at the University of Nevada, Reno, where he directs the Master of Judicial Studies degree program for trial judges. This program has nearly 100 trial judges from around the country enrolled, as well as a few from other countries. Professor Richardson teaches a course in scientific evidence in this program and he also published on evidence issues in law reviews and academic journals in this and other countries. He has also done considerable consulting in trial situations and has served as an expert witness a number of times as well, in the U.S., Australia, England, and Russia. Address: Masters Program in Judicial Studies, University of Nevada, Reno, NV 89557, Telephone: 702-784-6270, Email: jtr@scs.unr.edu

WAYNE ROTH-NELSON, Ph.D., University of London, is founder and chair of the Risk Science & Law Specialty Group within the International Society of Risk Analysis. His credentials are in environmental health science and policy. He is a Diplomate of the American Board of Forensic Examiners and serves as consultant and expert witness in toxic injury lawsuits. His independent practice, Roth-Nelson Risk Science (Boulder, CO), specializes in science in support of risk regulation and litigation. He analyzes human health risks from toxic chemicals in outdoor and indoor environments and in food and pharmaceuticals. Previously, he was health risk manager at Battelle Memorial Institute and Science Applications International Corporation, working throughout the U.S. Recently, Roth-Nelson served as expert witness for defendants in a civil lawsuit tried by jury in a federal district court and for plaintiffs in a state district court. His article "Risk Evidence in Toxic Torts," co-authored by Dr. Kathey Verdeal, was published in 1996 in The Environmental Lawyer (Vol. 2, No. 2) by the American Bar Association. His special interest, as leader of the Risk Science & Law Specialty Group, is to explore the interface between legal and scientific standards for evidence of disease causation or increased health risk from exposure to chemicals. Address: Roth-Nelson Risk Science, 8663 Hollyhock Lane, Lafayette, CO 80026-8923.

MERLE TROEGER has practiced as a trial attorney for twenty three years, litigating matters in the areas of insurance coverage, civil rights, commercial disputes, employer liability, medical malpractice, premises liability, products liability, and toxic tort. She has extensive experience defending catastrophic personal injury actions, managing and conducting discovery, preparing and arguing appropriate dispositive motions, carrying out settlement negotiations and trying cases before juries. These cases required a comprehensive knowledge of many medical issues including the diagnosis and treatment of head injuries, orthopedic and neurological injuries, selection and administration of general anesthesia, the emotional component of injury and vocational rehabilitation. Her extensive litigation and trial experience has made her a frequent lecturer in the areas of litigation practice, examination and cross-examination of expert witnesses, taking effective depositions, jury selection and achieving maximum jury impact. She has served as a faculty member and team leader for the National Institute of Trial Advocacy in New York State and Colorado. In addition, she has lectured regularly for bar associations, insurance companies and in-house programs on topics which include defending insurance coverage litigation, uninsured/underinsured coverage, defining the insurer's duty to the insured and liquor law liability. Ms. Troeger is admitted in New York State and Colorado and has practiced extensively in the U.S. District Courts. Address: Merle Troeger, Denver, Colorado.

KATHEY M. VERDEAL, Ph.D., University of Wisconsin, has served as consultant and expert witness in civil and criminal litigation, specializing in mammalian and environmental toxicology and industrial and forensic chemistry. She is a Diplomate of the American Boards of Forensic Examiners and Forensic Medicine. She was Laboratory Director at Colorado Forensics and Toxicology, Inc., before establishing her independent practice as Toxicology Consulting, Inc. (Boulder, CO). She has testified in numerous courts in Colorado as well as Alaska, Arizona, Iowa, Kansas, Nebraska, Oklahoma, Pennsylvania, Texas, Utah, and Wyoming. Her testimony has dealt with health effects of toxic substances in a wide range of environmental, occupational and product exposures. Address: Toxicology Consulting, Inc., Boulder, CO 80301.

TABLE OF CONTENTS

1 Science, Medicine and the U.S. Common Law Courts

Carl Meyer

CONTENTS

INTRODUCTION

Two recent U.S. Supreme Court decisions in *Daubert v. Merrell Dow Pharmaceutical, Inc.*[1] and *General Electric v. Joiner*[2] have given federal trial judges the power to determine the reliability of scientific opinions and have strengthened their discretion as gatekeepers of scientific evidence.[3] The Federal Judicial Center has provided a reference manual to assist trial judges with the implementation.[4]

---

[1] *Daubert v. Merrell Dow Pharmaceutical, Inc.*, 509 U.S. 579 (1993). Note that the Daubert decision consists of a series of cases, see Chapter 4.

[2] *General Electric v Joiners*, ____U.S.____; 118 S.C. 512 (1997)

[3] See Chapter 5.

[4] *Reference Manual on Scientific Evidence,* Federal Judicial Center, Washington, DC (1994). This manual offers suggestions for effective management of expert testimony and contains separate chapters on epidemiology, toxicology, survey

The stated purpose of these cases is clear and laudable - namely, to make it harder for forensic experts to present pseudo-scientific opinions to juries. The unstated purpose is more controversial - namely to make it harder for plaintiffs to win. The Daubert criteria are effective in achieving the latter, but the conflict between the two goals makes it difficult for trial judges to justify their decisions in terms of the first. Accordingly, the application of *Daubert* has been inconsistent, and the federal appellate circuits have been almost evenly split on where the border lies between scientific and non-scientific experts, whether Daubert applies to medical experts,[5] and whether clinical physicians can be evaluated with the help of the *Daubert* criteria. The U.S. Supreme Court has granted certiorari to resolve this matter.[6] In a parallel move, the National Conference of Commissioners on Uniform State Laws (NCCUSL) has submitted a proposed, revised version of Federal Rule of Evidence 702 to the federal judicial council,[7] but it will likely take several years before a new rule has been finalized and can be uniformly applied. In the meantime, the admissibility of scientific and other expert evidence will not be fully predictable. This uncertainty threatens an important purpose of law, namely, toS provide a predictable outcome.

It is now more important than ever that judges, experts and litigators better understand the strengths and limits of their own and each other's fields.

A BRIEF HISTORIC PERSPECTIVE

The first documented forensic expert was Antistius. He was asked to examine the corpse of Julius Caesar to determine the cause of his death and opined that only one of the 24 sword wounds was deadly, namely the one perforating his thorax.[8] Experts have been used in English courts since the 14th century, and in the common law courts of North America for more than two hundred years.[9,10]

The relationship between scientists and lawyers has always been uneasy, and scientific expert testimony has long been a thorn in the side of the courts, because experts are not only allowed to explain fact, but to express opinions, even when they concern the ultimate issues at trial. Many litigators and judges have long complained that some experienced expert witnesses have shamelessly abused this power. In fact, Wigmore, the father of much of our evidentiary law, is quoted as

---

research, DNA evidence, statistics, multiple regressions and estimation of economic loss in damage awards.

[5] See *Moore v Ashland Chemical*, 126 F.3d 679 *rev. en banc* ___ F.3d ___(5th Cir. Aug. 14, 1997)

[6] *Carmichael v. Samyoung Tire Co.*, 131 F.3d 1433 (11th Cir. 1997), cert. granted June 23, 1998.

[7] National Conference of Commissioners on Uniform State Laws (NCCUSL), *Federal Rule of Evidence 702* (rev. August 8, 1998).

[8] *Institute Justinian*, 529-533 A.D.

[9] Learned Hand, Historical and Practical Considerations Regarding Expert Testimony, 15 *Harv. L. Rev.* 40 (1901).

[10] William L. Foster, Expert Testimony. Prevalent complaints and proposed remedies, 11 *Harv. L. Rev.* 1 (1897).

stating in the early 1920s that the admission of expert opinions did more than any other rule of procedure to turn trials into a state of legalized gambling.[11] However, the nature of frictions has changed substantially.

Two hundred years ago it was still possible for an educated person to gain a satisfactory overview of the cultural world of his own society. Since the dawn of modern chemistry and physics, at the end of the 18th century, the amount of knowledge and the sophistication of tools have increasingly forced scientists to specialize and choose subfields of science, such as chemistry, or physics or biology. The scientific world is now so large that despite the intimate international contact among specialist groups, it is no longer feasible for a university professor or a head of an industrial laboratory to keep fully abreast in all subfields of his own academic specialty. Since the middle of the 20th century the rapid progress in the sciences has led to the proliferation of an increasing number of subspecialties which have only partly clustered into new interdisciplinary fields, such as the health sciences, the environmental sciences and science policy. Furthermore, in recent years, much of the research initiative has shifted back to industry, where public access is restricted for proprietary reasons.

Despite the tremendous scientific and social changes that have altered the practice of science, professionals still depend on close and regular personal consultation with their peers, to whose opinion they pay deference.

The same is true in the health care professions,[12,13] but progress has been slower. While fifty years ago, medicine was still primarily an art rather than a science, medicine is now interlinked with a plethora of technical and scientific occupations. The proliferation of information and specialties has become such that large health care providers now employ specialists in primary care, and farm out patients for further specialized treatment. In fact, some specialties have become so compartmentalized that surgeons, chemotherapists and radiation specialists no longer feel comfortable weighing the advantages of competing treatment modalities for certain types of diseases, such as cancer of the uterus or prostate gland.[14,15]

---

[11] American Law Institute, *Model Code of Evidence*, American Law Institute, Philadelphia, 1942

[12] Starr, P., *The Social Transformation of American Medicine*, Basic Books (1982).

[13] Rodin, *Medicine, Money and Morals* (1993).

[14] Andy Grove and Bethany McLean, Taking on Prostate Cancer, *Fortune Magazine*, p. 56-81 (May 13, 1997).

[15] *Cal. Health and Safety CODE* §109277. Notice of alternative treatments; breast cancer or biopsy, and §109282. Notice regarding alternative treatments; prostate cancer or biopsy. (Added by Stats. 1996,c. 1023 (S.B. 1497), eff. Sept. 29, 1996). Requires physicians and surgeons treating cancer patients to post a 8.5 x 11" sign that advises patients that their doctor has been urged to provide them with a written summary of alternative treatment methods that has been prepared by the State Department of Health Services. The summary is updated every five years by the State Cancer Advisory Council, consisting of 9 physicians, 3 non-physicians, 2 non-profit cancer research institutes recognized by the National Cancer Institute, and the Director of the Cal. Dept. of Health Services.

Furthermore, even though clinical training increasingly adopts international standards, the practicing physician has become so overburdened with paper work and information about new treatment modalities that he defers to the authority of oral, local peer consensus to make treatment decisions.

Another complicating factor is that clinicians are licensed by the State, and are subject to the jurisdiction of the State Board of Medical Examiners, and are disciplined if they do not follow the local standard of care. The difference between local standards of care is often substantial, because the State Boards of Medical Examiners belong to a privately operated Federation[16] that jealously promotes the independence of these State Agencies, and there is no formal mechanism for coordinating the standard of care between the local clinical community, academic medicine, the State medical licensing board and the American Medical Associations. A similar situation also exists in the other health care professions,[17] that are regulated by virtually autonomous state licensing boards whose members are usually appointed by the state governor.

In law the trend has been different. While scientific and medical research are truly international, law has retained its national origin. Attempts to unify the common law of North America and Great Britain with the civil law of continental Europe move slowly, and even though the European Union has harmonized a substantial part of its laws, the legislative trend in the U.S. has been towards increased delegation of legislative and regulatory power to State and local jurisdictions. The trend has not only affected procedural matters, which have proliferated to such an extent that many local courts, and even individual departments, set their own procedural rules, but also affects many important substantive matters, such as whether certain crimes should be punished with the death penalty, and whether the death penalty will be enforced.

What triggered the Daubert decision

The current attitude toward expert testimony reflects the uncertainty that has been created by the rapid implementation of progress in science and technology. The U.S. Supreme Court decisions in *Joiner* and *Daubert* reflect the efforts of industry to change public policy and reduce the liability of manufacturers for defective products. This battle is being conducted in the media, the legislatures, the public arena and the courts, and has already significantly reduced the consumer rights that were promulgated during the more prosperous post-World War II period. This backlash is partly due to economic forces and partly due to the unfulfilled and

---

[16] Federation of State Medical Boards, Euless, TX 76039-3855

[17] Robert W. McCluggage, *A History of the ADA, A Century of Health Service*, ADA, Chicago (1959), at 67-89; B. Friedland, B. and R.W. Valachovic, R.W., The regulation of dental licensing: the dark ages? 17 *Am. J. Law and Med.* 249 (1991); The author argues that it makes sense to maintain licensing for harbor pilots, because each harbor has a different topology, but that changing dental standards along state lines is excessively restrictive, because the human anatomy does not change along political borders; Jay W. Friedman and Kathryn A. Atchison, The Standard of Care: An Ethical Responsibility of Public Health Dentistry, 53 *J. Pub. Health Dent.* 165-169 (1993).

exaggerated promise that science, if lavishly funded, would rapidly produce cures for all types of cancer and other diseases. This uncertainty is being further fueled by sensationalism in the media, especially television, which currently selects news reports primarily on the basis of their entertainment value,[18] rather than their accuracy [19] or relevancy[20] to the public.

Furthermore, many of the tensions between science and the courts are due to tensions between science and the underlying legislation or regulation.[21]

Among the factors that shape current changes are:

- ► Experts occupy an unique position among witnesses, because the Rules of Evidence allow experts to interpret data and express opinions, even if these opinions address the ultimate issues that are in dispute.
- ► Science has occupied a unique position in modern society in that it is embraced as a point of reference in many areas of activity which are not themselves scientific. The power of science can be compared to that of the medieval church,[22] because many of those who now invoke the power of science, including most politicians, do not understand science, but call upon it as a matter of faith. Many believe that science has become too powerful, and blame science, scientists and experts for problems that have nothing or little to do with science.
- ► The overwhelming majority of legislators, and the public, including business leaders, lack the mathematical and scientific foundation that is necessary to recognize the difference between science and pseudo-science.
- ► Business leaders, the chemical industry and many manufacturers feel that environmental law and product liability law have given consumers too much power and have unduly restricted industry's freedom. Some would like to return to the principle of "caveat emptor," i.e., consumers should be responsible for the products they use.

---

[18] Bok, Sissela, *Mayhem, Violence as Public Entertainment*, Perseus Books, MA (1998).

[19] Achenbach, J., Reality Check; *Washington Post*, December 4, 1996, at C-1 (The information age has one nagging problem: Much of the information is not true).

[20] Foster, K.R. and P.W. Huber. *Judging Science: Scientific Knowledge and the Federal Courts*. Cambridge, MA: The MIT Press (1997).

[21] An example of legislation that is inconsistent with science is the classification of ammonium nitrate as fertilizer. During World War II, when this chemical was used for manufacturing bombs, it was classified as an explosive. When it was shipped under the Marshall plan to Europe, after the war, the exact same product was reclassified as fertilizer. This led to the careless handling that is responsible for the April 17, 1947 explosion in the harbor of Texas City that claimed 600 lives and led to fifty years of litigation.. See, e.g., *In re Texas City Disaster Litigation*, 197 F.2d, 771 (5th Cir. 1952), *Petition of Republic of France v. U.S.*, 290 F.2d 395 (5th Cir. 1961) and underlying cases.

[22] Greer, A.L. and Meyer, C., Explaining Science to Judges and Jurors, *The Chemist*, 19, 35-44 (Spring 1998).

▶   While science, medicine and law depend on each other, because their issues frequently overlap,[23] each of these fields obeys different laws and has different goals. Each of these fields has areas in which it commands priority over the others. This leads to a power struggle.

▶   Law, science and medicine are large and increasingly complex fields that not only require extensive education and training but extensive practical experience. Even some of the most outstanding attorneys are functionally illiterate in medicine and law,[24] and most scientists and physicians are functionally illiterate in law. This leads to communication problems.

     While most litigators and judges readily admit that they lack the basic scientific training necessary to decide technical issues that come before them,[25] many judges do not recognize it when decisions involve scientific issues.

▶   Considering the differential skills and conflicting cultures, it is not surprising that lawyers, scientists and physicians do not feel comfortable when dealing with each other. [26]

---

[23] The recent decision in *Flue-Cured Tobacco Cooperative Stabilization Corporation, the Council for Burley Tobacco Inc., Univer Incorporated, R.J. Reynolds Tobacco Company, and Gallins Vending Company Sal Leaf Tobacco Company Incorporated, Philip Morris. v. U.S. EPA*, No. 6-93 CV 00370,_ F. Supp. _ (M.D. N.C. July 17, 1998) offers a powerful example: In order to determine whether EPA had overstepped its authority in issuing its report on the effect of second-hand tobacco smoke, judge Oosten had to determine whether EPA had committed a material procedural errors, in this case, whether EPA's omission of industry experts on the panel determining the biological plausibility of a carcinogen constituted a material error. Whether the exclusion was material depends on the scientific nature and importance of the issue. Thus, in order to grant the plaintiff industry summary judgment, J. Oosten had to find fault, and severely criticized EPA's scientific decisions and conclusions, as well as its procedures.

[24] Scientific literacy depends on familiarity with some basic mathematical skills that are traditional acquired in junior high school and high school courses, such as the ability to solve story problems, fundamentals of algebra, differential calculus and statistics. These courses are still required of all University-bound students in Europe, but have been traditionally optional in U.S. High schools.

[25] See e.g. *Ethyl Corp. v. EPA*, 541 F.2d 1, 67 (D.C. Cir.) *cert. den.* 426 U.S. 941 (1976) (Because substantive review of mathematical and scientific evidence by technically illiterate judges is dangerously unreliable, I continue to believe we will do more to improve administrative decision-making by concentrating our efforts on strengthening administrative procedures) and *International Harvester Co., v. Ruckelshaus*, 478 F.2d 615, 651 D.C. Cir. 1973) (I recognize that I do not know enough about dynamometer extrapolations, deterioration factor adjustment, and the like to decide whether or not the government approach to these matters was statistically valid.)

[26] See e.g., Bear, L.A., ed. *Law, Medicine, Science and Justice*, C, Thomas Publishers, Springfield, IL 1964. and Gerber, S., *Physician in Courtroom*, L. Adelson, ed., Western Reserve U Press, 1954, Typically, physicians don't understand the scientists' preoccupation with causation, their lack of compassion

- ▶ Communication between science and law does not take place in a vacuum, but is influenced and moderated by vested interest groups, such as trade associations, that sometimes promote their own agenda, while ostensibly serving as intermediaries for third parties. An example of the power of these intermediaries is shown by the fact that the American Association for the Advancement of Sciences and the New England Journal of Medicine are recommended as brokers for "neutral" scientific advice in Justice Breyer's concurring opinion in *Joiner*,[27] even though both organizations openly promote self-serving, partisan positions,[28] including the protection of industry and the medical profession against litigation by consumers.[29]
- ▶ Litigators are advocates. The importance that assign to science or medicine depends on whether science supports their side in a pending dispute.
- ▶ The frictions between the sciences and the courts are more pronounced in North America than in the civil law countries of continental Europe. While the vast majority of North American scientists do everything possible to avoid court testimony, most leading European scientists consider it an honor to be called to testify as an expert witness. One of the reasons for the different attitudes is that the U.S. common law court requires experts to provide oral testimony in open court and withstand vigorous cross-examination during which opposing counsel not only tries to discredit the expert's testimony, but also his personal integrity. As explained in Chapter 6, the civil law courts of Continental Europe rely heavily on written expert reports that are reviewed by peers selected by the opposing parties; they do not take testimony under oath, and do not rely on cross-examination to flush out covert biases, and therefore provide a more friendly atmosphere for expert testimony.

---

and their failure to accommodate the subjective needs of others, and the differential between the level of certainty at which a physician needs to intervene and the much higher level of certainty that the court and scientists require when reviewing whether a diagnosis is accurate and final and supports causation.

[27] See also, "The Interdependence of Science and Law," Associate Justice Stephen G. Breyer, Supreme Court of the United States, Address at the 1998 American Association for the Advancement of Science Annual Meeting and Science Innovation Exposition, Philadelphia, Pennsylvania, February 16, 1998

[28] See, e.g., Angell, M., *Science on Trial: The Clash of Medical Evidence and the Law in the Breast Implant Case,* Norton (1996) (Dr. Angell is executive director of the New England Journal of Medicine and has acted as expert witness), and Philip H. Abelson, Toxic Terror; Phantom Risks, 261 Science, 407 (1993); Philip H. Abelson, Pathological Growth of Regulations, 260 Science; 1859 (1993). Philip H. Abelson, Risk Assessment of Low Level Exposures. 206 Science 1507 (1994). Letters responding to this editorial were published at 266 Science 1141-1145 (1994). Dr. Abelson was the editor of Science magazine for many years.

[29] The problem with professional self-discipline is that professional ethics are a scheme of law enforcement...by private policemen where privately declared laws are punished by penalties imposed by private "judges" after privately conducted trials. *Fashion Originator's Guild v. FTC,* 312 U.S. 457, 463 (1941). Adv. Op. Dig. 128 (1967-70) Trade Reg.Rptr. ¶ 17950 at 20,329 (FTC 1967).

WHAT MAKES THE *DAUBERT* DECISION UNUSUAL?

There are several problems with the *Daubert* decision, and its application.

First, the *Daubert* and *Joiner* decisions suggest two incorrect assumptions about science, namely: (a) that in the natural sciences, "reliable" knowledge can be fully explained and has no "analytical gap," and (b) that the existence of a rational explanation makes scientific arguments reliable.

If the first were true, there would be no need for patents. To be patentable, a discovery must, *inter alia,* be novel[30] and non-obvious,[31] i.e., the invention must produce unexpected or surprising results that were not anticipated by those skilled in the prior art. Most technology is in use long before the reason for its functioning is understood; the quantum theory and wave theory have successfully co-existed for more than seventy years, even though the reason for the duality is not yet understood.

If the second assumption would be true, the rule of Alchemy would have been several hundred years earlier.[32]

Second, the *Daubert* decision suggests that there is a bright line between science and art, but fails to define the borders of "science." This contradiction is explained above, i.e., that most scientific fields are far too complex to be fully articulated, and practical experience plays a much bigger role in science than is commonly appreciated.

Third, litigators, judges, and most jurors do not sufficiently understand the science that underlies an expert opinion, to recognize the border between legitimate art and pseudo-science.

Fourth, the *Daubert* decision is silent about testimony of treating physicians and clinical toxicologists, the two areas that are often the weakest link in the chain of toxic causation. The myth that medical semiology and clinical toxicology should be evaluated as exact sciences unduly distracts from the reliability of these well-established medical arts,

Fifth, the U.S. common law system does not provide sufficient room for a meaningful scientific exchange to explore scientific issues, because expert opinions

---

[30] An invention is novel if it differs from prior art when no single prior art describes all of the invention's elements. 35 U.S.C. § 102.

[31] 35 U.S. Code § 103.

[32] The phlogiston theory was based on the correct observation that carbon and other fuels disappear during combustion, and on the logical and rational conclusion that if the fuel disappeared, so did the chemical matter. It took the genius of Lavoisier to demonstrate that carbon did not lose weight, but that, in the contrary, carbon gained weight during the combustion, by combining with oxygen. The fact that the public and our politicians still do not comprehend the basic chemical mechanism of combustion is proven by the fact that power companies and other energy users are taxed for the use of cooling water, but not for the consumption of oxygen that they extract from the ambient air.

are filtered by attorneys before they reach the trier of fact.[33]

Sixth, one goal of the *Daubert* decision is to abate "junk-science," a term that some define as pseudo-science, while others define it as any type of science that yields results that are adverse to their own interests.[34]

Seventh, the rules set down by *Daubert* for recognizing and excluding pseudo-scientific reasoning are not applicable to several fields that fall under the broad definition of the term "science," such as clinical medicine.

Eighth, *Daubert* implies that giving judges the power to rule that scientific evidence is not reliable will serve as an adequate substitute for scientifically illiterate litigators,

Ninth, the *Daubert* rules unduly discourage competent scientists – especially physicians, clinical toxicology and in other areas where experience and art are important factors – from serving as expert witnesses for the plaintiff, because few will be willing to take the risk of letting a scientifically untrained judge declare their professional opinion as "unreliable," merely because the judge does not understand the border between legitimate art and pseudo-science.

Tenth, it subscribes to the believe that judges are better qualified to recognize pseudo-scientific arguments than jurors.

If the "reliability" of science is to be decided by the judge, rather than the jury, i.e., if it is a question of law rather than a question of fact, it would seem more practical and candid – and it would improve the relation between scientists and lawyers – if the courts would use legal terminology and devices, rather than pseudo-scientific rules and arguments, to exercise their discretion to exclude what the court perceives to be far-fetched scientific evidence by using, say, the time-honored concept of proximate causation as defined in Palsgraf:

> What we do mean by the word "proximate" is that, because of conve-nience, of public policy, of a rough sense of justice, the law arbitrarily declines to trace a series of events beyond a certain point. This is not logic. It is practical politics.[35]

WHAT JUDGES, SCIENTISTS, ENGINEERS, PHYSICIANS AND OTHER EXPERTS SHOULD KNOW ABOUT EACH OTHER.

Science, Engineering, Medicine and Law all fall under the legal definition of "sciences," in that they use a rational approach to resolve complex multifactorial

---

[33] The U.S. common law system differs from the European civil law system. Contrary to widely held belief, in the latter, the court does not choose "neutral" experts to educate the court bilaterally. Instead, expert reports are circulated among professional peers, selected from a list submitted jointly by both parties, and peer responses are presented together with the opinions, to be reviewed by the trier of fact. This peer review discourages both sides from advancing pseudo-scientific arguments, and provides the trier of fact with unfiltered access to what working scientists consider relevant strengths and weaknesses in each other's arguments, rather than with opinions that have been filtered by counsel or experts.

[34] See Chapter 7.

[35] *Palsgraf v Long Island Railroad*, 248 N.Y. 339, 162 N.E. 99 (1928)

problems.[36] However, the successful practice of these professions also involves a substantial amount of practical experience[37] that cannot be acquired solely by reasoning.

Furthermore, experience in one field does not translate into others. Lawyers cannot discuss legal issues with people who do not have a law degree, regardless of whether they are undergraduate students or Nobel chemistry prize winners whose achievement is reflected in hundreds of research publications and many patents. Likewise, a medical doctor cannot intelligently discuss his clinical reasoning to a person who lacks clinical experience, and a research chemist cannot fully share his scientific reasoning with someone who lacks personal research experience as a post-doctoral fellow.

The gap between the professions also reflects their handling of emotions. Science and engineering are governed by facts and based on rational thought. These professionals learn early to keep emotions separate from their work. In contrast, physicians need to balance rational reasoning with a willingness to negotiate, show compassion toward patients and respect for the consensus of mentors and peers. Litigators go a step further. They pick and choose facts, and call upon emotions to bolster their arguments.

Science The laws of nature have universal and eternal validity; they take preference over human law; they are not negotiable; they are self-enforcing; their implementation is not discretionary, and they do not provide for equal rights and due process. The science community has an strongly elitist structure that is based on professional competence and seniority, and scientists are notorious for trampling procedural rights. However, scientific findings can be tested anywhere anytime by anyone who possesses the appropriate facilities. Interpretations of facts are rejected unless they fit each link to pre-existing knowledge. The fit of data and compliance with pre-existing science must be 100%. Scientists look for answers that are right or wrong. For scientists, time is not of the essence.

Engineering While research scientists search and test the limits of natural laws and rules in order to expand the known universe of science, engineers must operate within a closed universe, and strictly obey professional standards and rules, or they will lose their license.

Medicine Medical research uses scientific methodology, while clinical medicine remains an art that is largely based on experience and observation. The goal of the treating physician is to heal the patient, or, at least, to reduce his suffering. A requisite to success is diagnosis. Diagnosis is difficult because many diseases have similar symptoms. Diagnosis is based on history, physical exam, diagnostic tests and response to treatment. The fact that diagnosis is more of an art than a science does not distract from its potential reliability.[38]

---

[36] See *Webster* and *Manual of Scientific Evidence.*

[37] By way of example, the discovery of scientific applications often precedes a scientific explanation. If the application of science would not be an art, and would strictly rest on natural laws, science would not require patent law, because natural laws cannot be patented.

[38] As Jacobs explains it, a large part of the knowledge of medical practitioners consists of cultural and occupational experience that is individual and does not exist in libraries. See: Jacobs, J.M., *Doctors and Rules, a Sociology of Professional*

Physicians do not have the luxury of time; they deal with individuals, and they cannot conduct statistically significant testing on their patients. Regardless of their often extensive scientific training, physicians must be able to act before all facts are in, in the face of uncertainty. They do so by relying on tradition, the advice of mentors and consensus among local peers, rather than scientific independent analysis.[39] In practice, physicians are often more concerned about treating symptoms – such as mending bones, controlling pain, or controlling an infection – rather than with determining causation. Treating physicians must rely to a large extent on subjective symptoms presented by the patient, and they cannot obtain compliance with the prescribed treatment plan unless they negotiate with the patients, and obtain their consent.

The field of medicine has become so large that it is virtually impossible for specialists to stay abreast of the relative merits of treatment.[40]

Law   The goal of the law is to protect the interests of society and the individual. It does so by preserving public peace and safety, settling individual disputes, resolving conflicting social interests, maintaining the security of expectations, and by channeling social change.[41] Even though the news media cover worldwide events with lightening speed, man-made law remains distinctly national and local.

The power of law depends on the weight, trust and confidence the citizen puts on peaceful coexistence. While most nations agree, at least in principle, on certain basic rights, such as property rights, and the freedom of the individual from bodily intrusion, there is such a deep disagreement on many matters , such as individual freedom, that war, rather than legal adjudication is still a recognized method for resolving disputes among nations.

Since people tend to change their notions how their country should be governed, national and local law are subject to change.[42] In democratic countries, such as the U.S., where the legal philosophy of different population groups are often conflicting, a shift in political mood can lead to rapid reversal of public policy and public law. Furthermore, in most countries and jurisdictions the printed word and actual practice of law differ for economic, political and other reasons.[43]

The practice of U.S. law is determined by a complex hierarchy of Federal,

---

Values. Routledge, London (1995).

[39] See Starr, P., *The Social Transformation of American Medicine*, Basic Books, 1982, and Chapter 4, infra. Note that the standard of care is enforced by autonomous state licensing boards.

[40] See Grove, A. and McLean, B., *Taking on Prostate Cancer*, FORTUNE MAGAZINE, May 13, 1997, at 56-81.

[41] See e.g. Jones, H. W., An Invitation to Jurisprudence, 74 *Columbia Law Review* 1023 (1974).

[42] In a nucleus, national legal system systems belong to one of at least three different concept: common law, originating in the Anglo-Saxon countries, civil law, originating in continental Europe; and communist law, originating in Russia.

[43] See e.g., Neumayer, K. H., Fremdes Recht aus Büchern, fremde Rechtswirklichkeit und die funktionelle Dimension in the Methoden der Rechtsvergleichung, 34 *Rabels Zeitung,* 411 (1970).

State and local laws and regulations, some of which may be partly inconsistent. During the past twenty years, the trend towards national standardization of state laws has been reversed. Furthermore, local procedures and their implementation differ significantly, and many courts, and even individual judges, promulgate their own procedural rules. Generally, State courts must take judicial notice of common law, constitutions and public statutes of the United States, of each State, territory and jurisdiction of the United States and of the official compilation of Codes, rules and regulations of each state. Courts may take judicial notice of private acts and resolutions of Congress and of State legislatures, ordinances and regulations of officers, agencies or government subdivisions of the States or the U.S., as well as the laws of foreign countries or their political subdivision under the principle of comity, i.e., courtesy among foreign countries.

Conflict of laws and choice of law are important areas of litigation. An example dealing with the limit of the application of the full faith and credit clause of the U.S. Constitution is offered in *Baker v. General Motors*.[44] As part of the settlement of a law suit between Ellsworth, a former employee of General Motor and his former employer, Ellsworth agreed that he would not testify against his former employer. The question remained whether this agreement was valid outside the jurisdiction of the court. The U.S. Supreme Court determined that a settlement agreement made in a Michigan court could not be enforced in a Missouri litigation by parties not involved in the Michigan settlement, because a Michigan Court could not control the actions of a court in another jurisdiction.

The Role of the Court The role of the judge is to resolve disputes by balancing the interest of the litigants, and that of the litigants with that of the public in a manner that is consistent with the law. In a jury trial, the judge determines legal issues, and the jury determines the facts. In a non-jury trial, the judge determines both. The reason why trial lawyers like the jury system is because it relies on the common sense of the individual juror to balance the rational and emotional content of the information presented by the parties by comparing it on the basis of their personal life experience and their personal balance of rational and emotional factors.

The procedural function of the judge is twofold: First, he acts as a procedural referee to ensure that each party gets a fair and full hearing; and second, he acts as an evidentiary gatekeeper to ensure that the parties focus on the issues that need to be and can be adjudicated by the court. However, before a judge presides at trial, he will do everything possible to get the parties to settle without the need for a trial, and if this is not possible, the judge will likely decide the case in such a manner that both parties are disappointed with the outcome.

In the U.S. common law system, the judge is not an investigator or a researcher, but must rule on the basis of the evidence presented by the parties. In fact, judges are charged with using evidence rules to narrow issues, by excluding anything that is not directly relevant to the case at bar. As Shasanoff defines it, the strength of the legal proceeding is its ability to produce localized, content-specific epistemological and normative understandings that are not subordinate to

---

[44] *Baker v. General Motors,* 86 F.3d 811 (8th Cir. 1996), rev'd. 118 S.Ct. 657 (1998).

inappropriately universal claims and standards.[45] Frictions arise when the courts seek nationally consistent solutions, for example; in class actions concerning the liability for products such as breast implants or asbestos.

An example of the type of balancing in which common law judges excel is offered by product liability law, which developed during the 1940s and 1950s in California as the result of judicial concern over finding a balance between the interests of consumers, manufacturers and the public: [46] As Justice Traynor stated it in his opinion in *Escola v Coca Cola Bottling Co. of Fresno:*[47]

.... public policy demands that responsibility be fixed wherever it will most effectively reduce the hazards to life and health inherent in defective products that reach the market. It is evident that the manufacturer can anticipate some hazards and guard against the recurrence of others, as the public cannot. Those who suffer injury from defective products are unprepared to meet its consequences. The cost of an injury and the loss of time or health may be an overwhelming misfortune to the person injured, and a needless one, for the risk of injury can be insured by the manufacturer and distributed among the public as cost of doing business. It is to the public interest to discourage the marketing of products having defects that are a menace to the public. If such products nevertheless find their way into the market it is to the public interest to place responsibility for whatever injury they may cause upon the manufacturer, who, even if he is not negligent in the manufacture of the product, is responsible for its reaching the market. However intermittently such injuries may occur and however haphazardly they may strike, the risk of their occurrence is a constant risk and a general one. Against such a risk there should be general and constant protection and the manufacturer is best situated to afford such protection.

It is noteworthy that product liability law has since followed the trend, and that common law has been increasingly replaced by statutory law that reflects the power that special interest groups have on legislation.

A basic premise is that the trier of fact acts free of bias. Webster defines bias as a distortion of one's judgment owing to a prepossession of any sort, i.e., a fixed conception in the light of which anyone or anything is judged.[48] However, as explained in Chapter 7, the term bias is a term of art; in the litigation context it relates only to judgment concerning issues that are in dispute. Being unbiased indicates a willingness to make a rational and reasoned decision based on law rather than on other interests.

---

[45] Jasanoff, S., *Science at Bar*, Harvard University Press, 222 (1995).

[46] See e.g. *Greenman v. Yuba Power Products*, 59 Cal.2d. 57 (1963)

[47] *Escola v Coca Cola Bottling Co of Fresno*, 24 Cal.2d 453, 150 P.2d 436 (1944).

[48] *Webster's New Collegiate Dictionary* (6th ed.), Merriam Publishers, Springfield, Massachusetts, 1993.

What Makes an Expert "Scientific?"

Science is knowledge attained through study or practice.[49] The courts distinguish scientific and non-scientific, or experiential, expert witnesses:

> The distinction between scientific and non-scientific expert testimony is a critical one. By way of illustration, if one wanted to explain to a jury how a bumblebee is able to fly, an aeronautical engineer might be a helpful witness. Since flight principles have some universality, the expert could apply general principles to the case of the bumblebee. Conceivably, even if he had never seen a bumblebee, he still would be qualified to testify, as long as he was familiar with its component parts.
>
> On the other hand, if one wanted to prove that bumblebees always take off into the wind, a beekeeper with no scientific training at all would be an acceptable witness if a proper foundation were laid for his conclusions. The foundation would not relate to his formal training, but to his first-hand observations. In other words, the beekeeper does not know any more about flight principles than the jurors, but he has seen a lot more bumblebees than they have.[50]

In the context of expert witnessing, the term science includes physical scientists, social scientists, engineers, physicians, other health care professionals and even lawyers.[51] However, each of these fields requires not only much formal education, but many years of practical experience.

Close cooperation between litigators and experts is crucial, because the litigator must determine what scientific information a party needs to present, and the expert determines how to explain it. Thus, the expert need not only understand the science he wishes to present, but he should be able to apply it to the facts of the case, understand the needs and viewpoint of his audience, translate scientific facts and opinions accurately from professional scientific jargon so that the trier of fact will comprehend it, and recall the testimony at the time of the decision making.

As explained, there is a distinct difference between scientific experts and treating physicians because the latter deal with individual cases, i.e., anecdotal evidence, their diagnosis and treatment plan depend on a patient's presentation of subjective symptoms and their decisions rely on informal peer consensus.

SCIENCE, LAW, POLITICS AND THE PUBLIC INTEREST

Science, law and politics belong to different cultures.[52] Science is dedicated to finding facts; law is more interested in justice than in facts, and politics puts

---

[49] *Webster's New Collegiate Dictionary*

[50] *Berry v City of Detroit*, 25 F.3d 1342, 1349 (6th Cir. 1994).

[51] *Reference Manual on Scientific Evidence*, Federal Judicial Center, Washington, DC (1994).

[52] Peter H. Schuck, Multi-culturalism Redux: Science, Law, and Politics. 11 *Yale Law & Policy Review* 1-46 (1994)

consensus over fidelity to facts and individual values. The relation between the three can be visualized as forming a triangle in which science and law have a strong orientation towards politics but only very little direct connection between themselves. Furthermore, the field of science is broad and consists of a large number of subfields that differ in size, stage of development, and, therefore, in "reliability." This has led to the development of the field of science policy that acts as an intermediary, and sometimes as a filter, between the sciences and the outside world. The need for scientists to work with politicians derives from the fact that much of modern science is conducted by scientific teams that require extensive and expensive facilities.

The link between law and politics is even stronger. First, all criminal law and administrative law is based on legislation. Since the legislative process is driven by politics, it is vulnerable to economic pressures. What is unique about the U.S. legislative system is the tension between state and federal law, and frequent reversals in public policy. The death penalty, minimum sentencing laws and gun laws are examples of laws that have reduced judicial independence. Many tensions between science and the courts are due to tensions between science and the underlying legislation, or due to regulations that are triggered by legislation.

Second, special interest groups and some legislators have become increasingly partisan in criticizing the decisions of judges and jurors in individual cases, for example, when they feel that the latter excessively favored plaintiffs in civil cases[53] or criminal defendants.[54] Some members of Congress have declared that it is their "responsibility to oversee judges and their performances on the bench," and "go after judges in a big way." This is not empty oratory. During 1996, the then majority leader of the U.S. Senate, and the Majority Whip of the House of Representatives pressured a federal judge in the Southern District of New York to change his decision in a pending criminal matter by threatening him with impeachment proceedings, and the President followed up by suggesting through a spokesman that he would ask the judge to resign if he would not yield to the threats.[55] The American Bar Association's Commission on the Separation of Powers and Judicial Independence has documented several similar cases of political intervention with pending cases. It feels that this trend is increasing, and it has formed an eleven member committee, chaired by a former federal judge and director of the FBI to find means to better protect judicial independence.[56]

Third, State and Municipal judges must periodically stand for re-election. This makes them vulnerable to local power brokers. These pressures are

---

[53] Marcia Angell, *Science on Trial: The Clash of Medical Evidence and the Law in the Breast Implant Case*, Norton (1996). Peter W. Huber, *Galileo's Revenge: Junk Science in the Courtroom,* 18 (1991).

[54] Anonymous, To solve a fatal rape a judge issues a controversial order, *Britain Today*, 150, (9), British Embassy, Washington D.C. (Sept. 1, 1997).

[55] Commission on separation of powers and judicial independence. *An Independent Judiciary*, report by the American Bar Association committee on separation of Powers, Chicago, November 1997.

[56] Special Committee on Judicial Independence, American Bar Association, Chicago, IL (1997)

accentuated by the fact that judicial election campaigns require expensive television advertisement budgets, because judicial elections are not considered newsworthy, and are rarely covered by television. Thus, between 1994 and 1996, the average cost for the election campaign of Nevada State Supreme Court Justices was more than half a million dollars, even though the campaign was not unusually controversial. This is about five times the annual salary of these justices. The average campaign for a seat on the State district court was over $120,000.00, i.e., larger than the annual salary for the position.[57]

Fourth, we live in a period of rapidly shifting values. Short-term business profits are currently rated more important than consumer relations, and a large fraction of the public also rates individual freedom higher than loyalty to their society. A comparison of the public attitude toward crime investigations proves this point: In England the police may take DNA samples – blood or a bit of flesh from the inside of each cheek – from any criminal suspect. The British Forensic Science Service keeps 16,000 DNA profiles from convicts and 160,000 from suspects, and claims that since 1995 it has found more than 7,000 criminal matches. Large-scale screening of DNA has been used in England for some time: It was used in 1995 to convict the murderer of 15-year old Darid Owen in South Wales, and DNA testing of 7500 truck drivers was commenced in 1996, during the investigation of the rape and murder of 17-year old French student, Celine Figard, during a visit in Great Britain. In France, in 1997, after Caroline Dickinson, a thirteen-year-old British tourist was raped and murdered while she and her school class visited Plaine-Fougère in the Bretagne, a French court ordered all 258 men[58] living in the town to provide saliva samples for DNA testing. All, except six men were found and complied. Similar testing has been conducted in Germany since 1994.

U.S. police departments are now building DNA data bases for convicted felons, and the U.S. Department of Justice strongly supports the use of DNA testing,[59,60] but testing of the general population remains unthinkable in the U.S. for political reasons, and because the testing lacks "probable cause."

SCIENCE IN THE COURTROOM ARENA

The court is a battleground where people with conflicting goals and aspirations and different means and skill clash in an emotionally charged setting full of traps. It is the last resort for people who have found it impossible to resolve their

---

[57] Testimony of Assemblyman Jack Close before the Nevada Legislature, March 27, 1997.

[58] Swardson , Anne, Court Orders French Villagers to Undergo DNA Tests in Effort to Find Killer, *Washington Post*, Friday, August 15, 1997; Page A3; Anonym., L'Affaire Dickinson: 252 hommes aux tests sur 258 convoqués. *L'Humanité,* Paris, Nov. 24, 1997, p. 1.

[59] *Convicted by Juries, Exonerated by Science: Case Studies in the Use of DNA Evidence to Establish Innocence After Trial ,* National Institute of Justice, Research Report (June 1996).

[60] *The People vs. Sergio Venegas, 98 Daily Journal D.A.R.* 4901 (May 13, 1998) ___ CA __, (1998)

problems otherwise. While some people come to the court with the hope of finding a rational solution of their disputes, a large number of people come for one reason only, to win. However, half of the litigants lose outright.

To protect the rights of all parties, to manage disgruntled litigants, and to bolster the power of the judge, the U.S. courts draw heavily on the symbolism of high drama to support its power. The emotional power and impact of the architectural design, the ceremonial pomp and the oratory that starts when the bailiff, acting like a town crier calls out "all rise, the Court is now in session" are far more powerful on those who are thrust into the role of participant in this ritualistic, medieval tournament setting, than that perceived by television observers who remain at a safe distant from the jurisdiction of the gavel and the grip of the bailiff who is always ready to use his handcuffs to subdue any defiant actor, and take convicted criminals into custody.[61]

Oral proceedings in open court have been the foundation of the U.S. common law court since its inception. Oral hearings derive from English procedure including trial by jury and the right to cross-examine all witnesses whose testimony forms the basis of the decision.[62] The psychological foundation and operational effectiveness of cross-examination as a tool in search for truth depends on the spontaneity of an oral response to a question in front of the triers of fact. Part of the effectiveness of traditional cross-examination is to cater to sensationalism.[63]

Clearly, the court room setting is the opposite of the environment that scientists and physicians cherish when they practice their professions. However, as will be discussed later and in other chapters, the court offers scientists a unique forum to test their professional skills against the common sense standard of the public, on whose support science depends.

Whether an experienced scientific expert can profit from this authoritarian atmosphere in the courtroom depends on his level of knowledge, character and personal skill.

In the courtroom the trial lawyers fulfill a variety of roles. They serve as advocates for the parties and as sworn officers of the court. They act as intermediaries between the parties, as coaches and as spokespersons. Their role is shaped by law, the client, and the attorney's own initiative. During pre-trial, litigators collect, select, and shape facts, very much like a playwright; when they prepare and call witnesses in court, they act as stage director; and during other phases of the trial, such as when they present their opening statement or argue legal points at the

[61] See, e.g., Asthma, David E., *Courtroom Majesty and Defendant Frames: a Theater of Powerlessness*. Master thesis in sociology and criminology, Department of Sociology, Northern Illinois University, Carbondale, Illinois (1995).

[62] A full cross-exam of a witness upon the subject of his examination in chief is the absolute right, not the mere privilege of a party and a denial of this right is a prejudicial and fatal error, *Gilmer v. Higley*, 110 U.S. 47, 50, 3 S.C. 471, 28 LED 62 (1910). See also *Lindsey v. U S*, 133 F.2d 368, (D.C. Cir. 1942), *overruled on other grounds* by 405 F.2d 1352, 1359 (D.C. Cir. 1968), and Hammelmann, Expert Evidence, 10 *Mod. L. Rev.* 32 (1947), and Homburger, Functions of Orality in Austrian and American Civil Procedure, 20 *Buffalo L. Rev.* 9-39 (1970).

[63] As Webster defines it, sensationalism is the use and effect of subject matter and literature treatment calculated to arouse excited interest and emotional response.

bench, they turn into actors.

When both parties are represented by equally competent counsel, the presence of litigators helps a fair resolution of the case. When counsel are not equally skilled, the better counsel can strongly affect the outcome of almost any matter.

Communications between counsel and judges rely heavily on technical, and sometimes archaic language. Even the modern court encourages oratory and professional jargon, and some commonly used terms assume specialized meanings. The terms evidence and facts serve as examples.

As used in the legal phrase "finding of facts and conclusions of law," the term "fact" does not refer to the actual, underlying facts, but only to those facts that were presented by the parties as admissible evidence at trial. Thus, in this context, the term "facts" corresponds to what a French judge would call the "assumptions" that the judge uses to make his decision.[64]

Note that the term evidence is also a term of art. The definition of evidence used in the State of California is:

"Evidence" means testimony, writing, material objects, or other things presented to the senses that are offered to prove the existence or non-existence of a fact. Cal. Ev. Rule 140.

WHAT DETERMINES WHETHER EVIDENCE IS ADMISSIBLE?

The *Daubert* criteria and their application are described in Chapter 5. A detailed discussion is found in the Reference Manual on Scientific Evidence.[65] The underlying definition of the expert witnesses is provided in Sections 702 of the Federal Law of Evidence and in the corresponding definitions of the Law of Evidence in every State:

(Revised) Rule 702. Testimony by Experts (Revised August 8, 1998, by the National Commission on Uniform State Laws, and submitted to the Federal Judicial Council).

If scientific, technical, or other specialized knowledge will assist the trier of fact to understand the evidence or to determine a fact at issue, a witness qualified as an expert by knowledge, skill, experience, training, or education, may testify thereto in the form of an opinion or otherwise.

(a) General rule. A witness may testify in the form of opinion or otherwise if the following are satisfied.

(1) Basis for testimony. The testimony is based on scientific, technical, or other specialized knowledge.

(2) Assistance to trier of fact. The testimony will assist the trier of fact to understand evidence or determine a fact at issue.

---

[64] David, R., Kindred, M., *French Law: Structure, Source and Methodology,* Louisiana State Univ., Baton Rouge, LA (1972). Devries, H. P., *Civil Law and the Anglo-American Lawyer*, Oceana Publications, Dobbs Ferry, NY. (1976).

[65] Berger, M. A., Evidentiary Framework, Chapter 5 in *Reference Manual on Scientific Evidence*, Federal Judicial Center (1994).

(3) Qualification of witness. The witness is qualified by knowledge, skill, experience, training, or education as an expert in the scientific, technical, or other specialized field.

(4) Reasonable reliability. The testimony is based upon principles or methodology which is reasonably reliable as established under subdivision (b), (c), or (e).

(5) Reliably applied to facts of case. The witness has applied the principles or methodology reliably to the facts of the case.

(b) Reliability deemed to exist. A principle or methodology is deemed reasonably reliable if its reliability has been established by controlling legislation or judicial decision.

(c) Presumption of reliability. A principle or methodology is presumed to be reasonably reliable if it has substantial acceptance within the relevant scientific, technical, or specialized community. A party may rebut the presumption by proving that it is more probable than not that the principle or methodology is not reasonably reliableas provided in subdivision (e).

(d) Presumption of unreliability. A principle or methodology is presumed not to be reasonably reliable if it does not have substantial acceptance within the relevant scientific, technical, or specialized community. A party may rebut the presumption if it is more probable than not that the principle or methodology is reasonably reliable as provided in subdivision (e).

(e) Other reliability factors. When determining the reliability of a principle or methodology, the court shall consider all relevant additional factors, which may include:

(1) Testing. The extent to which the principle or methodology has been tested;

(2) Research methods. The adequacy of research methods employed in testing the principle or methodology;

(3) Peer review. The extent to which the principle or methodology has been published and subjected to peer review;

(4) Rate of error. The rate of error in the application of the principle or methodology;

(5) Experience of expert. The experience of the witness as an expert in the application of the principle or methodology; and

(6) Acceptance within the field. The extent to which the field of knowledge has substantial acceptance within the relevant scientific, technical, or specialized community.

It remains to be seen how much of this revision will change during the coming comment period.

Qualification as an Expert Witness

(a) A person is qualified to testify as an expert if he has special knowledge, skill, experience, training, or education sufficient to qualify him as an expert on the subject to which his testimony relates. Against the objection of a party, such special knowledge, skill, experience, training, or education must be shown before the witness may testify as an expert.

(b) A witness's special knowledge, skill, experience, training, or education may be shown by any otherwise admissible evidence, including his own testimony. (1965 ch. 299)[66] Cal Rules of Evidence § 720

In contrast to the academic setting, the strongest source of testimony for a person's qualification is the expert himself.

Qualification as a Medical Expert Witness

Medical experts need to be licensed.   Most courts have liberalized the rules and no longer require that experts be locally licensed, or have personal knowledge of the standard of care at the time when the alleged malpractice occurred. While a layperson may not base his testimony on a medical text book, a physician is free to do so. [67,68]

WHAT TYPE OF TESTIMONY IS PERMITTED?

Rule 703: Bases of Opinion Testimony by Experts: The facts or data in the particular case upon which an expert bases an opinion or inference may be those perceived by or made known to the expert at or before the hearing. If of a type reasonably relied upon by experts in a particular field in forming an opinion or inferences upon the subject, the facts or data need not be admissible in evidence. FRE 703.

Rule 704 (a). Opinion on Ultimate Issue: (a) Except as provided in subdivision (b), testimony in the form of an opinion or inference otherwise admissible is not objectionable because it embraces an ultimate issue to be decided by the trier of fact.

According to Webster's New Collegiate Dictionary, the term "opinion" implies a belief stronger than an impression and less strong than positive knowledge.[69] Rule 704(a) has been the focus of strong criticism since the inception of the rule. Wigmore, the father of evidence law, stated that this rule would convert trials to a lottery.[70]

---

[66] *Cal Rules of Evidence § 720 (1998)*

[67] *Brown v. Colm (1974) 11 Cal.3d 639 [114 Cal. Rptr. 128] (does witness have skill or experience sufficient so that testimony will aid jury)*

[68] *Mann v. Cracchiolo* (1985) 38 Cal.3d 18 [210 Cal. Rptr. 762, 94 P.2d 1134] (abuse of discretion to find insufficient foundation where witness has disclosed knowledge sufficient to assist jury)

[69] *Webster's New Collegiate Dictionary*, 798 (8th ed. 1981).

[70] Wigmore opposed this rule: "it has done more than any one rule of procedure to reduce our litigation towards a state of legalized gambling" cited by Edmund M. Morgan, Foreword to the ALI Model Code of Evidence, 34 (1942).

This matter of opinion is a peculiar one, anyhow. First the expert witness gets on the stand and gives his opinion that if such and such is the case, then such and such must be the result, that is his opinion; then the lawyer gives the jury the benefit of his opinion as to the opinion of the expert; and then the jury is called upon to give their opinions of the opinions of the lawyer and the expert, and it is only an opinion after all.[71]

We have already discussed the fact that during the past five years the U.S. courts have tightened the rules for screening the testimony of experts before it can be presented to the jurors. While some of the State courts in the United States still follow the evidentiary rules set out in Frye, the Federal Courts and an increasing number of States now use the trial judge as a "gatekeeper" to screen expert testimony before it reaches the jury,. Furthermore, the recent decision in *General Electric v. Joiner* has not only expanded the discretion of scientifically untrained trial judges to determine the relevance and reliability of the scientific methods used by experts, but also to determine whether the scientific methods used by experts for interpreting the data have "too large an analytical gap."

Rule 705. Disclosure of Facts or Data Underlying Expert Opinion:
The expert may testify in terms of opinion or inference and give reasons therefore without first testifying to the underlying facts or data, unless the court requires otherwise. The expert may in any event be required to disclose the underlying facts or data on cross-examination.

Evidence rests upon our faith in human testimony as sanctioned by experience, that is, upon our general experience of the truth of the statements of men of integrity, having capacity and opportunity for observation, and without apparent influence from passion, or interest to pervert the truth. This belief is strengthened by our previous knowledge of the narrators, reputation for veracity; by the absence of conflicting testimony; and the presence of that which is corroborative and cumulative. It is upon this faith that the court or jury in a trial are largely obliged to rely.[72]

WHEN IS SCIENCE RESPECTED IN COURT, AND WHEN IS IT REJECTED?

Every scientist has heard of the outcome of some litigation that was allegedly inconsistent with scientific facts. There are several possible reasons for this. One is that it is much easier to explain scientific findings to a peer than to a layperson. The criteria that determine whether legal decisions are compatible with science depend on several factors. Among them are whether (a) the underlying scientific theory is solid, (b) the theory is related to the issue before the court, (c) the expert

---

[71] J. Joel M. Longenecker, Chicago, March 1, 1894, cited in Mundo, A.L., *The Expert Witness*, Parker & Baird Co., Los Angles, 1938.

[72] Greenleaf, cited in Mundo, A.L., *The Expert Witness*, Parker & Baird Co., Los Angles, 1938.

witness fully understands the science, (d) the expert applies the scientific principles correctly to the facts of the case, (e) there is sufficient data to support its application, (f) the expert witnesses can effectively communicate with the audience, (g) counsel understands and promotes the opinion correctly, (h) the judge rules that the scientific opinion is relevant and reliable, i.e., admissible, (I) the theory and the expert appear credible, (j) the trier of fact comprehends the theory and expert opinion, and (k) the trier of fact remembers the expert's testimony at the time of decisionmaking, and (l) the trier of fact fits it into the decision matrix.

Overlaying all this is that legal proceedings are adversary, science usually favors one side, and the disfavored party has an interest in confusing the trier of fact about the content and accuracy of the scientific findings.

Since lawyers and parties are not scientifically trained, they are not in a position to judge the quality of science, but they know whether the results are helpful to them. Note that in any litigation there are inevitably losers who will look for reasons to be critical of the jurors, the judge and the experts.

THE ROLE OF AUTHORITY

The rule of law depends on the delegation of authority to the State.[73] A person's authority can derive from his personal qualifications, or from his position.

The court bestows experts with much institutional authority, but, in the U.S. common law system, the link between an expert's authority and his subject matter competence is uncertain, because the expert's competence is reviewed by attorneys, rather than by scientists, and oral communication skills are as important in the selection of an expert as his understanding of the subject matter.[74]

Furthermore, judges are elected or appointed by people who are not fellow professionals, and the contact between judges and the constituents is usually short. The same difficulties exist concerning the qualifications of litigators and law firms, especially for large firms, where much of the work is performed by junior law clerks who have no direct contact with clients.[75]

The situation is different in the sciences, because authority is, at least partly, determined by peers who have worked with their colleagues, often for many years.

---

[73] The Preamble of the U.S. Constitution states: We the People of the United States, in order to form a more perfect union, establish justice, insure domestic tranquility, provide for the common defence, promote the general welfare, and secure the blessings of liberty to ourselves and our posterity, do ordain and establish this Constitution for the United States of America.

[74] The Civil Law system of continental Europe relies strongly on written review of expert reports by professional peers, i.e., scientific competitors who know the expert professionally and share with him a continuing interest in the scientific issues. Their reports are discoverable, and are reviewed by the court. In contrast, the U.S. common law system puts stronger emphasis on oral criticism by professional expert witnesses whose scientific opinions are not subject to scientific scrutiny by scientific peers, i.e., people on whom the future of their scientific credibility depends.

[75] Fleming, M., Lawyers, *Money and Success*, Quorum Books, Westport, CT (1997).

Thus, in academe, the link between a scientist's competence in his chosen professional field and the authority of his position is almost always strong, while the link between a professor's teaching ability and his academic rank is less certain, because colleagues do not normally attend each other's classes, and student do not work with their professors over long periods.

The same type of consideration applies in clinical medicine. The authority of mentors is strong, because it is based on experience shared over a long term; the authority of peers is less powerful among doctors who do not treat the same patients.

The weight of authority on court decisions is apparent when one compares its impact on the standard of proof in civil and criminal cases. While in a civil case, the plaintiff's burden of proof is by preponderance of evidence, i.e., a probability of 51%, in criminal cases the State must prove that the guilt is proven "beyond reasonable doubt," i.e., the standard is much higher, perhaps more than 90%. On first blush it would seem that it would be far more difficult to obtain a criminal conviction than to win a civil case, especially in criminal cases where the State must rely on circumstantial evidence, or the testimony of a paid informer, or a convict who has been promised a more lenient sentence for his own criminal activities if he testifies against the accused.

In reality, in civil trials, the plaintiff wins in only about 30% of the cases, while in criminal cases the State obtains conviction in more than 95% of cases. This is because most of us, including jurors, respect the power and authority of the State that are felt in every court room by the national and state flags that decorate the room, by the presence of armed bailiffs, and other insignia. It is relatively easy for this authority to undermine the trust in an isolated individual when he is accused by, and faces the presence of such powerful authority. Judges, and we all, give more weight to evidence presented by a person representing authority, than to evidence proffered by an defendant of uncertain societal ranking, especially when the latter appears in handcuffs and in chains.

The same effect is observed when a physician testifies in Court, and when a patient sues his physician for malpractice, because the public tends to respect the health care professions, and gives great weight to a physicians' opinion.

A difficult issue arises when an expert voices an opinion about a party's mental propensity to truthfulness, such as when a psychiatrist testifies that plaintiff has a borderline personality disorder, or is an alcoholic, and that all persons belonging to these groups cannot be trusted to testify truthfully.[76]

EXPERTS HAVE TO COMMUNICATE WITH DIFFERENT AUDIENCES

Experts need to be able to communicate effectively with five different types of audiences: their clients' attorneys, the opposing attorneys, the judge, the jury and with other experts for both sides. Each of the five audiences has distinct needs and strengths and weakness, and each requires a different approach.

---

[76] See Sutherland, P.K., Henderson, D.J., Expert Psychiatrists and Comments on Witness Credibility, 34 *Trial*, (7) 82-88 (July, 1998)

Communications with Attorneys for whom the Expert Testifies

Communications between attorneys and their experts should start as early as possible. For the plaintiff, this means before a complaint is formulated and filed. For the defendant, this is as soon as the defendant suspects that he might become the target of a lawsuit.

One cannot emphasize enough the importance of early and thorough communication between an expert and the attorney for his party, because, as explained in Chapter 7, there is nothing more deadly to an expert's impact than "friendly fire," i.e., being shot in the back by one's own counsel. Trial lawyers are advocates for a cause, and are hired to win. This is not the same as finding and promoting full and accurate facts. Furthermore, litigators are accustomed to picking and selecting facts that suit the situation best. Their instinct to find grey areas, shade interpretations and exercise discretion is so deeply ingrained that most subscribe to the mistaken belief that a scientific fact is nothing more than the collective judgment of a specialized professional community.[77]

Experts must make a conscious effort not to be drawn into a partisan and unrealistic assessment of the facts and legal issues in a case. One way of avoiding this is to insist on having access to and reviewing all records – including those available from the opposing party – before accepting an appointment. Another tool is to insist on prepayment of a sufficient retainer, so that the expert does not live under the fear that he will not be paid if his opinion is not satisfactory.[78] Trial lawyers are always in a hurry, and since experts usually account for a large part of the litigation expense, clients want to minimize their costs and experts virtually never are afforded the luxury of time they would need to thoroughly resolve problems.

In most cases, experts are selected and hired by the party's attorney rather than by the party. The expert should realize that even though the party's attorney represents the experts in motion hearings and at depositions, the attorney has a latent conflict between the interests of his client and his expert. Such conflicts can surface when an expert discovers that his report is not favorable to his party, or that the opposite party has a more valid scientific argument.

Communications with Fellow Experts and Opposing Experts

If a case involves more than one expert, it is essential that each expert knows all facts, and as many of the other experts' opinions as feasible, including those of all opposing experts. The most ignored interdisciplinary barrier is that between scientists and physicians. Even though scientists and physicians regularly join forces at trial regarding toxic causation and toxic injuries, their value systems and methodology are fundamentally different. While opinions in the field of molecular toxicology can be supported and falsified by testing, symptomatology and clinical toxicology usually cannot be falsified, because they are based on art. This should, however, not distract from the potential reliability of the latter.

---

[77] Peter W. Huber, *Galileo's Revenge: Junk Science in the Courtroom,* 18 (1991)

[78] Note that it is common among treating physicians to accept liens against a case, but that the same is considered unethical for scientific experts.

It is important to resolve the communication gap between the professions before trial; otherwise, the different language of the two groups may lead the trier of facts to the conclusion that the two groups disagree. By way of example, while a molecular toxicologist finds strong evidence for causation, a clinical toxicologist may conclude that a causal link to the toxic source might be that the molecular toxicologist has direct evidence for the presence of the poison, while the clinical toxicologist deals with a disease, i.e., a pattern of symptoms, say headaches, tiredness, inflammation of tissues and similar generic symptoms that can be evoked by many agents and not only the poison in question. The disagreement might be enhanced by general caution between the specialists, as explained in Chapter 6.

The Expert Deposition

While under old procedural rules it was common for parties to keep their theories secret and then ambush the opponent at trial with an expert, the modern tendency has been to open up discovery so that the parties can better understand each other's side, and hopefully settle without the need for a trial. There are many books that explain the procedures that take place at depositions.[79] Experts need to be aware that the primary purpose of depositions is not only to thoroughly discover the opinion of the opposing expert, but to prepare for impeachment.

If an expert is not fully prepared by counsel for his deposition he will likely contradict himself at trial and be impeached. Alternatively, his deposition may be used to exclude him or the controversial part of his testimony at trial.

Pretrial Hearings Before the Judge

The judge's job is to resolve disputes in the fairest and most efficient manner so that everybody can go on with their activities and lives. This is done by balancing the conflicting goals of our pluralistic and politically diverse society. The strength of the legal proceeding is its ability to produce localized, content-specific epistemological and normative understandings that are not subordinate to inappropriately universal claims and standards.

The judge is required to provide parties with a fair hearing. In the U.S. common law system, the judge is restricted to evidence presented by the parties. Furthermore, the judge has wide discretion to exclude facts that he does not deem to be relevant, and if the opposing counsel request striking of irrelevant material, and it is irrelevant, the judge must do so.

The Role of Evidence Rules

Scientist and physicians are often puzzled by the fact that U.S. attorneys spend much time arguing whether evidence is admissible. So are litigators from civil law countries. Obviously, the role of evidentiary rules depends on the type of law under which a country operates. As Wigmore stated:

---

[79] Bronstein, D.A., *Law for the Expert Witness*, Lewis Publishers, Boca Raton, 1993, and Matson, J.V., *Effective Expert Witnessing* (2nd edition) Lewis Publishers, Boca Raton, FL (1994).

The apportionment of the task of adducing evidence is one of the most characteristic features of the Anglo-American System. It is wholly placed upon the parties to the litigation; it is not required or expected of the judge. In this respect, the emphasis is in contrast to the continental system [of Europe].[80]

In civil law countries, the judge is in charge of the investigation and shapes the scope of a litigation by his own investigation and formal requests for information to the parties. In the common law system, the court must make its decision on the basis of the evidence presented by the parties. The latter's tool for shaping issues is his decision whether the evidence that is proffered is admissible or not admissible As far as expert testimony is concerned, the most important criteria are whether evidence is relevant and reliable. This subject is explored and explained in Chapter 4.

Whether the Daubert and Joiner rules apply depends on the jursidction. Among the rules that currently apply in Federal court are:

FRE 401. Definition of "Relevant Evidence." Relevant evidence means evidence having the tendency to make the existence of any fact that is of consequence to the determination of the action more probable than it would be without the evidence. FRE 401

and,

FRE 403. Exclusion of Relevant Evidence on Grounds of Prejudice, Confusion, or Waste of Time. Although relevant, evidence may be excluded if its probative value is substantially outweighed by the danger of unfair prejudice, confusion of the issues, or misleading the jury, or by considerations of undue delay, waste of time, or needless presentation of cumulative evidence. FRE 403

The recent rule that the judge should expand the *Daubert* inquiry and determine whether expert opinions are "reliable" or whether the "analytical gap between the data and the expert opinion is too large" is not statutory law, but was established by the U.S. Supreme Court in the decision of *General Electric v Joiner.*[1] See Chapter 4.

Another difference between the common law judge and his continental brethren is that the first does not conduct any independent investigation. However, the common law judge is empowered with a great deal of discretion to screen evidence and determine which of the evidence is admissible. When attorneys do not provide him with what he needs, FRE 706 provides him with the power to appoint his own expert. This procedure is built on legal theory that goes back to 1794:

---

[80] Wigmore, J. H., *Evidence in Trials at Common Law*, (9th edition, Chadbourne, D. H., ed.), par. 2483, p. 276. Little Brown (1981).

It is the duty of the Judge to receive every offer of evidence, apparently material, suggested to him, though the parties themselves through negligence, ignorance, or corrupt collusion, should not bring it forward. A judge is not placed in that high situation merely as a passive instrument of parties. He has a duty of his own, independent of them, and that duty is to investigate the truth. However, the common law judge is not merely a referee between the parties.[81]

However, until recently, this power has been very rarely used.[82] Several parties have called for increased use,[83,84] and the *Joiner* decision now expressly encourages federal trial judges to make more extensive use of this option. The problem with the use of so-called neutral experts is that the judge and jury have no opposing expert to point out limits and weaknesses in scientific opinions.

Testimony Before the Jurors

As explained in Chapter 2, most litigators believe that jurors are more competent to decide cases that involve scientific issues, if counsel do a competent job.

Some of the communication problems with jurors are that (1) part of the communication is a one-way street, (2) much of the communication takes place under time pressure, and (3) the communication takes place in an adversarial setting where destruction of arguments and raising doubts take precedence over collaborative thinking. But as shown in Chapters 2, 3, 7, 9, 11 and 12, there are well- established techniques for effectively communicating with juries.

While scientists apply rational valid methodology and seek universal answers, jurors are charged with deciding a case in accordance with local law and prevailing community standards. They do this by (a) judging the credibility of experts, and (b) using common sense based on their own life experience to balance conflicting priorities and irreconcilable information. Whether this procedure is appropriate depends on the nature of the case before the court. Common sense is suitable, say, to determine to what extent a community which suffers a shortage of physicians might want to condone an isolated case of medical negligence.

Common sense would tell such a community to be somewhat more tolerant than a community that suffers from a surplus of physicians. However, common sense and common sense rationalizations are a ticket to disaster when applied to

---

[81] Burke, E., *Report of Committee on Warren Hastings' Trial*, 31 Parl. Hist. 348 (1794)

[82] Cecil, J.S., in *Reference Manual on Scientific Evidence,* Federal Judicial Center, Joe S. Cecil, Carol E. Drew, Marie Cordisco, Dean P. Miletich, EDC. (1994).

[83] Carnegie Commission on Science and Technology, *Science and Technology in Judicial Decision Making: Creating Opportunities and Meeting Challenges* (1993).

[84] The National Council of Lawyers and Scientists was established in 1984. Half of the members are appointed by the AAAS, half by the ABA section on Technology. The reports are not available to the public or AAAS members (personal observation of the author, March 1996).

scientific problems. As indicated above, chemistry offers many examples, because chemistry not only requires careful experimental planning and keen observation of experiments, but the ability to put aside perceptions and use theoretical reasoning to interpret the results. Thus, the volume of two mixed liquids is not the sum of the combined volumes, but is determined by intermolecular forces. For example, in a mixture of ethyl alcohol and water, the total volume is smaller than the sum of the two separate volumes. Another example is the combustion of coal. For more than a thousand years chemists believed that the carbon released phlogiston during combustion and thereby lost weight, until Lavoisier demonstrated that during combustion carbon combines with oxygen and gains weight.

CONCLUSIONS

The frictions that arise at the interface between science, medicine and the courts are symptoms of cultural problems that started during the Renaissance and the Enlightenment - periods that encouraged medicine to think of itself as scientific, and people to perceive themselves as independent individuals. This led to an over-emphasis on technical specialization that neglects the interdependence of science, medicine and law.

The frictions are enhanced by the fact that the practitioners of science, medicine and law are initiates who understand their own field better than anyone else can, and who are reluctant to share control with non-initiates. The rivalry is further complicated by the fact that, while scientific laws have eternal and universal validity, and take precedence over legislation, the interpreters of legislation, i.e., the courts, have a more complete knowledge of their field and enjoy statutory power over the interpreters of the sciences.

The conflict between science, medicine and the courts is most acute in toxic injury cases and class actions,[85] where the methodology necessary to find the universally valid answers that science needs[86] is in conflict with the purpose of the

---

[85] The breast implant cases offer a good example of the problems. First, the law favors litigation against only one of the potentially responsible parties, the product manufacturers. It does not reach the cosmetic surgeons who continued to recommend implants after 1974, when manufacturers started warning them that the average lifetime of the implants would be shorter than that of the patients. Second, the emphasis of the litigations on immunity issues belittles other issues, such as whether the patients gave fully informed consent. Third, the class action format did not always allow adequate distinction between the causation experienced by individuals; and fourth, scientific questions concerning immune system damage are not suitable for adversary adjudication by trial, or by panels of select scientific experts. For an overview of the more than 27,000 cases, and the status of the class action see, e.g., the Internet site maintained by the Federal Judicial Center that provides current information and links to other sites. <http://www.fjc.gov/ BREIMLIT/ mdl926.htm>

[86] The question of whether it would be better to resolve scientific questions with the help of regulatory action under the Administrative Procedure Act – which offers a more open and far better scientific discourse – raises issues that go beyond the scope of this chapter.

courts, i.e., to produce localized, content-specific epistemological and normative understandings that are not subordinate to inappropriately universal claims and standards.[87] This is regrettable, because the legal system is an important and unique tool for balancing the cost of defective goods between the manufacturer and the buyer, and for giving manufacturers an incentive to control the quality of products sold to consumers.

The *Daubert* and *Joiner* decisions reflect the fact that the oral, adversary setting of the U.S. common law courts is not conducive for solving interdisciplinary problems, that litigators and judges lack the facilities and the basic scientific training necessary to handle scientific issues that arise in our contemporary society, and that scientists lack the basic training in social sciences necessary to understand the importance of their participation in the legal process.

Neither *Daubert* nor any other legal rule can substitute for the lack of functional scientific literacy of litigators who have avoided mathematics and science courses since junior high school, but, nevertheless, take it upon themselves to litigate scientific issues. Basic scientific literacy cannot be solved by courses on scientific issues that are currently in litigation. It requires at least rudimentary scientific education for litigators and judges, and an equally basic education in civics for scientists.

In the meantime, the *Daubert* and *Joiner* rulings present judges, experts and litigators with a new challenge in communication. Each group needs to become better aware of the scope, strength and weakness of its own, as well as the others' professions. This requires effective communication; effective communication requires knowledge of the audience; knowledge of the audience requires respect and understanding for the position of other people, and the latter requires that we overcome the overly adversarial attitude that has taken over current society, and has been accentuated by the commercial sensationalism of the media.

The present situation could be improved if professional experts would put more emphasis on scientific content than on adversarial rhetoric, and if counsel would more frequently use active scientists as scientific experts and for evaluating expert reports rather than specialists in persuasion. Civil and criminal litigation offers good scientists an opportunity to demonstrate to the court and the public the value of rational reasoning.

---

[87] Jasanoff, S., *Science at Bar*, Harvard University Press, 222 (1995).

2 Are Jurors Smart Enough to Understand Scientific Evidence?

By Patricia M. Ayd and Merle M. Troeger

CONTENTS

INTRODUCTION

> *The jury system puts a ban upon intelligence and honesty, and a premium upon ignorance, stupidity and perjury. It is a shame that we must continue to use a worthless system because it was good a thousand years ago. I desire to tamper with the jury law. I wish to so alter it as to put a premium on intelligence and character, and close the jury box against idiots, blacklegs, and people who do not read newspapers.*
> Mark Twain, *Roughing It*[1]

Many lawyers and scientists are tempted to agree with Mark Twain's disdain for the jury system. Dissatisfaction with the jury system is often expressed when jurors are asked to evaluate scientific evidence. People ask the question, "Are jurors smart enough to understand scientific evidence and to apply that evidence to arrive at just resolutions of disputes?"

The answer to this question will depend upon the respondent's underlying beliefs about the intellectual ability of the American public, the value of the jury system and the roles of judges, jurors, attorneys, and experts in that system. Whether the answer is "yes" or "no," the underlying basis for the belief should be explored. Is the answer based on review of empirical data, positive or negative personal experience, rumor, personal opinion, or gut instinct?

If one concludes that jurors are not smart enough to understand scientific evidence, then who in society is going to resolve disputes between citizens or

---

[1] Mark Twain's *Roughing It*, New York, Harper (1913).

between the government and the citizens? Do we entrust scientists, lawyers, judges, politicians, or only the college educated to resolve these matters? Are these individuals, alone or in concert, better suited to arrive at informed and just decisions than a jury representing a cross-section of the population?

REASONS OFFERED TO JUSTIFY RESOLUTION OF DISPUTES WITHOUT JURIES

The following reasons are commonly offered to explain why jurors should not be involved in the resolution of disputes, especially those involving scientific or other complicated evidence.

- Jurors do not have the intellectual capacity to learn necessary information
- Jurors are uneducated and thus lack basic skills needed to understand and learn complex information
- Jurors are not sophisticated enough to evaluate evidence critically
- Jurors have short attention spans and are not able to focus long enough to understand complicated evidence
- It is too difficult to break down complex information into simple units for jury comprehension
- Jurors are easily swayed by irrelevant factors such as:
    The physical appearance of witnesses or parties,
    Prejudice against certain organizations or persons,
    Sympathy for the plight of the injured plaintiff,
    Paper credentials of the witnesses,
    The slick presentation of the evidence rather than the content of the information, and
- Jurors will ignore the law in favor of their own personal preferences and beliefs.

REASONS OFFERED TO SUPPORT USE OF THE JURY SYSTEM

In spite of the occasional bad press created by seemingly incomprehensible verdicts, the jury system is not without its supporters who contend the jury system:

- Provides a needed balance between the rule of law and the wisdom of the common man,
- Insures that the general public maintain active involvement in the development and application of our laws,
- Creates public confidence in the legal system,
- Promotes the concept of justice with reasoned application of the law,
- Creates a dynamic system of law which reflects the values of the general public,
- Prevents judges, the legislature, or the intellectual class from exercising too

much power, and
- Allows the voice of the people to be heard in our legal system.

SEVENTH AMENDMENT TO THE UNITED STATES CONSTITUTION

The seventh amendment to the United States Constitution, which is unlikely to be changed in the foreseeable future, specifically grants citizens the right to a jury trial.

Amendment VII

In suits at common law, where the value in controversy shall exceed twenty dollars, the right of trial by jury shall be preserved, and no fact tried by a jury, shall be otherwise re-examined in any Court of the United States, than according to the rules of the common law.

Given the constitutional mandate, the jury system in some form is here to stay unless participants to a dispute voluntarily choose another mechanism of dispute resolution.

THE JURY'S ROLE IN THE RESOLUTION OF DISPUTES

The role of the jury is to render a verdict based only on the evidence and the law presented at the trial to resolve a dispute between the parties who are before them in the courtroom.[2] The role of the jury is not to decide public policy, resolve disagreements between scientists, or settle similar disputes between other parties.[3]

---

[2] The fact that it is the role of the jury to render a verdict for the parties in the courtroom is not to say that individual jury verdicts involving issues of importance to the general public cannot affect the manner in which business is conducted in this country and around the world. One verdict in favor of a woman burned by hot coffee at a fast food restaurant can result in a change in the industry standard for the temperature of coffee. A jury verdict finding birth defects from a particular drug can affect the use of that drug by medical providers. However, the fact that there is a verdict against a manufacturer of a drug in one instance does not mean that there must be a verdict in the next instance. Jury verdicts are not based on the scientific process. They are the result of numerous factors throughout the trial and deliberation process. No two juries are the same.

[3] Though the jury is deciding a dispute between individuals, in this day of instant communication, there is no doubt that results of individual jury trials involving issues of public concern can affect how those cases are viewed by parties involved in similar litigation or the general public. However, it is clear that the results of one trial do not dictate the results in another. Tobacco companies have lost and won suits by smokers who claim that they were misled or injured. Not every breast implant case, or toxic exposure to a particular chemical, results in the same

THE ROLE OF SCIENCE IN THE LEGAL SYSTEM

Scientific facts, principles, and theories are simply evidence, along with all the other evidence, to be considered by the jury and do not necessarily control the jury's decision in a case. The jury may understand and believe all the science, but return a verdict for the opposing side because they were convinced by other evidence which did not relate to a scientific issue. For instance, a jury may not believe that the plaintiff was exposed to the chemical he claims caused his injuries. They may even believe that the plaintiff was not injured at all.

Admissibility

The expert is a witness called into the courtroom to help the jurors understand the scientific evidence. Scientific facts, principles, and theories are presented and explained to the jury through expert testimony. Expert witnesses testify according to the Rules of Civil Procedure. The standard for admitting expert testimony is:

If scientific, technical, or other specialized knowledge will assist the trier of fact to understand the evidence or to determine a fact in issue, a witness qualified as an expert by knowledge, skill, experience training, or education, may testify thereto in the form of an opinion or otherwise.[4]

Credibility

The fact that a scientific expert's testimony is admitted into evidence does not mean the jury will rely upon or even believe that testimony. Jurors are free to consider all of the evidence in a case and to believe or disbelieve evidence based on a many factors including credibility of the witnesses – even expert witnesses. Specifically, jurors are given an instruction which states in some manner:

You have heard evidence in this case from witnesses who have testified as experts. The law allows experts to express opinions on subjects involving their special knowledge, training and skill, experience or research. The jury shall determine what weight, if any, should be given their testimony as with any other witness.

---

resolution. These verdicts reflect the fact that jurors do pay attention to the evidence presented and can make independent decisions based on that evidence. These verdicts may also reflect the failure of judges and attorneys to insure that the jurors have sufficient and comprehensible evidence to resolve the dispute presented to them.

[4] Federal Rules of Civil Procedure Rule 702. The rules for introduction of expert testimony in state courts generally follow this rule in substance if not form.

In one of the few studies examining the believability of experts,[5] the researchers found that jurors' perception of an expert's impartiality is a dominant factor in the expert's credibility. The more impartial an expert seemed to a juror, the more believable they reported that expert to be. Jurors who participated in the study had no difficulty rejecting or ignoring the testimony of experts they believed were "hired guns."[6]

Weight of Testimony

Even if jurors find the scientific experts credible, they may not rely on the scientific testimony in reaching their verdict. While many cases tried by jurors involve scientific concepts of one type or another, from simple physical principles involved in an automobile accident, to complex causation of injury in toxic tort cases, the impact of the scientific evidence in the jury's resolution of the case may vary greatly.

Experts may believe that their testimony should be given special consideration, but a juror is free to consider their testimony equally with all of the evidence. In fact, jurors in a study conducted by the American Bar Association ("ABA")[7] were almost uniformly unimpressed with the experts who testified in the four study cases. Even in the most complex case involving trade secrets, the jurors concluded that the experts added little to the case. Despite the technical and scientific sophistication required to understand and follow the testimony concerning the processes involved in manufacturing hydrocracking catalysts, jurors recognized the points on which expert opinions differed. Still, an expert who "explained the chemistry mess well" and "put things in perspective for the layman" reportedly had little influence on their decisions.[8]

The weight given to the scientific evidence will depend on how effectively the expert presents that evidence to the jury. The ABA study concluded:

> Experts who had an impact on the jury were those who had an independeent involvement with the subject matter of the case, had spent time and worked to become familiar with it, and were able to give testimony that was helpful to the jury and presented in words that they could under-stand.[9]

---

[5] Shuman, D. W., Champagne, A., Whitaker, E., Assessing the Believability of Expert Witnesses: Science in the Jurybox, 37 *Jurimetrics* 23.

[6] *Jury Comprehension in Complex Cases*, Report of the Special Committee on Jury Comprehension of the ABA Section of Litigation, 40 (1989).

[7] *Jury Comprehension in Complex Cases, supra.*

[8] *Jury Comprehension in Complex Cases, supra.*

[9] *Jury Comprehension in Complex Cases, supra,* 42.

JURY RESEARCH

Though complaints of the jury system abound, surprisingly little research has been conducted by social scientists to help trial lawyers and experts understand how jurors acquire and evaluate scientific evidence. A jury deliberates in strict privacy. Federal law (18 U.S.C. §1508) forbids videotaping the deliberations of actual jurors. The ABA study of jurors included videotaping a group of alternate jurors while the regular jury deliberated behind closed doors. During the trial, none of the jurors knew during the trial who would serve as regular jurors and who would serve as alternates. All jurors sat in the same jury box, heard the same case, listened to the same lawyers, considered the same expert testimony and received the same jury instructions.

[The] videotapes revealed that jurors were often bored and frustrated, and had difficulty understanding the instructions on the law. Nevertheless, the jurors in these cases seemed capable of assisting each other in correcting omissions and mistaken impressions; and despite the sometimes chaotic nature of their deliberations their final verdicts appear to be fair.[10]

In the ABA study, regular jurors and alternate jurors in each of four cases were interviewed following their verdicts. In a sexual harassment case, the judge had told the ABA interviewers that "he was on the fence" about the verdict, but if the plaintiff prevailed, the damages would be in the range of $25,000 to $50,000. Demonstrating the judge's prediction that the verdict could go either way, the regular jury returned a verdict for the plaintiff in the amount of $50,000, and the alternate jury reached a defense verdict.[11]

In an antitrust case, the judge told the interviewer that if he had been the fact finder, he would have rendered a verdict for the defendant. Of the eleven real and alternate jurors interviewed, a majority favored the defense case. Most jurors were able to apply portions of the jury instructions and explain the basis for their decision.

In sum, jurors reached a reasoned verdict and came to that decision by considering the crucial facts and applying the relevant, albeit somewhat confusing, law. A modest number of jurors were clearly out of their league and ill-equipped to understand the issues. Both the real and alternate juries had at least one member who clearly grasped those issues and who could educate the others. The more able jurors directed the discussion and a seemingly sensible verdict resulted.[12]

---

[10] *Jury Comprehension in Complex Case, supra,* 60.

[11] *Jury Comprehension in Complex Cases, supra,* 12, 13.

[12] *Jury Comprehension in Complex Cases, supra,* 16.

In an insurance fraud case, both the regular jury and the alternate jury reached a guilty verdict. All jurors concluded that the circumstantial evidence pointed to the defendant's role in the conspiracy to defraud. They compared the two interpretations of a given event and tried to determine which was more plausible.

To give the defendant the further benefit of any doubt, the jury attempted to reconstruct his version of events and argued its validity. "There were about 6 different instances where the defendant had disagreed with what a government witness had said and we took each one and tried to determine which one would have the reason to lie. ."
This method of resolution suggests that jurors were diligent in evaluating the government's charges. They seem to have carefully reviewed the instructions and tried very hard to accurately reconstruct the witnesses' testimony. . . The data indicates that the jurors grasped the legal concepts involved in the case, interpreted the facts in a reasonable way and reached a justifiable verdict.[13]

The most scientifically complex case studied by the ABA Special Committee was a claim for misappropriation of trade secrets that included highly technical scientific evidence concerning the manufacture of hydrocracking catalysts (used to break down crude oil molecules), and subtle differences between patents for similar chemical processes. The trial consumed six weeks and twenty-five witnesses testified. In addition to the plaintiff corporation's claims against the defendants (which the judge dismissed during the trial), the defendants asserted numerous counterclaims against the plaintiff. The regular jury deliberated for ten hours and returned a verdict for the counterclaiming defendants on all except one count. That jury also found one scientist liable for disclosing trade secrets and awarded $100,000.00 in damages. The alternate jury returned a verdict against the same scientist, but on different grounds (breach of employment contract with each of the corporate counterclaimants and misappropriation of trade secrets), and, in contrast to the regular jury, awarded total damages of $5,000,000.00. Post verdict interviews with all jurors showed that most jurors viewed the case quite similarly, but that the give-and-take of the deliberative process, coupled with a desire to reach a verdict, led to compromise. The investigators noted

The two juries' sentiments about the case were not as disparate as they may appear at first blush. Although the regular jury found for the [counterclaimants] on only one claim, and the alternate jury found in their favor on three claims, five of the six regular jurors argued for the latter verdict. These five jurors finally agreed to withdraw their proposed verdict for the [counterclaimants] on the two breach of contract claims if

---

[13] *Jury Comprehension in Complex Cases, supra,* 19, 20.

a sixth holdout juror, who was opposed to any findings of liability, went along with them on the breach of fiduciary duty claim. Their desire to resolve the case as a group ultimately led these jurors to compromise with one holdout who saw things in a different way.[14.]

The ABA study involved only four complex cases, and there were disparities in the results reached by the regular and alternate juries. We can speculate about why these disparities occurred: The same evidence may support more than one reasonable result. The interpersonal dynamics of each group undoubtedly differed. Perhaps the alternates were less committed to achieving a "right" result than the regular jurors. The individual jurors on the two panels may have had different levels of education and skill which resulted in different understanding of the information presented, Certainly, different individuals reacted differently to the same information and material.

CONCLUSION

Unlike the sciences, where replication of results demonstrates that a hypothesis tends to be correct, replicating a jury verdict result does not carry the same meaning. A jury verdict represents a collective understanding and evaluation by a particular group of people who share a common experience of jury service but may share little else. If a verdict is supported by a reasonable interpretation of the evidence, it is acceptable.

Although jurors are generally not educated in the law or science, they bring to the courtroom assorted backgrounds of life experience, education, intelligence, attention level, memory capacity, world view, and understanding that deserve respect. Jurors should participate in legal decision making, even when scientific or technical issues are involved.

By and large, the jury system works well when attorneys and expert witnesses recognize, respect, and improve the capabilities of jurors. Actual experience with jurors and juror commitment leads us to conclude that, in all but the most complex cases, jurors readily understand and weigh scientific evidence when it is well presented.[15]

---

[14] *Jury Comprehension in Complex Cases,* supra, 21-23.

[15] In those few cases where the information may be so complex that it is anticipated that a juror cannot understand, it should not be assumed that a judge is going to understand either. Judges, as a group, have no more scientific knowledge than jurors as a group. In actuality, a jury panel often may include one or more individuals who have some scientific background. Judges often are judges because they were lawyers, and they were lawyers because they didn't understand science. If a case involves complicated scientific evidence that cannot be broken down into understandable information for the nonprofessional, then perhaps that is the case in which to seek agreement with opposing counsel to resolve the matter through some

Other chapters in this book offer many practical ideas for presenting scientific evidence persuasively. These suggestions recognize the jurors' individual learning styles, life perspectives and their collective desire to render a fair verdict. Jurors can understand scientific evidence when attorneys, experts and parties remember that it is their responsibility to provide understandable information to the jury.

---

other process. Utilize the talents and skills of the clients and attorneys to come up with an innovative process that works. Consider an arbitration panel which is composed of a judge and two scientists. The judge is knowledgeable about the legal procedure and evidence. The scientists can educate the judge about the scientific issues. Other creative avenues can be used in those rare cases where a jury or judge trial is not the appropriate forum to resolve the dispute.

3 The Fundamental Differences Between Science and Law

Robert A. Bohrer

CONTENTS

INTRODUCTION

For at least twenty years, there has been a significant debate about the difficulty of incorporating science into legal decisionmaking[1] and, more recently, that difficulty has become part of the very heated debate over the impact of tort litigation generally, and product liability litigation in particular, on our economy and society. So-called "Mass Tort Cases," such as the Bendectin cases and, most recently, the Silicone breast implant cases, have been highly publicized and politicized examples of the difficulties of integrating science into judicial decisionmaking.[2] My perhaps overly ambitious goal for this chapter is to try to reveal something of what lies at the core of the difficulty and that which I believe accounts for so much of the current frustration over the role of science in the courtroom. The title "The Fundamental Differences Between Law and Science" is intended to convey that this chapter is not about solutions to these issues, but rather an attempt to describe more fully the nature of the problem. The first section of the chapter will describe the three basic differences between the world of science and the world of law: science is digital, replicable/general, and objective/universal; law is analogical, unpredictable/particular, and normative/contingent. Part II provides examples of scientific and legal reasoning, as illustrations that underscore and clarify the fundamental differences discussed here. The conclusion provides a brief discussion of the Silicone breast implant litigation as a short case study in which the fundamental differences between law and science are manifested. The conclusion reached in Part III is that, in a great many toxic torts cases, the

---

[1] See Goldberg, S., *Culture Clash: Law and Science in America* (1994); Bernstein, A., Essay: Formed by Thalidomide: Mass Torts as a False Cure For Toxic Exposure, 97 *Colum. L. Rev.* 2153 (1997).

[2] Bernstein, *supra* note 1.

fundamental differences between science and law require a distortion of the concept of the legal causation, which is traditionally individual and particular, and is an essential element of our sense of justice or fairness.

Part I. The Fundamental Differences Between Law and Science

There are at least three fundamental differences that need to be understood. First, science, at least the business of doing research and gathering data and analyzing and evaluating results, is a "digital" process. Digital is used here to indicate that scientific research is generally intended to examine variables that are discrete, well-understood, and have quantitative attributes that allow the results of experiments to be quantitatively reported, even if only in a binary, 0 or 1 sense.[3] Clearly, this is a generalization, but law is analogical, at least the business of courts deciding cases is leaving aside what legislators do for the moment. The variables, such as "negligence," or "intent to do harm," or "material non-disclosure," are "soft" conceptual categories that have no fixed boundaries and need reinterpretation in every difficult or interesting case.

Second, science, by virtue of the nature of its variables (they must be attributes that are shared by a number of subjects, e.g., weight, or pH, or more complex, aggregated categories, such as "protein") aims at replicability and generality. Science is only science if it is predictable (that is, replicable and general; the same experiment under the same quantitatively defined conditions should yield the same, predicted results).   Law, on the other hand, by virtue of its variables (e.g., reasonable care) is particular and of very limited predictability.   The "soft" variables of law require an analogical process of comparing similarities and differences to determine the best fit between a case that needs to be decided and the universe of prior cases (precedents) and their "rules."

The replicability of science is well known, but the closely related "generalizing" function of science is equally fundamental, but rarely considered. Science is inherently incapable of making a coherent, scientific statement about what attributes of an individual are "unique" in the sense that they are not shared with any other individual.[4] It is a scientific truism that everyone's fingerprints are unique, but in order to make a prediction about the relationship between one's fingerprints and one's, let's say, susceptibility for cancer, you must first decide what COMMON patterns of fingerprints should be categorized and looked at for correlation with cancer rates. The uniqueness of a fingerprint is meaningless to science;[5] its shared

---

[3] For example, a researcher may be investigating the question of whether a particular chemical signal to a cell is delivered by a protein molecule or a non-protein molecule. If the particular messenger is isolated and purified, the categories of protein and non-protein are "digital," 0 or 1 variables in the sense used here.

[4] Percy, W., *Message in the Bottle* (1984).

[5] Uniqueness is meaningless to science except as a replicable prediction – i.e., "if the fingerprints of a thousand different individuals are compared, no two individuals will have identical fingerprints," is the predictive, scientifically meaningful form of the statement that individual fingerprints are unique. The statement "this individual's fingerprints have a unique whorl that is precisely 2 mm. in diameter" is either a simple statement of fact without scientific significance or, alternatively, the

attributes with other fingerprints is the beginning of the possibility of scientific inquiry.[6]

Law, however, must acknowledge uniqueness. It is not a nonsense statement for a court to say "this is a case of first impression." Rather, it is an admission that the particular case presents facts and questions that have never before been considered by the court and, in important dimensions, is unlike any previous precedent in the universe of cases that came before. At such a juncture, a court will consider its similarity and differences to a number of other cases, ultimately deciding the case by its goodness of fit (or perceived relationship of fairness and justice) to one strand of precedents rather than another. The only "binary" variable that can describe the intended result is the maximally "soft" category of "fair" or "unfair" result.

Third, and closely related to the distinction between science's future-oriented, generalizing nature and law's past-oriented, particularizing nature, is the distinction between science's goal of objectivity and universalism and law's inherent normative and contingent nature. Science aims, although history is filled with sad exceptions,[7] at discovering and applying categories that are objectively derived, and which not only permit the prediction of future events, but can do so universally— that is, the results of the experiment should not vary whether it is done in Las Vegas or on a moon of Jupiter, provided that the conditions are properly controlled. By contrast, law is inherently normative-- its categories can only be as universal as the values of the community from which the category is derived, which is generally not universal at all.

A distinguished scientist and good friend of mine, Dr. Clifford Grobstein, whose principal career was as a developmental biologist, late in his career turned his efforts to issues of science and public policy, writing a book entitled *Science and the Unborn: Choosing Human Futures* (1988). It was a very well done effort to shed some light on the debate over abortion in our society. Grobstein's approach

---

implied scientific statement that a search of a database of fingerprints would not turn up an identical whorl (a predictive, replicable, binary statement).

[6] For example, to actually do fingerprint identification with today's technology requires that variables representing a variety of non-individually unique fingerprint characteristics:

> Finger imaging is the process of using computer equipment to scan fingerprint impressions and to extract identifiable characteristics. This is done in sufficient detail to enable the computer to distinguish a single fingerprint from images of thousands, or even millions, of fingerprints that have been stored in the computer's memory through the automated process. The computer's scanning and mapping algorithms convert the spatial relationship of a fingerprint's minutiae points as well as the ridge direction and ridge contour information into a digitized representation of the fingerprint.

Constance, Jennifer K., Comment: Automated Fingerprint Identification Systems: Issues And Options Surrounding Their Use to Prevent Welfare Fraud, 59 *Alb. L. Rev.* 399, 401 (1995) (citations omitted).

[7] See, e.g., Gould, Stephen J., *The Mismeasure of Man* (1996).

to abortion attempted to relate particular objective criteria that he believed philosophically could be tied to the acquisition of legal rights, such as the ability to feel pain and self-consciousness, to what science could tell us about the stages of fetal development. Of course, Cliff's effort was largely doomed to fail,[8] because the objective scientific evidence concerning fetal development has little to do with the normative and socially contingent category of legal person. Almost all Americans were appalled at the recent news of a young college student who killed her baby, or the high school student who gave birth to her baby and killed it during her high school prom. Yet we know that there are large areas of the world where infanticide is not only not shocking, it is expected.[9] Science can tell us how many chromosomes are in the nucleus of a normal human cell, but science cannot tell us what it is to be a normal human, a question for law, with all its normative and contingent difficulties.

Part II. Paradigmatic Examples of Law and Science

It may be useful to use a few examples of science and law to illustrate the fundamental differences described in Part I. I have included only a single example from science, from a recent issue of *Science*, because I feel that the basic features of scientific inquiry, as I have attempted to relay them here, are relatively easily understood and well represented by the example. The August 8th issue of *Science* contained a Technical Comment entitled "Basal Forebrain Neuronal Loss in Mice Lacking Neurotrophin Receptor p75."[10] The purpose of the research was to determine the effect on brain development of the neurotrophic ligands to the Neurotrophin Receptor p75. The hypothesis was that if the ligands to the receptor were significant to the normal development of the mouse brain, mice lacking the receptor, and thus, unable to respond to the stimuli of the receptor's ligands (primarily NGF, or nerve growth factor), would show detectable physiological or behavioral differences from normal mice. The central findings of the research were presented in a table in which the variables are all nicely represented in quantitative form – the septal volume of the mice forebrains in cubic micrometers, the number of Choline Acetyltransferase positive and tyrosine receptor kinase A (trkA) positive neurons, as well as the total number of neurons. The numbers are reported in terms

---

[8] By this, I mean that abortion debaters took little note of what he wrote and his book is now out of print. A recent Lexis search of legal periodicals yielded 5 citations to *Science and the Unborn: Choosing Human Futures* and of those only two seemed to deal seriously with his argument, rather than using his book as a technical reference. *See*, Ronald Dworkin, Unenumerated Rights: Whether and How Roe Should be Overruled, 59 U. *Chi. L. Rev.* 381 (1992); John A. Robertson, Reproductive Technology And Reproductive Rights: in The Beginning: The Legal Status of Early Embryos, 76 *Va. L. Rev.* 437 (1990).

[9] Clark, *Two's company, three's allowed*, The Sunday Telegraph Limited, May 3, 1998, at FEATURES; p.04. ("Polyandry has been forced upon Himalayan peoples by the high rate of female infanticide, which naturally results in a shortage of females in later life, but it is primarily seen by anthropologists as a means by which a society short of land can reduce its birth-rate.")

[10] Peterson, et al., *Science*, 277, 837 (8 August 1997).

of Mean, variance, p value and change between wild type controls and p75 negative mutants. However, I picked this example not only because it is such a clear, one-variable experiment that examines a number of endpoints in such nice digital form, but because the results are vigorously debated in a Response[11] that I believe even further underscores my basic generalizations. The response deals with the limitations of the experimental methodology in determining the endpoints reported on in the main comment, principally whether the counts could be accurate given the problems of different methods of counting one-dimensional sections of a three-dimensional area. This is, I believe, a perfect example of science as I have argued it. It is digital: it is about variables that lend themselves (more or less) to quantification, about the relationship between two variables (the p75 receptor and neuronal forebrain development); and, it is about doing experiments that are replicable and predictable. Perhaps, it is even more important for purposes of this discussion, to recognize that it is NOT about why any individual mouse in either the wild-type group or the mutant group had more neurons than another individual mouse in the same group.

Now, for some examples from law. One of the best examples of the lawyer's art might be the famous opinion of Justice Blackburn in the intermediate appellate court in *Fletcher v. Rylands* (L.R. 1 Ex. 265, 1866) dealing with water collected in a reservoir that had broken through an underground abandoned mine shaft, and flooded a neighboring landowner's mines. Justice Blackburn drew on cases of cattle escaping and doing damage, cellars being invaded by filth from neighboring privies, and habitations made unhealthy by the fumes from neighboring alkali works to produce the conclusion that

> ...the person who for his own purposes brings on his lands and collects and keeps there anything likely to do mischief if it escapes, must keep it in at his peril, and, if he does not do so, is prima facie answerable for all the damage which is the natural consequence of its escape....And upon authority, this we think is established to be the law whether the thing so brought be beasts, or water, or filth, or stenches.

So, by analogizing water in a reservoir to cattle in an enclosure and waste in a privy, Justice Blackburn created the "soft" category of "things likely to do mischief" to provide analogical guidance to future generations of lawyers, each concerned not just with the similarity of their problem (be it natural gas deposits or water from a broken pipe) to *Fletcher v. Rylands*, but also the differences, and not with predicting the future, but with satisfying our sense of justice about the past.

As a second example of the lawyer's analogical art, let me share with you an exercise I impose on my first-year law students in their study of Torts, the course which is primarily concerned with individual claims for compensation for personal injuries. One of the first cases we study is entitled *Garratt v. Dailey*, 304 P.2d 681 (Wash. 1956), which was a suit by a woman against a boy who was five years and nine months old when he pulled away a chair as she was about to sit down upon it, causing her to fall to the ground and break her hip. The case was brought as an action for battery, which required the plaintiff to prove that the defendant boy had the intent to cause her to have a harmful physical contact (in this case with the

[11] Hagg, Van Der Zee, et al., *Science*, 277, 839 (8 August 1997).

ground). The point of the case then becomes that the requirement of proving intent in the case meant proving that the boy "knew with substantial certainty" that the consequence would result (her attempting to sit followed by harmful contact with the ground). A few classes later we read the case of *Ploof v. Putnam*, 71 A. 188 (Vt. 1908) which involves a suit by a boat owner against the owner of an island and dock for trespass to the boat and for negligence. The boat owner, during a sudden and violent storm, tied his boat up to defendant's dock, to save the boat and its passengers (the plaintiff and his family) from "destruction or injury." The defendant had his servant untie the boat from the pier, which caused the boat to be driven into the shore and the plaintiff and his family to be tossed into the lake and injured. Now the discussion of the *Ploof* court, as guided by the lawyers in that case, was entirely about whether the defendant could justify his action because the plaintiffs were trespassers, or whether their trespass was privileged by necessity and therefore could not be used as a justification by the landowner for "trespassing" against their boat or line.

What I ask my students to do with *Ploof* is to ignore the analysis of the court and to recast the plaintiff's case as a battery action. What some of them see is that the case can be analogized rather nicely to the *Garratt* case, and that the line and boat are to the plaintiffs in *Ploof* more or less as the chair was to the plaintiff in *Garratt,* and that the same issue is presented: Did the defendant know with substantial certainty that the action of untying the boat would result in the harmful contact of plaintiff or his family with the storm and water? In other words, how good is the analogy between the boat line and the chair? Can we put them both in a soft category of "objects upon which the plaintiff's physical integrity relies?" One can certainly argue that the defendant's intention in *Ploof* was less than the intention of the boy in *Garratt*, but that is always the problem of law and one of its fundamental differences from science; new cases inevitably are like precedents in some ways and unlike the same precedents in other ways that we may also believe are important. We can only approach each case on its own merits and hope that reasonable people would generally agree on the justice of the outcome. The digital, universal, predictable, and replicable method of science, in which P75 receptors can be studied in relationship to numbers and types of neurons, is not concerned with individuals within a group; the analogical, particular, individual and retrospective method of law is concerned above all with whether the individual can be fairly placed within a loosely defined group.

Part III. Silicone Implants, A Case Study in the Fundamental Differences

Using the framework of fundamental differences developed in Part I, this last section will examine some of the problems that are created when science is brought into the courtroom to answer the question, "What happened to this plaintiff?" The example chosen here is the current mega-litigation in the U.S. over silicone breast implants.[12] The cases have generated a fair amount of scientific research, with an increasing amount of epidemiological data, mostly negative,[13] and a fair amount of

---

[12] *In Re Breast Implant Cases*, 942 F. Supp. 958 (E.D. and S.D. N.Y. 1996).

[13] Silverman et al., Reported complications of silicone gel breast implants: an epidemiologic review, *Ann. Intern. Med.* 1996 Apr 15;124(8):744-756 "Studies of scleroderma and other defined connective tissue diseases suggest that implant

immunological data which is mostly suggestive of the possibility of a positive association between silicone exposure and autoimmune disease.[14] What are we to make of these conflicting types of scientific studies? Epidemiological evidence ought to show an increase in disease among the exposed population if the immunological evidence suggestive of the *possibility* of causation means that systemic exposure to silicone really "*does*" cause autoimmune disease.

Why does the serum of women who have been exposed to silicone implants and have more severe symptoms of autoimmune disease contain much higher levels of anti-polymer antibodies[15] if the immunological response to silicone which produces the antibodies is unrelated to their disease? One possible reason is that the effects of silicone exposure are only pathogenic in a relatively small subset of exposed women and produce an otherwise relatively common disease in those women. (DES caused vaginal cancer only in a very small subset of the exposed daughters, but because the disease it caused was extremely rare in that population, the increased incidence was easily detected.)[16] Autoimmune syndromes are relatively common in the general population (arthritis, lupus, scleroderma, and so on) and particularly in women as they age beyond 30.[17]

So let us assume, just for the purposes of illustration, that silicone is harmless to most women, except for those who have a relatively infrequent and rare genetic variation, or perhaps infrequent combination of different immune-system-related genes, which hypothetically occurs in about one of every thousand persons. The variant genotype renders them particularly sensitive to silicone and results in the variety of autoimmune disorders that are complained of by the plaintiffs in the silicone implant cases. This genotypic variation is, we will assume of no other consequence to persons with the genotype, other than in the event of unusually high exposures to systemic silicone (and perhaps other related chemicals which rarely, if at all, are introduced into the body at high concentrations). That would mean out of the three hundred and seventy-five thousand or so women who are now registered with the court in the class action, 375 are likely to have disorders due to the silicone and the rest are simply suffering from the same incidence and probability of autoimmune disorder as the general population (a staggering 15-20%!),[18] and are blaming the silicone implant manufacturers for what is, in fact, random fate. Now epidemiology would almost certainly not find such a low frequency, but definite,

---

recipients have no substantially increased risk for these disorders; however, the epidemiologic literature is insufficient to rule out an association between breast implants and connective tissue disease-like syndromes."

[14] Tenenbaum et al., *Lancet* 1997 Feb 15; 349 (9050): 449-54.

[15] *Id.*

[16] Herbst, A. L., Clear cell adenocarcinoma and the current status of DES-exposed females, *Cancer* 1981 Jul 15; v. 48 at 484-8.

[17] Helmick, et. al., Arthritis and other rheumatic conditions: who is affected now, who will be affected later? National Arthritis Data Workgroup, *Arthritis Care Res* 1995 Dec;8(4):203-211. "The prevalence rate of self-reported arthritis and other rheumatic conditions in the United States is projected to increase from 15.0% (37.9 million) of the 1990 population to 18.2% (59.4 million) of the estimated 2020 population."

[18] *Id.*

causal link (375 silicone-derived cases out of an estimated 67,500 "expected" cases in the exposed population).[19]

In fact such a genotypic variation is so close to unique that it is of little interest in science. When the Human Genome Project is completed, and the "normal" alleles of those genes are established, persons with the "Silicone Sensitivity" alleles would be able to determine that they had a variant of the "normal" genotypic pattern of immune-system related genes that was not known to be of any significance and, correctly, not to worry about it. One in one thousand people has the genotype, and less than one in 720 of those people is at risk for high-dose exposure to silicone. So a person who has the genotype is unlikely to be exposed to high levels of circulating silicone or related compounds and suffer from the disadvantage of their genotypic variation's effect.

The purpose of law, of course, is to worry about what to do in precisely such cases, and the fact that it may be unknowable, scientifically, whether silicone has an adverse affect on a small percentage of the population is why the conclusions of science are less than fully satisfying for problems of law. When we do a clinical trial of, for example, a new cancer drug, we may get results something like this: Control group – 150 patients, survival at 18 months – 36% (54 patients). Treatment group – 150 patients, survival at 18 months 52% (78 patients). Of course, the scientist's concern is whether this drug shows efficacy; that is, whether the difference between the two groups is statistically significant and unlikely to be due simply to chance. But those numbers tell us that even if the excess number of 18-month survivors is likely due to the drug's action, the majority of those in the treatment group would have survived anyway. We are generally unconcerned with determining which of those in the treatment group owed their life to the drug and which to their own recuperative power. Similarly, the epidemiologist who finds a possible slight increase in relative risk, a possibility of 103 deaths in the exposure group where 100 would be predicted in an unexposed group, cannot tell us which 3 owe their premature demise to exposure. It is not within the epidemiologist's power to tell us, nor is science devised to answer such questions,[20] yet our fundamental desire for law is to know the answer to the question of who has been

---

[19] Furthermore, as argued below, even where the causal link is established, it is only in cases where the condition is virtually non-existent, absent exposure, in a particular population, that we can ever identify the true victim from the random sufferer.

[20] There has been a significant scholarly discussion of the problem created by toxic substances which cause increases in the rate of disease that are less than 100%, e.g., Daniel A. Farber, Toxic Causation, 71 *Minn. L. Rev.* 1219 (1987) (arguing that the damages due to the percentage increase in disease be distributed to the most likely victims, rather than among all exposed persons with the disease). Farber, however, acknowledges that "Plaintiffs must still establish by a preponderance of the evidence, the facts needed to recover; namely, their exposure to a toxic substance and the statistical effect of that substance on the cancer rate. Establishing these facts entitles them to a remedy..." *id.* at 1241.

harmed.[21] If, as I argue here, science can rarely, if ever, answer the question: "Who are the real victims?" then any solutions the law devises to compensate persons who may or may not have been injured necessarily leaves us frustrated. We can compensate the "most likely victims"[22] or give recovery to all exposed persons for the risk imposed upon them[23] or for their emotional distress.[24] All of these solutions attempt to grapple with the central dilemma of doing justice where the fundamental differences between science and law mean that scientists cannot answer the questions that law asks. The reason for the variety of solutions and the continuing debate over the right solution is that none of them can bridge the unbridgeable gap between digital, universal, predictive science and analogical, particular, retrospective law.

What are we to do then, in cases like the silicone breast implant cases, where injuries are caused, at a level beyond the power of epidemiology to detect with scientific certainty, or even cases in which epidemiology can find the relationship, but cannot discriminate between victims and random "normal" sufferers? Two things are certain: First, the courts will reach verdicts – persons will either be compensated or they will not. Second, whatever the result, we will feel a sense of frustration, realizing that we have not satisfied our desire for individual justice. Science is digital and deals with the shared, the collective sample, the universal and predictable. Law is analogical, it seeks the truth of the individual, the particular, the normative, and the socially contingent. Scientific causation is probabilistic, legal causation is individual and particular. Science is universal in the replicability of good experiments. Universal justice can only be done one case at a time.

ACKNOWLEDGMENTS

I wish to thank Professor Daniel Farber of the University of Minnesota College of Law, Professor Celia Wasserstein of Hebrew University's Faculty of Law, and Professor Richard Fink of California Western School of Law for their helpful comments on earlier versions of this manuscript.

---

[21] Richard W. Wright, Causation, Responsibility, Risk, Probability, Naked Statistics, and Proof: Pruning the Bramble Bush by Clarifying the Concepts, 73 *Iowa L. Rev.* 1001 (1988). Wright discusses the difference between probabilistic causation (which I have equated with scientific causation in this discussion) and actual causation (which I equate with traditional legal responsibility, as does Wright).

[22] Id.

[23] Christopher H. Schroeder, Corrective Justice And Liability For Increasing Risks 37 *UCLA L. Rev.* 439 (1990).

[24] Bohrer, R., Fear and Trembling in the Twentieth Century: Technological Risk, Uncertainty and Emotional Distress, 1984 *Wis. L. Rev.* 83 (1984).

4 The End of Splendid Isolation: Tensions Between Science and Practice

Ann Lennarson Greer

CONTENTS

INTRODUCTION

> *The very success of science has ended its splendid isolation.*[*]
> Robert Sinsheimer[1]

It is a tribute to the power and charm of science that it has become a consistent and important reference point for far older institutions, including medicine and, in many of its concerns, the law. Legitimate decision-making in these latter domains now requires that they incorporate scientific findings. The means to do this, however, remain controversial. That medicine does not correspond more closely to science has become a major concern of policy-makers, educators, managers and payers of health care. All are investing immense energy in efforts to achieve closer conformity. In law, argument surrounding the value of scientific testimony in court proceedings has frayed nerves and led the U.S. Supreme Court to accord trial judges wide latitude in deciding not only whether such testimony is relevant but to employ legal reasoning to decide whether it is reliable. My focus is on the struggle over the role of science in medicine with the thought that analogous professional difficulties may exist in the judicial process. Between medical science and medical practice, problems arise because the two activities have different goals, cultures, and operating codes.

---

[*] The research upon which this chapter draws was funded by The Agency for Health Care Policy and Research Grant #R01 HS 06065 and # R01 HS 03238 and by the National Institutes of Health #FO6 TW00986.

[1] Robert Sinsheimer was quoted by Banta, H.D., Behney, C.J., Sisk-Willems, J. *Toward a Rational Technology in Medicine.* New York: Springer, 137 (1983).

In undertaking careers in science, scientists embrace commitments and methods which distinguish them as a group and differentiate them from others. The same is true of physicians who undertake careers in clinical medicine. For each group, professional work is a central life commitment with criteria not subject to compromise. Each group believes that its work is understood correctly and should be evaluated only by others who share the same commitment, training, socialization, and experience. The organizational milieus in which these professionals work have evolved over time to be generally consistent with the nature of the work as the professional work force understands it. The efforts of medicine and the law to internalize science create unique problems for both legal and medical practitioners on the one hand, and scientists on the other.

Medical practice is far older than medical science. Western physicians swore allegiance to Hippocrates and other gods of healing some two thousand years ago. In doing so, they embraced commitments to patients whom they would endeavor to help, or at least not harm, and to their teachers and fellow practitioners with whom they shared a sacred calling and the close experience of bedside care. Today's physicians are trained in science and consider it integral to the contemporary effectiveness of their craft. Similarly, the public has taken to heart the belief that medicine and science are tightly connected. In fact, the two are locked in uneasy harness as the recent controversy over the poor correspondence of medicine to published science makes clear.

THE CONTROVERSY OVER SCIENCE IN MEDICINE

A serious awareness of the size of the gap between science and medical practice may be dated to 1972, when British epidemiologist, Archie Cochrane, published an eighty page essay entitled Effectiveness and Efficiency: Reflections on Health Services.[2] He noted that the activities of the health services rarely rested on decisive experimental design, in medicine referred to as the "randomized controlled trial" (RCT), despite the fact that medical scientists and practitioners agree that the RCT is the gold standard. Other prominent voices chimed in. Kerr White at the Johns Hopkins University, for example, estimated that only 15-20% of what doctors did rested on conclusive science. The debate accelerated when John Wennberg published studies showing that medical practice was highly variable from one small geographic area to the next, irrespective of shared population characteristics. Wennberg and Gittlesohn showed that the application of a particular treatment such as tonsillectomy might vary by a factor of ten in neighboring counties.[1] Subsequent research confirmed that such "practice variations" were broadly characteristic of medical practice.

Perceiving that the relative rarity of RCTs in biomedical research forced clinicians to rely on less than conclusive evidence, the leading founder of biomedical research, the U.S. National Institutes of Health (NIH), created an Office of Medical Applications Research (OMAR) to concern itself with the application of science in practice. To clarify the 'state of the art' in various areas of controversy, it pursued a strategy of Consensus Conferences wherein expert panels met

---

[2] Greer, A.L., Scientific Knowledge and Social Consensus. *Controlled Clinical Trials*: Decision, Methods, and Analysis, 431-436 (1995).

in Bethesda, Maryland to agree on best practice. Following the first conference in 1977, consensus activities and the issuing of guidelines incorporating consensus became popular activities of governments, medical specialty societies and other groups in the U.S and elsewhere.

The effectiveness of such initiatives was impaired, however, by the continuing lack of solid science documenting the effects of medical practices, new and old, on patients. By 1991, it appeared that another step was needed and the U.S. Congress created the Agency for Health Care Policy and Research (AHCPR) with a mandate to deliver, through new research, the missing information on outcomes of medical practices. This high aspiration has faltered in recent years. Many now look to the more modest objective of knowledge appraisal along the lines suggested by Cochrane in 1972.[1] Under the tag "evidence-based medicine," methodologies of meta-analysis are employed to systematically review and cull conclusions from published research. Reviewers weigh the contribution of each study according to its scientific quality so that, in the words of Ian Chalmers, the director of the Cochrane Center in Oxford, England, "we know what we know."

As researchers generated guidelines and literature assessments by the hundreds, a second problem became obvious: studies revealed that doctors were more likely to be aware of findings and recommendations than to be using them in practice.[3] A new wave of activity ensued as numerous demonstration projects sought to identify effective models of guideline dissemination. AHCPR required all grantees doing "outcomes research" to develop means to disseminate their findings. Dissemination demonstrations were carried out under auspices as well, including the continuing education arms of medical schools, federal and state government agencies, and medical societies. Health Maintenance Organizations (HMOs) and health insurance companies have used the existence of practice variation to defend their own literature reviews and use of the results to disallow payment for many treatments recommended by doctors for their patients.

All this activity suggests that we might question what exactly we ordinarily mean when we speak of medical practice as scientific. The new initiatives obviously introduce a demand for certainty and consistency which has hitherto had no such salience. The evidence of wide practice variation came as a surprise to most doctors who had themselves assumed that their activities were a good deal more consistent than they turned out to be. At the same time, the task of significantly reducing practice variations proves to be difficult. While science sits confidently at the table of medical practice, it does not sit comfortably.

To describe the movement of science and technology into medical practice, I ordinarily use the term "diffusion of innovation," which has deep research roots in the social sciences. More activist terms are also used including "technology transfer" in the physical sciences and engineering, and "implementation" in the management literature.[4,5]

---

[3] Cochrane, A.L., *Effectiveness and Efficiency: Random Reflections on Health Services*. London: Nuffield Trust (1972).

[4] Greer, A.L., Advances in the Study of Diffusion of Innovation in Health Care Organizations. *Milbank Q* 55, 505-532 (1977).

[5] Rogers, E., *Diffusion of Innovations*, New York: The Free Press (1995).

METHOD

Over the last two decades, I have interviewed physicians regarding their decisions to adopt new medical technologies, including both new equipment and new procedures. When I began my research in 1975, the coming storm surrounding practice variations and the relationship of evidence to treatment was far from visible. But my research affords a window into decision-making in medical practice and the role of science in it. Since 1975, I and my associates have conducted more than 500 personal interviews with physicians in ten medical specialties in the United States and approximately 100 interviews in Britain and other western countries. These were lengthy interviews, averaging one and one-half hours with each transcribed interview filling approximately twenty single-spaced pages. In these interviews, physicians described the attitudes and actions of themselves and others in relation to adoption of new technologies. I have used a strategy of "analytic induction" to systematically examine coded transcriptions for patterns. The data reviewed for this analysis consist of approximately 300 physician interviews conducted between 1984-90. Findings are consistent with published analyses of earlier interviews.[6]

THE TWO CULTURES OF BIO-MEDICINE: SCIENCE AND PRACTICE

Activity to link practice more directly to science often assumes that physicians are miscreant scientists whose hands should be slapped or whose statistical education be improved so that they might more quickly incorporate the latest scientific findings. My interviews show that these problems have little to do with physicians' slow embrace of new science. Rather, physicians suspect new knowledge. Pledged to "do no harm," practicing physicians must carefully consider not only the question "what is good science and what is junk science?" (to use the phrase of contemporary legal controversy) but does it apply to this case? Should it be used in this setting? Who should use it? These questions add multiple levels of uncertainty to the physician's embrace of new findings and parallel those asked after the fact by juries: Could it have been used? Should it have been? Was it used appropriately in this case?

These are not issues of science. The goal of science is the advancement of knowledge. Scientists approach uncertainty as a problem for research, for the formulating of a research design which isolates effects by controlling confounding variables. Probabilities measured against chance justify acceptance of a proposition into the canon. Scientists around the world evaluate new evidence and revise theories in terms of a shared method, language, and standard of judgment. Science is at once universal, cumulative, and provisional.

Clinical medicine is concrete and specific and action oriented. The case of a particular patient presents manifold interactions which confound certainty of diagnosis and selection of treatment. Often a decision must be taken and acted upon when there is uncertainty regarding the nature of the problem, the means to address it, and even the goal. Not only are patients bundles of uncontrolled

---

[6] Greer, A.L., The State of the Art vs. the State of the Science. *Int. J. Technol. Assess. Health Care,* 4, 5-26 (1988).

variables, they also have minds of their own and they live in social settings that may not reinforce the doctor's plan. Nor are the many health professionals whose actions come together around a patient under the doctor's control. These, too, have their own goals and methods. Physicians must make decisions with incomplete information, patients who may balk at recommended treatments, and co-workers with independent professional goals.

In the respect that the clinician must balance and integrate medical assessment with psychological, social, and organizational factors to develop a treatment plan, his role may have affinity with that of the judge or juror who must balance conflicting values to decide a legal dispute. Just as medicine refers to science but is local and adaptive, jury decisions refer to public law, but are "localized, content-specific epistemological and normative understandings that are not subordinate to inappropriately universal claims and standards." [7,8]

Uncertainties of Scientific Information

Physicians are skeptical of articles which appear in the biomedical literature. These contain the findings which have been subjected to peer review. They are, in principle, the best sources of information. But there are many false starts and many wrong turns. Findings which may constitute legitimate steps toward greater certainty in the minds of scientists may not constitute compelling reasons for a change in patient care. Science may be self-correcting over time; medical treatment do not afford this luxury. One physician said:

> There is much inconsistency from one study to the next and from one month to the next. Research is difficult. Research in a test tube is easy, but a clinical study is hard to do. It's hard to control all the variables. For a study to be dependable, it has to be large, be well done, double blind. It's hard to do. It's somewhat like your field [sociology] where it's even harder to control the relevant variables. And when you do manage to control many variables, it's hard to relate the findings to your own patients because those other variables are very likely to be considerations. I think, because of this, the key thing we look at is the concept. (030309; 1989)

A concept is more flexible than a scientific result. The latter depends upon conditions and procedures which should not vary by laboratory. Generalization is difficult when the many circumstances of implementation are unknown. For example, an anesthesiologist said:

> Sodium pentobarbital has been around for fifty years. They keep trying to replace it. But there is always some kind of a problem. And then there

---

[7] Meyer, C., Greer, A.L., Explaining Science to Judges and Jurors. *The Chemist* 75#2:15-19, p 222 (1998).

[8] Jasanoff, S., Science at the Bar, in *Law, Science and Technology in America.* Cambridge: Harvard University Pres (1995).

are problems that may not be problems [if you are in a research setting] where you have a lot of time – which we do not have at this hospital. (131309; 1989)

A physician will likely wait for expected controversy around a modality to emerge and to settle. Said one:

I go to different conferences and talk to people that are doing these new things and ask them the questions that are bothering me. [But] I usually wait to do it myself until enough have been done for me to see a trend in complication rates. I think that's a little bit safer. (131304; 1989)

The goal structure of science, as distinguished from the process of science, is a further problem as physicians consider published findings. One said:

You'll have to admit that the literature, the quest for literature gets to be ridiculous in the United States. You know, the old publish or perish performance. If you were to take the literature from medicine, . . . and survey it, with the jaundiced eye, you'd probably find that of all the articles, the articles published in a year, perhaps about 1% is really of any value and the rest are designed to prove that you're Ph.D. material or that you need tenure or that you're going to get into medical school or whatever. (090016; 1989)

The result is that the scientific literature is but one source of information for the practicing physician, used along with other sources, including conferences, advertisements, the lay press, and throw-away journals, to keep apprised of developments.

I suppose I usually become aware of new developments from the throw-away journals, not the kind we subscribe to, the kind that are supported by advertising and come to us for free. And they'll often have, you know, ...what I call "cheap" articles because somebody writes them for free, and submits them: "This is what we're doing. These are the problems that we had in trying to introduce it, etc." They write about their experience, somebody publishes it, so you get an idea: oh yes, such and such is coming down the line. Maybe it's reported out of a major university center somewhere, or a clinic where somebody is on the leading edge. You say, okay, what is this? And then pretty soon you'll get a flyer in the mail from a vendor. You begin to become aware that this new technology is out there, and little by little you feel this groundswell of peripheral information coming, and finally you say, gee, I think I need to know about this. (250013; 1989)

The opportunity for a momentum to move an individual from awareness to implementation depends upon much personal communication with colleagues who share information and experience about application.

Usually things come out first in one of the meetings. By the time an article is...is written and accepted by the editor, then published, it already is well known about. And especially since the time of the last meeting when somebody put up a poster or something. Evidence coming out of a reliable source, a clinical laboratory that in the past has done well, you tend to believe them. You find out what you can about their methodology by talking to them or other people you know, and then you talk to your own laboratory or hospital and find out how difficult this would be to set this up in your own hospital. You find that your colleagues that have the same sub-specialty, here in the city, generally [they] are doing the same thing, and you get together, usually over a can of beer (laughing), and talk things over. You find that some of your own colleagues that you have known in the past to be pretty reliable, they'll tell you what they have heard about it. You'll pass your information on and so by the time it hits the literature, most of the time you are already aware of it and some of the time you have already been incorporating it into your daily work. (040313; 1989)

When physicians speak about embracing concepts rather than prescribed steps, diffusion becomes quite flexible. If the question is not "has this been shown to be true?" but "does it make sense?," one draws for its evaluation, as the Goodwins' discuss, on one's understanding of disease process, one's experience, and the approach learned from a mentor.[9] A concept may be interpreted and modified to accommodate local values and local medical capabilities. Whether a new technology does fit the local technical configuration and way of working, including such things as tolerance for risk, is determined by the consensus of local colleagues.

Medical Capability: the Physician and his Setting

Medical care is delivered by particular people in particular facilities in particular places. In regard to both diagnosis and treatment, the skill of the medical personnel and the availability of equipment are factors. For example, Kosecoff et al. examined physician behavior in Washington state to determine the effect of published NIH recommendations. They found that physicians were more likely to order a diagnostic procedure in the sequence recommended if the technology were available in the local hospital. Physicians were less likely to comply if the patient had to be transferred to a hospital across the state.[10,11]
Wu interviewed surgeons to discover the reasons for the persistence of treatments of early stage breast cancer that are considered suboptimal by current

[9] Goodwin, J.S., Goodwin, J.M., The Tomato Effect: Rejection of Highly Efficacious Therapies. *JAMA* 251, 2380-2390, p.238 (1984).

[10] Kosecoff, J., Kanouse, D.E., Rogers, W.H., et al. Effects of the National Institutes of Health Consensus Development Program on physician practice. *JAMA* 258, 2708-2713 (1987).

[11] Greer, A.L., The Two Cultures of Bio-Medicine: Can There Be Consensus? *JAMA* 258, 2739-2740 (1987).

science, where optimal is either modified radical mastectomy or the less extreme lumpectomy procedure with an associated program of radiation. In such cases, the physician and patient need to balance two unpleasant alternatives and whether the fear of disease recurrence or the loss of a breast holds the greater dread for the patient. In some cases, surgeons chose officially suboptimal treatment. Explaining that he did sometimes do a lumpectomy without the requisite radiation, one surgeon explained:

> The only reason I do that is the patients are very, very high risk patients. I can do a lumpectomy with local anesthesia. They are too sick for a general anesthetic and a mastectomy, and they are too frail and sick for radiation.[12]

The expertise and skill of local colleagues are also considered in deciding what to do. In speaking of the success of surgical procedures, medical doctors commonly qualify their comments with the phrase "in his hands" or say that a particular surgeon has "good hands," as we might say of a concert pianist. A technique is possible for some but not for others. Such personal abilities influence a surgeon's willingness to take up new procedures and the willingness of other physicians to refer patients for them.

Experience is equally important. All physicians speak of difficulties which are expected in the early stages of the learning curve and of the fit of a new procedure to old skills. One surgeon described the different response of two specialties facing similar new technology, which worked through a needle inserted by the surgeon.

> That was the thing with the phacoemulsifier for the eyes. At the time it came out, a lot of ophthalmologists were very wary of being able to do it. It required a very steady hand or you could blind the patient. There was [patient] demand but most surgeons were afraid of it.

> In orthopedics, [it was different]. We had the experience of doing diskograms, which...[are] done by sticking needles into disks. In addition, I do most of my own epidural steroid injections, so I'm very familiar with sticking needles in and around the spine and I have very little apprehension about that. And, the anatomy is very straightforward, so the technique of actually getting it in there, I've had enough experience, that I'm not worried about that. (150026; 1989)

The experience of one's team members is also important. Medical insiders often advise patients to have complex surgeries performed at places that do many of the procedure because surgical teams at busy centers keep their skills in better trim than those that do fewer.

---

[12] Wu, Z., The Influence of Surgeon's Charactersitics on Treatment Recommendations for Older Women with Early Stage Breast Cancer (Dissertation). The University of Texas Medical branch at Galveston (1998).

The list goes on.[13] A cardiac surgeon described the effect of his own experience as a patient on his thinking about treatment.

> Until I had the surgery myself, I thought that if the surgery in the operating room was a success, our program was a success. When I was in as a patient, it changed my view. I had never thought about what happens after the patient leaves the operating room. I got depressed as hell when I got home. I had nobody to talk to. I thought my career was over. I realized that the coronary history is so long and the operation is such a small part of it.... The patient goes home to the same problems he had before his illness or surgery. He becomes depressed. [He does not follow the steps necessary to his recovery.] This is why we now have group therapy for patients.... It came about because I was a patient. (1114; 1976)

Developers of evidence-based guidelines seek to assure the broadest possible conformity of practice to science in units which can be isolated and compared. But the going is rough as local attitudes and complexities continually reassert themselves. I had occasion to listen to a planning session for a guideline implementation project. Participants were faculty physicians who had embraced the potential practice guidelines to improve medical practice. They were among the cadres seeking to identify means to transfer guidelines from development sites to sites of intended use. In this case, the target users were general practice doctors in rural communities. The topic was a guideline which had been issued by an NIH consensus panel on optimal steps for the diagnosis and treatment of high blood cholesterol. This conversation occurred:

> Physician #1: It says here that cholesterol should be measured in all adults 20 years of age and over... that doesn't make any sense. They must mean between 20 and 65 [writing the revision into his copy].

> Physician #2: You are supposed to begin treatment with dietary therapy. That's crazy if you have a cholesterol level of 400. Most patients won't comply. This must mean if the level is not too serious. What level would you think?

> Physician #3: If the "One Step Diet" doesn't work, the doctor is supposed to get a nutrition consult. [These rural doctors] ... do not have access to nutritionists. If they can not do that, I wonder if they are supposed to develop a diet themselves or [skip that step] and go on to drugs?

> Myself: Do you realize that, in sixty seconds, you have made three major changes to this guideline?

---

[13] Greer, A.L., The Shape of Resistance, The Shapers of Change. Joint Commission Journal on Quality Improvement, 21, 328-332 (1995).

Physician #4: The problem with guidelines is that they make no allowance for common sense.

This team felt it had to consider available resources to implement preferred steps including the capabilities of the physician and the availability of local resources. They also wondered how reliably the patient would follow the doctor's orders and how serious the consequences would be if they did not.

THE INFLUENCE OF THE PATIENT

The problem that the doctor must address is the one that has walked through the door, the patient with symptoms. The patient initiates a medical encounter because of a distressing breakdown or troubling symptom – back pain, for example. The physician depends on information provided by the patient on activity, diet, family history, use of drugs, physical abuse and many other factors to develop a diagnosis. A physician can recommend further testing to gain a level of certainty and protection against liability. Knowing that many medical problems, back pain among them, improve without any treatment the doctor might recommend "watchful waiting," the medically safest choice. But this may not appeal to a patient in a hurry to feel better. Various surgical procedures can be presented to the patient, with their various levels of risk, different probabilities of success, and different periods of recuperation. There are old and new drugs having different levels of evidence on results and side effects. Supporting data usually show that different patients respond differently to treatments but are not clear what differentiates the patients who benefit from those who do not. A laundry list of correlating factors quickly assembles but these await scientific support. Long-term effects are particularly elusive. Under these circumstances, what possible result is worth what risk? Does the patient understand? Or from the patient's perspective, does the doctor?

MEDICAL ETHICS: THE DOCTOR-PATIENT RELATIONSHIP

Western medicine has evolved around the idea of the ill patient who comes to a physician because he does not know enough or feel well enough to fend for himself. Medical codes of ethics assume that patients are vulnerable and that there is an imbalance of power in favor of the physician. This imposes on the physician a special obligation of trust. Sokolowski writes that a patient seeks "a trustful collaboration where his own human goals are joined with the specialized knowledge of the professional toward the goal of 'a good end.'"[14] Zaner says "The experience of illness, notable for its sense of peril and urgency,...makes prominent the need...for genuine trust so that decisions, at times critical and irreversible, can be made even when their basis is only relatively incomplete, uncertain, or ambiguous." Further, in a situation of human distress and desire for concerned

---

[14] Sokolowski: The Fiduciary Relationship and the Nature of the Professions, in Pellegrino, E.D., Veatch, R.M., Langan, J.P. (eds): *Ethics, Trust, and the Professions: Philosophical and Cultural Aspects*. Washington D.C.: Georgetown University Press, 27 (1991).

help: "It is hardly appropriate merely to cite statistical probability patterns for classes of diseases and/or persons...."[15] Pellegrino concurs: "Depending on his character and fidelity of trust, [the physician] may treat the patient as a statistical entity or he may be the patient's last protection against the 'system.'"[16]

In a research project in the mid-1980s, I asked a question of faculty and residents training in general internal medicine at a midwestern U.S. medical school. Just under 100 interviews were conducted. In these personal interviewees, I asked faculty and residents to identify the characteristics of their own role model in medicine, the doctor who came closest to their ideal. Their responses fell into two general categories. Physicians described either (1)personal character and commitment (honesty, integrity, compassion, caring, "working hard" for patients, and "compulsives" about getting it right); or (2) interpersonal skills (the doctor listens to patients, avoids an appearance of business with patients, elicits patient trust leading to better information and patient cooperation with treatment). Although characteristics like honesty and working hard for one's patients may imply keeping up with literature and operating from a base in science, no internist in this university group thought that ready access to or immediate use of new information distinguished the really good doctor, her own role model, from lesser figures. This was startling because this project was an evaluation of a demonstration of a computerized medical record. Yet no physician mentioned characteristics which were obviously enhanced by improved access to data such as the computerization project sought to deliver.

While this was one group of physicians at one site, and general internists at that, evidence in my interviews with other specialties in other sites and countries suggests that commitment to the patient's welfare is generally considered to be a first obligation. This commitment deeply conditions the practitioner's view of statistics and new science. Doctors caring for patients are as concerned with the nature of complications as with their frequency. A single terrible result leaves doctors feeling betrayed. A spine procedure, chymopapain, which was widely touted in the 1980s for back pain, spread rapidly but was short lived in most areas of the United States. It has not been rejected as a valid modality, but as one orthopedic surgeon explained:

> It's a good procedure and it is still being done in some places in the U.S., I think, and I know it's being done in Canada. But there was the potential for complications that were so horrendous. The occasional case of paraplegia or death was enough to discourage people from wanting to pursue it. (110041; 1989)

---

[15] Zaner, R.M., The Phenomenon of Trust and the Patient-Physician Relationship, in Pellegrino, E.D., Veatch, R.M., Langan, J.P. (eds): *Ethics, Trust, and the Professions: Philosophical and Cultural Aspects*. Washington D.C.: Georgetown University Press, 50 (1991).

[16] Pellegrino, E.D., Trust and Distrust in Professional Ethics, in Pellegrino, E.D., Veatch, R.M., Langan, J.P., (eds): *Ethics, Trust, and the Professions: Philosophical and Cultural Aspects*. Washington D.C.: Georgetown University Press, 75 (1991).

Although lawyers were undoubtedly involved in such cases, this merely underscores that, like the physician, the patient did not particularly care that this outcome was statistically rare.

THE PHYSICIAN'S SOLUTION

How scientifically deliberate medicine may become remains a question. British physician D.W.Young has suggested that characterized medicine embodies a approach to problem solving that is quite different than that now being advanced. He argues that the characteristic activities of a profession, such as the nature of its decision-making, attract or deter persons from entering that career. Of medical practice, he says:

> The clinical task varies both in the range of activities and variation in the same activity, dealing with people, coping with unexpected demands, irregular hours, freedom to choose when and to some extent what to do. Every patient, every example of a disease is different and this variability must be an attractive part of clinical practice....[The doctor's] key task is to make decisions usually on incomplete and uncertain information. Individuals who are not comfortable with this do not practice medicine.[17]

He compares the decision-making style of the physician to that of the chief executive of a corporation who pulls together disparate, incomplete, and ill-related information to chart the course for the company. Of the manila-folder medical records of most doctors, Young commented:

> The [paper] record is generally recognized to be disorganized, lacking in structure, incomplete, difficult to find specific pieces of information, hard to read, but in some strange way it reflects the hurly burly of daily medical practice.

Even as the computer becomes more and more a part of the medical world, the translation of data to individual cases will likely remain problematic. One physician in my study expressed his dismay:

> The number of probabilities that you might need for any one decision is astronomical....[He provides a lengthy example]. Most of the time we get away without probably knowing what those numbers are. You know what I mean? Where are we going to go? We're collecting information like mad. We're an information driven society. All of this is going into data banks. The question is: ... how do we improve physician or nurse, or PA behavior in appropriate fashion by utilizing all this technology, and all this information? (110040, 1989)

---

[17] Young, D.W., Can We Get Doctors to Use Computers? *Health Services Management* 87, 115-119, p. 119 (1991).

Another commented:

> Increasingly, I think, medical educators have tried as much as possible to make patient care and treatment decisions more deliberate, more logical, founded more solidly on good numbers, good data, what is known. The idea is to follow these algorithmic lines of decision-making depending on which groups of patients fall into which categories and so on and so forth.... The idea is to try to eliminate the casual decision, the one that is not based on sound data, and to maximize for the patient the most productive lines of diagnosis and treatment.

> But in a way, it's like being a mother. You can listen to your mother-in-law or to your mother tell you how to raise your kids, but basically, you raise your kids the way you're comfortable raising your kids and you can read all the books in the world about it, but when push comes to shove, you do what you feel most comfortable with and that's an experiential data base. (030009; 1989)

To select a course despite uncertainty, clinicians employ a familiar repertoire: repeating what has worked before, adhering to approaches of teachers and role models, conforming to the behavior of local colleagues, waiting for a new consensus to become evident. Physicians begin by assessing the credibility and integrity of promoters and end by seeking a consensus of local peers to confirm that a particular solution is right to embrace. These strategies, which doctors have learned from mentors and the past experience of their profession, may bear some comparison with the task of a jury.

Although the language "preponderance of evidence" is not a phrase ordinarily used by physicians, it may capture the balancing which occurs in medical decisions. This physician did use the term:

> I think the term that probably most applies is: at what point in time does the "preponderance of the evidence" point toward this as an accepted procedure. This is why I go to national meetings and look at the research that is being done by individuals at respected places. And what I feel are respected places may be different from somebody else. Somebody that trained in Texas may look at a separate set of institutions than I would....

> The other way to make a judgment would be to talk to other people in your own subspecialty and say, do they agree that this is a preponderance of the evidence? Everybody has their own flashpoint as to what they're going to accept or when they change and when they do not change. (250008; 1989)

ALIKE AND UNALIKE: SCIENCE, MEDICINE AND THE LAW

Science and medicine are very different activities. A good scientist limits himself to verifiable fact specified in terms of time and conditions. A good physician makes decisions in terms of a myriad of factors, which are medical, psychological, social and negotiated with the patient. The doctor must recompose what Whitehead called the "full concreteness" of the occasion, reintegrating factors which have been separated out for scientific study. Scott Greer says of the scientific abstraction which permits variables to be isolated:

> The process of abstraction is...double-edged. It is extremely useful if it is well-founded, if it corresponds to those aspects of the world in which we are interested. It allows us to avoid distraction by means of what is called 'partial analysis,' and if what we are interested in is itself relatively free from distraction, we are in a good position to understand it. But there is a price: you have excluded parts of the whole, and if those parts are important in your concerns, then you have built in a major error.[18]

Smith's analysis of the judiciary's reliance on doctrine and precedent suggests parallels with the problem of medical practice.[19] The courts would be paralyzed, he says, if the many values implicit in each case were actually articulated and definitively defined and measured. A prior case, a precedent, is a shorthand. The precedent embodies many factors, some of which are identified while many remain implicit. In accepting a prior case for comparison, a jury can reach an expeditious resolution of disputes in reasonable reference to the actual values of right and justice which are involved, but without arguing each in its own terms. The premise that this case is like another in important selected respects limits the demands of discourse while in a sense containing what has been excluded. Values must be related in context, where fact is important, but where an acceptable hierarchy among values is a goal.

Against these commonalities between medicine and law are important differences which stand in the way of ready sympathy or cooperation. Importantly, medicine is fundamentally a cooperative activity where collegial sharing of skill and information is normative. As a means of discourse, the adversary process is alien to both science and medicine. Scientific theories compete but science and medicine are fundamentally cooperative efforts of colleagues, where the sharing of skill and information is essential to the shared goal.

CONCLUSION

Over the years, specific professional goals have guided conduct within science, medicine, and also the judiciary. The contribution of science depends upon professional commitments and conduct which place it aloof from practical decisions. The very essence of medicine is a focus on a particular patient where complexities cannot be eliminated.

In its own terms, science is straightforward and compelling but a failure of

---

[18] Greer, S., *The Logic of Social Inquiry*. New Brunswick, NJ: Transaction Publishers, 73 (1989).

[19] Smith, J.C., Action Theory and Legal Reasoning, in Cooper-Stephensen, K., Gibson, E., (eds) *Tort Theory*. North York, Ontario: Captus University Publications, (1993).

other audiences to appreciate its strengths and weaknesses makes it a problematic actor in many situations. Carl Meyer attributes many problems that juries face in making use of scientific testimony to the "overselling of science." So, too, there has been an overselling of medical science. If medical treatment can be separated from the occasion, quantified and measured, the doctor's role in synthesizing and applying knowledge becomes problematic, as indeed it has. Insurance companies can assert roles for themselves in managing medical care, because its conduct is not well distinguished from science.

Science has gained great influence in many areas of activity where it is an important resource. It now provides reference points for patient care decisions and legitimates them in the public eye. At the same time, medical practice has its own roots and retains a decisional logic which is not that of science itself. As scientists are asked to contribute their knowledge to an ever-widening array of problems, it is important that the nature of the science and professional tasks be understood so that essential aspects of each are protected. To ask science to do more or less than that of which it is capable endangers the integrity of science – and also the practical decision.

5 Expert Testimony Involving Chemists and Chemistry

Richard Bjur and James T. Richardson

CONTENTS

INTRODUCTION

This chapter examines recent developments in the law of evidence that affect those offering expert testimony in legal cases and regulatory hearings. There is a special focus on the 1993 *Daubert* decision that is now the rule in all Federal and many state jurisdictions, with its four "guidelines" that involve falsifiability, error rates, peer review and publication, and general acceptance of the methodology used. This ruling developed out of efforts to assess the toxicity of chemical substances. A brief look at the history leading to *Daubert* will be offered, as will the impact of the Federal Rules of Evidence since their adoption. The chapter will end with attention paid to the importance of meeting the guidelines mentioned in *Daubert*, the gatekeeper role of the trial judge in determining the admissibility of scientific testimony, and the impact of *Joiner* on the standard of review.

Toxic effects of chemical substances on human health and concerns regarding chemicals in our environment have increasingly been involved in litigation in our state and federal courts. This growth of toxic tort litigation, which involves such substances such as Bendectine, Agent Orange, silicone, and PCBs, all of which have allegedly affected the health of thousands of people, has required that the courts develop new ways of handling cases which involve the use of extremely sophisticated scientific claims and counter-claims.[1] This chapter will focus on the

---

[1] For examples of major discussions of issues involving mass toxic torts, see Sheila Jasanoff, *Science at the Bar: Law, Science, and Technology in America* (Cambridge: Harvard University Press, 1995; Michael Green, *Bendectine and Birth*

evolution of substantive criteria for assessing proffered scientific evidence, along with attendant procedural developments that are integral to the assessment of scientific validity.

Available scholarship and case law in this area reveal that toxic tort litigation has been a major driving force behind the development of new rules and procedures for the assessment of scientific evidence throughout the legal system.[2] Jasanoff, for example, discusses the early history of toxic tort and environmental regulation and litigation, claiming that such cases became vehicles whereby the courts have played a role in developing ways to deal with increasing concerns about human activities that were apparently poisoning the environment.[3] She notes that the early history of mass tort and environmental litigation seemed to favor the plaintiffs, as the courts sought ways to allow redress for obvious problems derived from exposure to toxic substances.

Yet this litigation climate which was favorable to plaintiffs was not without controversy. Many claimed that the pro-plaintiff climate worked seriously to the disadvantage of American industry and made it costly to promote technological innovation. Jasanoff says, "Conservative economic and political analysts argue that the resulting rule changes - introduced case by case, without extensive consideration of their possible impacts - have created a costly bias against innovation in some sectors of the chemical industry."[4]

Whether this position is correct or not, it is clear that perceptions of the impact of mass toxic torts have fueled a move to limit access to the courts for many plaintiffs, a move that has sometimes included pressure to more carefully evaluate the science that underpinned many of the plaintiffs' claims of injury from exposure to chemical substances. Thus, we have seen congressional attempts to limit access, as well as actions in many state legislatures.[5] However, rarely have legislatures venture into the area of assessment of science by the courts, leaving this area generally to the courts to decide. And decide they did, with many significant cases being decided by the courts in the past two decades, as they grappled with the

---

Defects: The Challenges of Mass Toxic Tort Substances Litigation (Philadelphia: University of Pennsylvania Press, 1996; Jonathan Harr, A Civil Action (New York: Vintage Books, 1995); Peter Schuck, Agent Orange on Trial: Mass Toxic Tort Disasters in the Courts, Cambridge, Harvard Univ. Press (1987).

[2] See especially the books by Green and by Schuck and Chapter six of the Jasanoff book referred to in footnote 1.

[3] See Jasanoff, footnote 1.

[4] Jasanoff, footnote 1, p. 115.

[5] Jasanoff points out that federal efforts at tort reform have included "loser pays" laws, limits on punitive damages, and reform of product liability suits to encourage innovation. Efforts at state levels have included these and many other ideas, including alternative dispute resolution methods and even complete exemptions for certain behaviors (such as delivery of babies) from tort action.

rapidly growing load of tort actions involving allegedly toxic substances.[6]

THE *DAUBERT* DECISION

In 1993 the U.S. Supreme Court, after many years of criticism for ambiguous, outdated rules and procedures that allegedly allowed so-called "junk science" to pervade the courtrooms of America, rendered a decision that changed the rules dramatically.[7] That decision, rendered in a case involving the drug Bendectin, which was used by over 30 million women for pregnancy-related nausea, is causing a veritable revolution in American evidence law concerning use of science in the courts. We refer, of course, to the decision of the U.S. Supreme Court in *Daubert v. Merrell Dow Pharmaceuticals,[8]* which was decided on June 28, 1993.

The *Daubert* decision tossed out 70 years of law involving the admissibility of expert testimony, with its explicit statement that the famous 1923 decision in *Frye v the United States*[9] had been superseded by the Federal Rules of Evidence, which had been approved in 1975. The *Frye* decision, which held that a defendant in a murder trial was precluded from offering exculpatory evidence from a precursor of the lie detector, contained the following much-quoted statement:

> Just when a scientific principle or discovery crosses the line between the experimental and demonstrable stages is difficult to define. Somewhere in this twilight zone the evidentiary force of the principle must be recognized, and while courts will go a long way to admitting expert testimony deduced from a well-recognized scientific principle or discovery, the thing from which the deduction is made must be sufficiently established to have gained general acceptance in the particular field to which it belongs.[10]

This statement was transmuted over the decades into a "general acceptance" rule, which has been interpreted to mean that expert testimony should not be admissible unless and until the methods and principles on which it is based has achieved widespread acceptance in the relevant discipline(s). The rule had been

---

[6] A short list of some earlier influential rulings that demonstrate the courts grappling with proffered scientific evidence include: *American Petroleum Institute v. OSHA, 448 U.S. 607* (1980); *U.S. v. Downing*, 753 F.2d 1224 (1985); *In re "Agent Orange" Product Liability Litigation*, 611 F. Supp 1223 (D.C.N.Y. 1985); *In re Paoli R.R. Yard PCB Litigation*, 916 F. 2d 829 (3rd Cir. 1990).

[7] 113 S.Ct. 2786 (1993). Part of this discussion appeared in an earlier paper, Richardson, J., "Dramatic Changes inn American Evidence Law," in *The Judicial Review* (1994), 13.

[8] 509 U.S. 579 (1993).

[9] 293 F 1013 (D.C. Cir. 1923).

[10] Ibid at 1014.

adopted throughout the federal court system, as well as in a majority of state courts,[11] but was criticized as being a "short-cut" rule that allowed judges to avoid the necessity of understanding the proffered scientific evidence. In addition, this "general acceptance" rule was not uniformly applied.

Imwinklereid, a major critic of the *Frye* rule, has noted the illogical nature of not uniformly applying the "general acceptance" criterion in civil matters and with the so-called "soft sciences."[12] He has pointed out that not applying *Frye* in civil matters and "soft sciences" supposedly lowers the overall "costs" of using the rule generally, which he thinks are too high because of its conservative nature. But, he also notes the impact of the interaction of the level of proof with the application of the *Frye* rule. In civil matters in the U.S., the level of proof required is typically a "preponderance of the evidence," a lower standard than that required in criminal matters, which is "beyond a reasonable doubt." The compounding effect of a lower threshold of proof with a lower criterion for the admissibility of scientific evidence can result in unjust decisions through the acceptance of questionable science.

The *Frye* rule was also criticized as being a barrier to novel scientific ideas being offered in evidence, even if sound. Almost by definition, new ideas and results based on such ideas were precluded from being presented to juries in America.[13] Apparently, it was feared that juries would be incapable of discerning good from bad science, and would be stampeded to wrong decisions by novel science that was offered as evidence. On the other hand, prosecutors in criminal courts were increasingly frustrated in not being able to introduce novel scientific evidence that was believed to be based upon a reliable scientific foundation.

When the Federal Rules of Evidence were approved in 1975, the issue of *Frye*

---

[11] Admission of expert evidence varied widely, with some significant inconsistencies. For instance, in major criminal matters such as the penalty phase of murder trials, evidence has sometimes been allowed concerning alleged "future dangerousness," an area fraught with difficulty in terms of predictability, and about which there is considerable controversy among scientists in relevant fields of study. (J. Monahan and L. Walker, Social Science in Law, 2nd edition, Foundation Press, 1990, at 293-297). Thus, in these criminal cases where a life is at stake *Frye* has sometimes not been applied. See P. Giannelli, "Junk Science: The Criminal Cases," 84 The Journal of Criminal Law and Criminology (1993), 105-128.

[12] E. Imwinkleried, "Attempts to Limit the Scope of the Frye Standard for the Admission of Scientific Evidence: Confronting the Real Cost of the Acceptance Test," 10 Behavioral Sciences & the Law, (1992), 441-454.

[13] See P. Giannelli, "Forensic Science: *Frye, Daubert*, and the Federal Rules," 29 Criminal Law Bulletin, (1993), 428-436, at 432. Also see J. Richardson, "Expert Testimony by Social Psychologists: Issues and Experiences," Presented at annual meeting of the Western Psychological Association, Phoenix, Arizona, 1993.

was inexplicably left nebulous.[14] The Rules made no reference to *Frye*, but instead

---

[14] Following are some Federal rules especially relevant to this chapter:

FRE 702: Testimony of Experts. If scientific, technical, or other specialized knowledge will assist the trier of fact to understand the evidence or to determine a fact in issue, a witness qualified as an expert by knowledge, skill, experience, training, or education, may testify thereto in the form of an opinion or otherwise.

FRE 703: Bases of Opinion Testimony by Experts. The facts or data in the particular case upon which an expert bases an opinion or inference may be those perceived by or made known to him at or before the hearing. If of a type reasonably relied on by experts in a particular field in forming opinions or inferences upon the subject, the facts or data need not be admissible in evidence.

FRE 704: Opinion on the Ultimate Issue. Testimony in the form of an opinion or inference otherwise admissible is not objectionable because it embraces an ultimate issue to be decided by the trier of fact.

FRE 705: Disclosure of Facts or Data Underlying Expert Opinion. The expert may testify in terms of opinion or inference and give his reasons therefor without prior disclosure of the underlying facts or data, unless the judge requires otherwise. The expert may in any event be required to disclose the underlying facts or data on cross-examination.

FRE 706: Court Appointed Experts. (a) Appointment. The court may on its own motion or the motion of either party enter an order to show cause why expert witnesses should not be appointed, and may request the parties to submit nominations. The court may appoint any expert witness agreed upon by the parties, and may appoint expert witnesses of its own selection. An expert witness shall not be appointed by the court unless he consents to act. A witness so appointed shall be informed of his duties by the court in writing, a copy of which shall be filed with the clerk, or at a conference in which the parties have opportunity to participate. A witness so appointed shall advise the parties of his findings, if any; his deposition may be taken by any party; and he may be called to testify by the court or any party. He shall be subject to cross examination by any party, including a party calling him as a witness. (b) Compensation. Expert witnesses so appointed are entitled to reasonable compensation in whatever sum the court may allow. The compensation thus fixed is payable in funds which may be provided by law in criminal cases and civil actions and proceedings involving just compensation under the fifth amendment. In other civil actions and proceedings the compensation shall be paid by the parties in such proportion and at such time as the court directs, and therefore charged in like manner as other costs. (c) Disclosure of appointment. In the exercise of its discretion, the court may authorize disclosure to the jury of the seemed to require that the admission of evidence be solely based on the issue of relevancy. Thus, it was left to the courts to decide whether or not the "general acceptance" rule was still applicable to the implementation of the Federal Rules that are germane to the issue of expert testimony, or whether the *Frye* rule had been superseded by the rule of relevancy.[15]

The majority of the courts that had adopted *Frye* continued to do so after approval of the Federal Rules, still using the general acceptance test as a short-cut to understanding the substance of what was being offered. However, splits began to appear within the federal court system, with some federal courts explicitly overruling *Frye* and adopting a "general relevancy" standard, with others continuing to apply the *Frye* test. Differences also appeared in terms of the application of *Frye* to various areas of science.[16]

A mounting tide of criticism of the *Frye* rule and confusion about its relationship to the Federal Rules of Evidence, as evidenced by different rulings by the Federal Circuit Courts of Appeals, eventually forced the U.S. Supreme Court to take action.[17] The Court agreed to review the dismissal of a civil action in which it was alleged that Bendectin had caused birth defects in two children in the Daubert family. The case had been dismissed by the trial court, with the dismissal upheld by the Ninth Circuit Court of Appeals, solely on the basis that the plaintiffs' evidence did not meet the *Frye* standard. Thus, the case presented quite clearly the issue of continued viability of *Frye*, even though the case was a civil action (and one involving diversity jurisdiction, as well).[18]

---

fact that the court appointed the expert witness. (d) Parties' experts of own selection. Nothing in this rule limits the parties in calling expert witnesses of their own selection.

[15] Giannelli, note 12 *supra*, at 432 describes an effort of the Civil Rules Committee in 1991 to modify the Rules to speak explicitly to the issue of the relationship with the *Frye* test, and change the standard to one of "reasonable reliability." This effort proved to be controversial, as the issue of "junk science" being used in civil mass tort cases had erupted by this time, causing the effort to be abandoned.

[16] See P. Giannelli, note 12 *supra*, at 430 for a listing of the various courts which had ruled in different ways on acceptance of the *Frye* test. Also see P. Giannelli, note 1, *supra*, for a discussion of *Frye* versus *Daubert* in the criminal law area, and about the markedly inconsistent positions taken by the federal government on the use of more rigorous criteria in civil and criminal cases. The federal government under President George Bush implemented policies to make it much more difficult to admit scientific evidence in civil cases, but argued for a lower standard in criminal cases.

[17] 113 S.Ct. 2786 (1993), at 2791-2792.

[18] The Bendectin saga has been a long one in American legal history, which is instructive in a number of ways. See especially P. Huber, *Galileo's Revenge: Junk Science in the Courtroom*, New York: Basic Books, 1991, whose book has contributed much to public sensitivity about the issue of questionable scientific

testimony, and added the term "junk science" to the lexicon. Huber discussed Bendectin cases at length, citing claims of Bendectin as a teratogen as a major example of scientific fraud that has led to harm for the general public. Much of the brief summary that follows draws on Huber's work. Also see J. Sanders, "The Bendectin Litigation: A Case Study in the Life Cycle of Mass Torts", 43 Hastings Law Journal, (1992), 301-418.

Cases concerning Bendectin have been brought representing hundreds of individuals, with few successes at the trial level, some resulting in large damage awards (up to nearly $100 million in one case). Virtually all jury awards have been overturned at the appeal court level because of problems in establishing causation between ingesting Bendectin and subsequent birth defects, a problem illustrated as follows: It is estimated that over 30 million women have taken Bendectin, and about 100,000 children per year are born with some sort of birth defect in the U.S. Given the size of both those numbers, one would expect that these two universes would "overlap" to some extent, and some of the women giving birth to deformed babies would have ingested Bendectin, even if there was no causative connection. However, that could be purely coincidental, as only carefully planned epidemiological studies can establish causation. There have been about 30 such studies done to date, none of which established a causative link between ingesting Bendectin and subsequent birth defects. As discussed in the Supreme Court Opinion (at 2791), new types of evidence were being proffered in *Daubert*, however.

In the face of litigation, Merrell Dow withdrew Bendectin from the market in 1983. Since Bendectin was withdrawn, there has been no significant change in the incidence of birth defects, as measured by the birth defects monitoring program of the Federal Center for Disease Control in Atlanta. The withdrawal of the drug from the market has apparently resulted in a major problem for those having serious cases of morning sickness. The Journal of the American Medical Association reported in 1990 that hospitalizations had doubled for severe cases of nausea and vomiting in pregnancy since Bendectin was taken off the market. (Skolnick, "Key Witness Against Morning Sickness Drug Faces Scientific Fraud Charge," 263 Journal of the American Medical Association, (March 16, 1990), 1,468-1,473). The report added that severe nausea and vomiting can lead to dehydration and acidosis, which can threaten the health of both mother and fetus. Some cases have resulted in nutritional deficiencies and nerve damage for mothers and the report even suggests that birth defects could increase as a result of not having a drug to control severe morning sickness.

Merrell Dow has spent over $100 million dollars defending itself, and says that it would not reintroduce the drug under any circumstances, although it believes it to be safe. According to Huber, the Bendectin experience has brought a halt to virtually all research on medication for pregnancy related illnesses. The cases have been carried forward mainly through the efforts of a few scientists who believe there to be a connection between Bendectin and birth defects, although the work

When the case was granted certiorari, various organizations and individuals, including a number of major national scientific and legal organizations filed some 22 amicus curiae briefs.[19] The case even attracted attention in the mass media, with stories in major newspapers and newsmagazines pointing out implications of the pending case.

The Supreme Court ruling in *Daubert* was unanimous that *Frye* was no longer law in the area of expert testimony in federal courts. ("That austere standard absent from and incompatible with the Federal Rules of Evidence, should not be applied in federal trials."[20]) Seven justices also agreed to offer guidelines for deciding what proffered scientific evidence should be accepted. The implications of those "guidelines" are profound, and may be characterized as a revolution in U.S. evidence law, if they are implemented as written.[21]

Included as guidelines are:[22]

---

of those scientists has been severely criticized and was not published in peer reviewed journals. One of those scientists, Dr. William McBride, famous for his discoveries concerning Thalidomide, has since been accused of scientific fraud and has lost his right to practice medicine in his home country of Australia. He has written a book attacking Merrell Dow for allegedly destroying his reputation because of his involvement in Bendectin cases. See W. McBride, Killing the Messenger, Eldorado Books, 1994.

[19] One such brief, that of the Carnegie Commission on Science, Technology, and Government, as Amicus Curiae in Support of Neither Party, apparently served as the basis of much of the eventual decision. See R. Underwager and H. Wakefield, "A Paradigm Shift for Expert Witnesses," 5(3) Issues in Child Abuse Accusations, (1993), 156-167, at 164. The brief contained much of the reasoning used in the majority opinion's section which laid out guidelines for federal judges to apply in evaluating evidence. The brief discusses falsifiability, the requirement of testability, the need for replication and for examining error rates, and the idea of judges reviewing methodological matters such as study design and data collection in order to properly determine if the claims being made are truly scientific. Oddly, this brief was not cited specifically in the opinion.

[20] 113 S.Ct. 2786 (1993), at 2793.

[21] The author of the *Daubert* majority opinion, Justice Blackmun, was perhaps without peer on the Court in terms of his training as a scientist and his ability to articulate scientific and statistical issues. His retirement raises a question about the rigor with which the Court will enforce the *Daubert* criteria in subsequent opinions.

[22] The majority opinion lists those criteria, but also points out that sound criteria have been suggested in other sources, some of which they list, and says (113 S.Ct. 2786 (1993), at 2797, note 12): "To the extent that they focus on the reliability of evidence as ensured by the scientific validity of its underlying principles, all these versions may well have merit..."

(1) determining the "falsifiability" of a theory: is it testable and has it been tested;
(2) the "known or potential error rate" associated with applications of a theory;
(3) whether the findings have been subjected to peer review and publication; and
(4) the "general acceptance" of the science being offered.

JURIES AND "GATEKEEPING"

Before discussing the specific *Daubert* guidelines, a few general comments should assist in understanding the meaning of *Daubert*. First, Justice Blackmun explicitly stated that the decision does not just impact decisions about novel scientific evidence. He wrote that "Although the *Frye* decision itself focused exclusively on 'novel' scientific techniques, we do not read the requirements of Rule 702 to apply specially or exclusively to unconventional evidence."[23] This means that all proffered scientific evidence should be looked at anew, to discern whether it can meet the criteria listed in *Daubert,* an implication of considerable import.[24] Second, within the context of American law, with its widespread use of juries, the *Daubert* decision would appear to be a strong statement in favor of "let the jury decide," even in complex massive toxic tort cases. Indeed, there are comments in *Daubert* that suggest Justice Blackmun and other justices believe that juries can understand and apply scientific evidence, within the context of the adversarial system of justice.

> Respondent expresses apprehension that abandonment of "general acceptance" as the exclusive requirement for admission will result in a "free-for-all" in which befuddled juries are confounded by absurd and irrational pseudoscientific assertions. In this regard respondent seems to us to be overly pessimistic about the capabilities of the jury, and of the adversarial system generally.[25]

---

[23] 113 S.Ct. 2786 (1993), at 2796, note 11.

[24] Indeed, scholars such as Michael Saks have raised a serious question about why the legal system continues to accept certain types of scientific evidence when studies show some such traditional evidence has questionable validity and reliability. He has also asked why the legal system refuses to accept results from reliable techniques such as the polygraph. See his provocative discussion, with accompanying research data on reliability of various forensic techniques in M. Saks, "Enhancing and Restraining Accuracy in Adjudication," 51 Law and Contemporary Problems, (1988), 243-279.

[25] 113 S.Ct. 2786 (1993), at 2798.

This faith in juries may be questionable, particularly with cases dealing with emotional issues about which juries hold strong but poorly informed ideas that might be validated by questionable scientific opinions.[26]

Nonetheless, the Supreme Court's support of the traditional role of the jury in *Daubert* seems strong. Justice Blackmun's majority opinion does, however, indicate that limits can be placed on what jurors hear, based on decisions by judges that proffered testimony does not pass scientific muster.

> We recognize that in practice, a gatekeeping role for the judge, no matter how flexible, inevitably on occasion will prevent the jury from learning of authentic insights and innovations. That nevertheless, is the balance that is struck by Rules of Evidence designed not for an exhaustive search for cosmic understanding but for the particularized resolution of legal disputes.[27]

Blackmun also notes that Rule 403 may be used by judges to preclude relevant evidence, "if its probative value is substantially outweighed by the danger of unfair prejudice, confusion of the issues, or misleading the jury..."[28] He reminds, as well, that trial court judges can issue directed verdicts or grant summary judgments in cases in which "...the scintilla of evidence presented supporting a position is insufficient to allow a reasonable juror to conclude that the position more likely than not is true."[29] This detailed analysis by Justice Blackmun about the responsibilities of the trial judge to be a "gatekeeper" leads to a third general point: the *Daubert* decision places a considerable burden on judges to evaluate scientific evidence prior to its being presented to a jury. ("...the Rules of Evidence - especially Rule 702 - do assign to the trial judge the task of ensuring that an expert's testimony both rests on a reliable foundation and is relevant to the task at hand."[30]) Judges must be able to discern good from bad science, which in turn means that judges must come to some understanding of the history, philosophy, and sociology of science, and of scientific methodology. Justice Blackmun says:

---

[26] See J. Richardson, "Cult/Brainwashing Cases and Freedom of Religion," 33 *Journal of Church and State* (1991), 55-74 for one type of case dealing with controversial claims of "brainwashing," and J. Richardson, "Satanism in Court," in J. Richardson, et al. *The Satanism Scare* (1991), Aldine de Gruyter for claims having to do with alleged effects of subliminal stimuli embedded in recordings on behavior of listeners. Also, see S. Kassin and L. Wrightsman, *The American Jury on Trial*, New York: Hemisphere Press, 1988, for a more general discussion of problems jurors have with controversial and emotional cases.

[27] 113 S.Ct. 2786 (1993), at 2798-2799.

[28] Ibid at 2798.

[29] Ibid.

[30] Ibid at 2799.

Faced with the proffer of expert scientific testimony...the trial judge must determine at the outset, pursuant to Rule 104 (a), whether the expert is proposing to testify to (1) scientific knowledge that (2) will assist the trier of fact to understand or determine the fact at issue. This entails a preliminary assessment of whether the reasoning or methodology underlying the testimony is scientifically valid and of whether that reasoning or methodology properly can be applied to the facts in issue. We are confident that federal judges possess the capacity to undertake that review.[31]

DEFINING FALSIFIABILITY

A key passage of *Daubert* cites two of the most prominent philosophers of science, Sir Karl Popper, and Professor Carl Hempel, both of whom define science as empirical and require testing (and testability) of any theories claiming to be scientific.

Ordinarily, a key question to be answered in determining whether a theory or technique is scientific knowledge that will assist the trier of fact will be whether it can be (and has been) tested. "Scientific methodology today is based on generating hypotheses and testing them to see if they can be falsified; indeed this methodology is what distinguishes science from other fields of human inquiry."[32] "[T]he statements constituting a scientific explanation must be capable of empirical test."[33] "[T]he criterion of the scientific status of a theory is its falsifiability, or refutability, or testability."[34]

If judges do not understand the meaning of falsifiability, then the impact of *Daubert* may be the exact opposite of what the majority opinion apparently intended. The effect of *Daubert* could be the lowering of thresholds for expert testimony. After all, the plaintiffs in *Daubert*, who sought to overcome a motion to dismiss, did prevail, implying that plaintiffs seeking to offer novel even if questionable expert testimony should be allowed to do so.[35] Also, the Federal Rules

[31] Ibid at 2796. Federal Rule of Evidence 104(a) provides in part: "Preliminary questions concerning the qualification of a person to be a witness, the existence of a privilege, or the admissibility of evidence shall be determined by the court..."

[32] Green at 645 (1992). See also C. Hempel, Philosophy of Natural Science 49 (1966).

[33] C. Hempel, Philosophy of Natural Science 49 (1966).

[34] K. Popper, Conjecture and Refutations: The Growth of Scientific Knowledge 37 (5th ed. 1989).

[35] However, as noted by P Miller, B. Rein, and E. Bailey, Daubert and the Need for Judicial Scientific Literacy, 77 JUDICATURE 254 (1994) at 257, two decisions involving Bendectin were cited positively in the Daubert opinion, as examples of judges properly dismissing cases without substantial evidence to establish causation.

of Evidence do have a "liberal thrust," as indicated in the majority opinion's comparison of the Federal Rules with *Frye's* "general acceptance" principle. ("The drafting history (of the Rules) makes no mention of *Frye*, and a rigid "general acceptance" requirement would be at odds with the "liberal thrust" of the Federal Rules and their general approach of relaxing the traditional barriers to "opinion testimony."[36])

Bert Black, a prominent attorney, and Dr. Francisco Ayala, President of the American Association for the Advancement of Science and a member of the National Academy of Sciences, published a commentary on *Daubert*[37] in which they note: "...scientific knowledge is unique in the systematic understanding it provides of the world within and around us..." but that most people "...do not appreciate how science works through the formulation and testing of hypotheses, nor do they understand the institutional mechanisms science has developed for sharing and evaluating results." They state that *Daubert* "...marks the first time the high court has ever directly considered what standard should govern the use of science in the courtroom, and it has focused the spotlight of public attention on the judiciary's failure to develop clear and consistent guidelines for evaluating scientific evidence." They insightfully point out that "...neither the common law nor the Rules provide much guidance on how best to evaluate the validity and reliability of evidence that purports to derive from science." Ayala and Black conclude:

> Worse yet, the decisions of judges to allow scientists to give testimony based mostly on their personal biases may legitimate misunderstandings and groundless fears that can thwart progress and cause real harm. Verdicts based largely on quackery have driven some beneficial pharmaceuticals out of production and have greatly reduced research in fields such as contraception.[38]

Ayala and Black also state: "The solution to these problems is for courts to hold experts to the same standards scientists themselves use in evaluating each other's work."[39] Using the controversy over DNA typing as an example of what can happen when those in the legal system do not understand the intricacies of the scientific method, Ayala and Black develop a case for judges to learn more about the nature of science, which they describe as follows.[40]

---

[36] 113 S.Ct. 2786 (1993), at 2794.

[37] F. Ayala and B. Black, "Science and the Courts," 81 American Scientist, (1993), 230-239, at 230.

[38] Ibid.

[39] Ibid at 231.

[40] Ibid at 234.

Science shares the characteristics of explanation and systematic organization with other forms of systematic knowledge, such as mathematics and philosophy. But empirical science is distinguished from those other forms of knowledge by another principle: empirical testing. Because a scientific explanation must be subject to testing, it is always possible that it will be proven false. Indeed, many scientists consider falsifiability the most important characteristic separating science from other forms of knowledge. An explanation or hypothesis that cannot be subject to the possibility of rejection based on observation or experiment cannot be regarded as scientific.

These authors discuss some classic examples from the history of science where proper testing was either done or was ignored. Mendel's careful testing of ideas derived from experimenting with breeding various types of peas became the basis for modern genetics. This exemplary work, still used as an excellent example of the scientific method, is sharply contrasted to the ideas and efforts of, among others, Lysenko in the Soviet Union in the 1930s. Lysenko, for ideological reasons, promoted a theory of genetics that assumed environmental conditions were of crucial importance, and that acquired characteristics could be passed on to future generations. Lysenko's legacy was virtually to cripple the Soviet agricultural economy and destroy scientific genetics in his country. His theories achieved a strange sort of enforced consensus for a time in the Soviet Union ("general acceptance"), but the consensus did not rescue the ideas from the dustbin of history. Today the name Lysenko is mentioned only in scorn, as an example of science at its worst. This sharp contrast of examples:

> ...highlights the way in which ideology, hubris, overconfidence or just plain sloppiness can pervert science. It also explains why judges and other nonscientists who have to base decisions on scientific information need to understand the importance of properly formulating hypotheses and corroborating them through testing.[41]

Ayala and Black also discuss features of properly drawn hypotheses, citing: their internal consistency, their explanatory value, and their consistency with commonly held hypotheses and theories in a particular field of science. However, they also note that sometimes valid hypotheses are at odds with established theories. In the authors' words:

> ... a well-formulated hypothesis that explains observed phenomena and is consistent with accepted theories must still be tested empirically. Testing is accomplished by predicting what should be observed if the hypothesis is correct and then seeing if the predictions accord with what

---

[41] Ibid at 236.

is actually observed. Any meaningful test can result in the falsifying of a hypothesis, and it is only when a hypothesis survives such efforts at falsification that it becomes corroborated and accepted.[42]

Some commentators have used "bloodletting" to demonstrate the concept of falsifiability.[43] For about two hundred years, physicians believed that drawing blood could cure some diseases. An ill patient had a vein opened and a basin of the "bad blood" was drawn, a practice that apparently killed George Washington, who was suffering from a bad cold or flu. Physicians reasoned that if a patient recovered from the bloodletting, then the treatment had worked. If the patient died, then the patient was too sick to help or the bloodletting occurred too late. Such reasoning made it almost impossible to disprove the theory that bloodletting was helpful. Therefore, the theory of bloodletting had not been tested or shown to be falsifiable. Only later did medical research, based on germ theory, demonstrate with well-controlled studies that bloodletting was in fact a false theory.

ERROR RATES

The *Daubert* court also instructs trial judges to consider the "known or potential rate of error" of the scientific theory or technique offered as evidence, but it does not fully define what is meant by the term. In the context of the *Daubert* decision, "error rate" refers to the probability that the application of a particular technical procedure or theory leads to a mistake in the classification of an object, event, or person. The decision discusses error rates in terms of spectrographic voice analysis, citing cases that address the issue of admissibility of spectrographic identification evidence in criminal trials. The court notes that in considering the known or potential error rate of a technique, such as spectrography, the court should survey studies regarding the error rates of the specific technique (e.g., the probability of falsely identifying a voice), as well as the standards controlling the technique's operation (e.g., the established rules and procedures governing spectrographic analysis). Error rate analysis has obvious implications for litigation involving chemicals that allegedly cause harm. Errors can be made in identifying the substances that supposedly caused the harm, identifying the harm that was actually manifested, and determining whether or not this chemical substance in fact caused the harm identified.

Two types of error contribute to the error rate - false positives and false negatives. Someone mistakenly identifying a voice as being from a specific person illustrates the false positive concept, using the example from *Daubert*. A false negative is illustrated by someone claiming that a voice is not that of a specific person when in fact it is. While one can minimize one type of error by adjusting

---

[42] Ibid at 236-37.

[43] See R. Underwager and H. Wakefield, A Paradigm Shift for Expert Witnesses, 5 *Issues in Child Abuse Accusations*, 156 (1993).

the test parameters, one thereby increases the other type of error. In addition, a particular technical procedure or theory may be more prone to one type of error than the other, and in a given instance, the consequence of one type of error may be much more severe than the consequence of the other.

For example, a false negative error involving a drug test for substance abuse (erroneously not finding the drug in the sample) may mean that the person tested will not be found guilty, whereas a false positive finding (erroneously obtaining a positive test result) may mean that the person will be found to be guilty when he or she was in fact innocent. On the other hand, if a blood sample from a blood bank is being tested for the AIDS virus, a false negative error would be more serious than a false positive error since it would increase the chance that someone may be administered contaminated blood.[44]

PEER REVIEW AND PUBLICATION

Black and Ayala also explain the crucial institutional review processes that have been developed in different scientific areas of study to assist scientists in assessing new scientific claims. Their description of the functions and process of peer review is worth quoting at length.[45]

Peer review represents both an effort to police scientific claims and to attempt to assure their widest possible dissemination. The pressure on scientists to publish derives not only from narrow concerns about recognition and career advancement, but also from the desire of all scientists to learn of new developments that may guide their work. Because submitting a paper for peer review is the best way to establish priority for a new discovery or idea, the process serves to get new information out fast as well as to control its quality. The comments of peer reviewers help proponents of new hypotheses to improve their research and interpretations.

The review of scientific ideas takes place in a variety of contexts. Informal review can occur when scientists discuss their work with one another at the laboratory bench, during conversations and seminars, and at scientific meetings. Formal peer review is generally an integral part of the scientific publication process and the process whereby funds are allocated for the conduct of research. Any claim that would significantly add to or change a body of scientific knowledge must be regarded quite skeptically if it has not been subjected to some form of peer scrutiny, preferably submission to a reputable journal.

---

[44] See Green's explanation of the effects of the two types of errors, p. 317.

[45] F. Ayala and B. Black, "Science and the Courts," 81 *American Scientist*, (1993), 230-239, at 238.

However, Jasanoff offers a valuable word of caution in interpreting the process of accumulating knowledge in any field of science too idealistically.[46] Her sociology of science perspective assumes that science is socially constructed, a process not without some peril and which can sometimes go awry. Jasanoff's comments relevant to peer review are relevant as a corrective to the more idealized views of Ayala and Black. She says:

> The most significant insight that has emerged from the past 15 years is the view that science is social constructed. According to a persuasive body of work, the "facts" that scientists present to the rest of the world are not direct reflections of nature; rather, these "facts" are produced by human agency through institutions and processes or science, and hence they invariably contain a social component. Facts, in other words, are more than merely raw observations made by scientists exploring the mysteries of nature. Observations achieve the status of "facts" only if they are produced in accordance with prior agreements about the rightness of particular theories, experimental methods, instrumentation techniques, validation procedures, review processes, and the like. These agreements, in turn, are socially derived through continual negotiation and renegotiation among bodies of scientists.

Peer review also raises the obvious question of "who are ones peers"? This question is particularly perplexing in complicated toxic tort actions, which involve many different fields of inquiry that overlap each other.[47] This concern also has implications for publication, as refereed journals can be established by a subset of people within a field of inquiry, and such journals can publish material that is not accepted by the majority of practitioners in that field. Thus, the inquiry by the court into peer review and publication needs to go farther than just accepting assertions about such matters.

---

[46] S. Jasanoff, What Judges Should Know About the Sociology of Science, 77 *Judicature* 77 at 77-78.

[47] In a recent post-*Daubert* case involving breast implant litigation, Federal Judge Robert Jones of Oregon established a panel of experts to assist him in a 104(a) hearing about the scientific evidence being proffered in a multi-plaintiff case. He named to the panel an Ph.D. epidemiologist, an M.D. specializing in rheumatology, a Ph.D. specializing in immunology and toxicology, as well as a Ph.D. specialist in polymer chemistry. Judge Jones was assisted in electing this panel by an M.D., Ph.D. biochemist (*Hall v. Baxter Healthcare Corp.*, 947 F. Supp. 1387 (D. Or. 1996).

GENERAL ACCEPTANCE

The retention of the time-honored rule from *Frye* of general acceptance seems a clear indication that the court thought this a useful measure, but not by itself, and not as the defining guide to admissibility. This is just one of several guidelines offered by the *Daubert* court, and even then they add that the list is not exhaustive, and cite other cases that have developed criteria or guidelines for use in appraising scientific evidence. It is clear that this guideline is not to be used simply to toss out novel evidence, but it is a consideration that goes to the weight of any evidence proffered, especially if there has been time for the new findings to have achieved general acceptance but that has not occurred.

JUDGES AS EVALUATORS AND CONSTRUCTORS OF SCIENCE

The responsibility of judges to assess scientific evidence is controversial. Chief Justice Rhenquist was dismayed at the issue before the *Daubert* court, lamenting that it involves "matters far afield from the expertise of judges,"[48] and he urged caution in offering abstract advice on how judges should proceed in this area, "because our reach can easily exceed our grasp." His dissent (joined by Justice Stevens) closes with:

> I defer to no one in my confidence in federal judges; but I am at a loss to know what is meant when it is said that the scientific status of a theory depends on its "falsifiability," and I suspect some of them will be, too. I do not doubt that Rule 702 confides to the judge some gatekeeping responsibility in deciding questions of the admissibility of proffered expert testimony. But I do not think it imposes on them either the obligation or the authority to become amateur scientists in order to perform that role.[49]

Others have also expressed concern about the new role that has been defined for judges by *Daubert*. Jasanoff says:

> ...the analytic approach outlined in *Daubert's* criteria of testability and falsifiability will in their turn prove difficult to implement in courts of law...Trial courts may therefore soon discover that Chief Justice Rhenquist was not alone in his confusion over how to interpret the *Daubert* majority's criterion of falsifiability.[50]

---

[48] 113 S.Ct. 2786 (1993), at 2799.

[49] Ibid at 2800.

[50] Sheila Jasanoff, some of whose writing is cited in *Daubert*, is Chair of the Department of Science and Technology Studies at Cornell University. Her paper referred to herein is, "What Judges Should Know About the Sociology of Science,"

Jasanoff points out that when judges attempt to discern scientific truth they are actually participating directly in the social construction of that truth.

When judges exclude expert testimony, appoint their own expert witnesses, or render summary judgments, they inescapably give up the role of dispassionate observer to become participants in a particular construction... of scientific facts. They help shape an image of reality that is colored in part by their own preferences and prejudices about how the world should work. Such power need not always be held in check, but it should be sparingly exercised.[51]

Lawyers Miller, Rein, and Bailey, writing in *Judicature*, state:

To carry out the Court's purpose (in *Daubert*), each federal judge must achieve at least a basic level of scientific literacy. At a minimum, judges will have to become more conversant with the "sociology of science," with emphasis on such concepts as "the scientific method;" to understand the rudiments of statistics and probability theory; to obtain some appreciation of error factors and the implicit limitations of often-used means of scientific observation, measurement, and detection...[52]

DAUBERT GUIDELINES AND TOXIC TORTS

Plainly the four guidelines from *Daubert* have application to claims that chemical substances have caused harm to individuals. Jasanoff sums up the typical toxic tort claim requirements as follows:

...the plaintiff in a toxic tort action must identify the harmful substance, trace the pathway of exposure, demonstrate that exposure occurred at levels at which harm can result, establish that the identified agent can cause injuries of the kind complained of, and rule out alternative causes.[53]

Later she adds the additional crucial requirement of "specific causation," meaning that the chemical at issue did in fact cause the specific harm being claimed for an individual plaintiff.

To prove all these requirements means that much research must be done (or have been done) establishing the crucial links in the logical chain of events

---

77 *Judicature*, (1993), 77-82.

[51] Ibid at 82.

[52] See P. Miller, B. Rein, and E. Bailey, "Daubert and the Need for Judicial Scientific Literacy," 77 *Judicature* (1994), 254-260, at 254.

[53] Jasanoff, footnote 1, p. 119.

outlined. This means that many hypotheses must be developed and tested, using methods that are generally acceptable within the relevant disciplines. These tests must be such that the hypotheses can actually and convincingly be falsified. Such testing also requires considerable effort at proper identification of substances and effects, all of which may suffer from problems analogous to the error rate analysis offered above. Mistakes can be made, thus requiring careful review of every step of the research.

Applying such rigorous criteria can and does have a dramatic impact, particularly as case law has been developing in the toxic tort arena. Schuck in his detailed treatment of the Agent Orange litigation (which occurred prior to *Daubert*, but which used similar assessment criteria) and Green in his thorough discussion of the impact of the Bendectin and Agent Orange cases agree that the threshold may have been moved too high to allow justice to those bringing toxic tort claims. Others are saying this about the breast implant litigation, especially after the expert panel conclusions in *Hall v. Baxter Healthcare* led Judge Jones to grant a summary judgment motion to defendants.

At issue here is the question of what kind of data are acceptable in the post-*Daubert* world of litigation. Put another way, what methods of research produce valid results that are relevant to the key issues being raised in toxic tort litigation? At a minimum, these data must be able to survive a summary judgment motion, a case management tactic that seems to be growing in favor with the courts in mass tort litigation.

Green's excellent treatment of the Bendectin cases contains a primer on the types of research methods that are used in mass tort cases. His chapter entitled, "The Science of Determining Toxic Causation" lists epidemiology, animal studies, *in vitro* testing, chemical structural analysis, and case reports as being acceptable ways to produce relevant evidence in such cases. He agrees with much of the case law and the opinions of other commentators that epidemiological evidence is the best to have, if it is available. However, this is not inconsequential issue.[54]

Green has also discussed at length some of the potential methodological problems with epidemiological research, a point completely overlooked in some major cases that declare it the method for determining causation in toxic tort actions.[55] Green has also presented balanced discussions regarding the other approaches he lists, noting their problems (for instance, the external validity problem with animal studies), but he refuses to disregard these other methods entirely for gaining relevant knowledge pertaining to the issue being decided, as

---

[54] Also see Jasanoff, footnote 1 on problems of dependence on epidemiological evidence.

[55] See especially Judge Jack Weinstein's very influential opinion in the Agent Orange case listed in footnote 6.

some case law has done.[56] What Green and others, including Jasanoff and also Schuck, are concerned about is the move in the courts to accomplish tort reform by fiat, with rulings (and interpretations of rulings) that make it more difficult to carry toxic tort cases in the future, even though real harm has been done to potential plaintiffs by exposure to toxic substances. This legacy of *Daubert* and other case law in this area may not work to achieve justice, according to these commentators, as they represent policy decisions implementing the agenda of those interested in tort reform.[57]

THE POST-*DAUBERT* ERA

The concerns just mentioned about the conservative thrust of *Daubert* has recently been amplified in *General Electric Company v. Joiner*.[58] This case involved the standard of appellate review that can be applied to a trial court's exclusion of expert scientific testimony and dismissal of the case on a summary judgment motion in a case that alleged certain deleterious effects of PCB exposure.

The trial court had rejected the plaintiff's expert testimony, including both epidemiological studies and the results of some animal studies, and had ruled that Joiner's experts had failed to show that there was a link between exposure to PCBs and the small cell lung cancer which Joiner had claimed had been promoted by PCB exposure.[59] The trial court maintained that the testimony of Joiner's experts did not rise above "subjective belief or unsupported speculation." The appeal court offered some rather harsh criticisms of the trial court's dismissal, saying that the trial court had abused its discretion in granting the summary judgment motion, and that it had "crossed the line" and made judgments about the correctness of conclusions rather than just assessing the methods used. The appeal court also was much more respectful of the testimony of the treating physicians and considered the animal studies to be relevant and not subject to dismissal out-of-hand.

---

[56] See Green, footnote 1, Chapter 17, "The Legacy of Bendectin for Toxic Tort Causation," in which Green laments the growing use of a threshold requiring good epidemiological evidence in order for plaintiffs in a toxic tort action to survive a summary judgment motion. He is critical of Judge Weinstein's Agent Orange (footnote 6) decision, which established that standard which has since been used in a number of cases. Also, see Schuck's critical discussion of the motives behind Weinstein's decision, which Schuck suggests were not pure and were designed to protect the settlement that Judge Weinstein had forged in the Agent Orange cases.

[57] There is a major controversy over the implementation of *Daubert* as demonstrated by the writings and actions of some prominent plaintiffs attorneys such as Barry Nace, who claim that *Daubert* is being interpreted in a quite conservative manner by the courts, when its holding can be interpreted in a more liberal fashion.

[58] 118 S.Ct. 512 (1997).

[59] 864 F.Supp. 1310, 1329 (N.D.Ga.1994)

The appellate court ruling was based on a liberal view of *Daubert*, which made it easier to present legitimate conflicting views to the jury. The appeal court also stated that the trial court should limit its role to determining the "legal reliability of proffered expert testimony, leaving the jury to decide the correctness of competing expert opinions."[60] By reversing the appellate court decision and upholding the original trial court ruling, the Supreme Court held that the question of admissibility of expert testimony is reviewable under the "abuse of discretion" standard. The Court also held that in this case the trial court had not abused its discretion and that the appellate court had not given "the trial court the deference that is hallmark of the abuse of discretion review." In one sense, this ruling promotes what seems to be an agenda of the Court, that it appears to want more limited access to the courts in mass tort litigation, and also seeks to regain a modicum of control over the science that seems at times to be overwhelming the court. In another sense, it clearly returns control of the trial to the trial court judge and places the responsibility for determining both the admissibility and the sufficiency of the proffered evidence on the trial judge or "gatekeeper" as well.

It is clear that the *Joiner* ruling will have a major impact on how frequently chemists testify in court and exactly what they might testify to when acting as an expert witness. It is also clear that a chemist must clearly link the data being presented with the specific factual issue being decided by the court, and be able to present a reasonable nexus between the data and the conclusions that have been reached. While the Federal Rules give the expert witness great latitude in presenting expert opinion, the *Daubert* and *Joiner* decisions restrict that latitude and limit the data and the conclusions that can be drawn from such data, and place the control of such decisions in the hands of the trial judge. This requires the trial judge to have a reasonable understanding of the scientific process to insure adequate reliability. Thus, it is clear that Sheila Jasanoff's point that the courts are involved in the construction of science is well illustrated by the *Daubert* and *Joiner* decisions.

---

[60] 78 F.3d 524 (1996), at 533.

6 The Role of Experts in German Environmental Law

Claus-Peter Martens

CONTENTS

INTRODUCTION

Experts are witnesses who provide a court, a public authority or private individuals with the special knowledge they lack for the assessment of facts.[1] The expert furnishes the court with this special knowledge by means of written opinions, which he prepares on the evidential issue at the request of the court. In German environmental law, significant importance attaches to the role of the expert, not only in administrative proceedings in court but also in administrative procedures. Apart from the courts, public authorities and private individuals can also ask an expert to prepare an opinion.

The function of an expert is distinguished by whether a suit is based on civil law or on public law. These two areas of law follow different principles in the course they take, and these principles are also decisive for the role of the expert or the function of the opinion he has prepared.

---

[1] Kopp, F. O., *Verwaltungsverfahrensgesetz,* München, 1996, § 26, 19.

THE ROLE OF THE EXPERT IN COURT PROCEEDINGS

The Expert in Administrative Proceedings in Court and in Administrative Procedures

Contentious administrative proceedings are, for example, decisive in a court action against sovereign measures for the warding off of danger. Among other things, this applies to the action by the operator of an installation against a public authority order under the terms of § 17 of the Federal Immission Control Act *(Bundesimmissionsschutzgesetz - BImSchG)*. The authority can make such a subsequent order if the general public or the neighborhood is not sufficiently protected from harmful adverse effects on the environment or other dangers by the operation of the installation (§ 17 para. 1 sentence 2 BImSchG).

These proceedings are also decisive in the case of measures in accordance with the police and public order statutes of the law of the individual federal states, such as, for example, in the case of a public authority order to remove residual pollution or the consequences of an accident involving oil. Frequently, it is disputed in such cases whether the authority can impose on the owner of the property the costs for cleaning it up.

The Inquisitorial System

The administrative proceedings are characterized by the inquisitorial principle: the courts are obliged to investigate the facts and circumstances *ex officio.* They are not restricted to the submissions and offers of evidence of the participants.[2] Rather, in contrast to the principle of party presentation which applies in civil proceedings (where the parties must submit the relevant facts and evidence in the oral proceedings), it is assumed in administrative proceedings that the public interest in a correct decision demands an objectively correct and complete investigation of the facts and circumstances. The legality of the decision to be taken also depends on the proper and accurate investigation of the facts relevant for the decision. However, the inquisitorial principle cannot be put into practice in its complete form in the face of a lack of specialist and financial resources. Thus, for example, the courts are often prevented from commissioning expensive opinions and analyses. In this way, parties who themselves are in a position to introduce such sources of expertise into the proceedings have an advantage.

Together with the courts, the administrative authorities are also bound by the inquisitorial principle. The following comments also apply for administrative procedures.

The inquisitorial principle places an obligation on the court to carry out an objective clarification of the facts. If it fails in this duty, there will be a procedural error.[3] If the factual assessment of the facts and circumstances of the case

---

[2] Maurer, H., *Allgemeines Verwaltunqsrecht,* München, 1997, 436.

[3] Kopp, F. O., *Verwaltungsverfahrensgesetz*, München, 1996, § 86, 7.

presupposes special expert knowledge, the court must consult an expert or must demonstrate its own special knowledge in the judgment. The duty of proper clarification of the facts and circumstances can, in individual cases, make the consultation of several experts necessary.

The comprehensive duty of clarification and the inquisitorial principle are limited by the principles of reasonableness and proportionality.[4] In particular, this threshold is reached by incapacity, inaccessibility, or the wrongful use evidence. The same applies to the obviousness of an alleged fact.

Taking Evidence by the Appointment and Hearing of an Expert

In principle, it lies within the discretion of the court to determine whether evidence shall be used and, if so, which evidence. Offers of evidence by the participants can be refused and other evidence taken into consideration. The discretion is, however, restricted insofar as an unbalanced course of action which accords advantages to one of the participants constitutes a breach of the inquisitorial principle. This means, for example, that even circumstances which are favorable to the private individual must be cited and taken into consideration against the organ of sovereign power. Overall, an objective clarification of the facts and circumstances must be carried out. One of several possibilities of taking evidence which are provided for by statute is the consultation of an expert.

The court is under an obligation to appoint and hear an expert if it does not itself have any special knowledge for the assessment of a case from a factual point of view.[5] However, if the court has "a treasury of experience" accumulated in the course of frequent assessment in repeated, similar cases, the appointment of an expert in new proceedings may not be necessary. In addition, obvious facts and principles derived from experience can be taken as such without evidence being required. In difficult, complex questions, "advice" by experts can be desirable, if a distinction between factual and evaluating points of view cannot be drawn from the outset and the assessment of factual circumstances requires special expert knowledge.

The involvement of an expert does not necessarily presuppose that the chosen specialist is in a position to guarantee a "right" decision or a decision which is "more right" than that of the special authority or the court. Where questions are involved which are scientifically disputed or which depend on uncertain factors that cannot be exactly determined, it often cannot be assumed that there is any one "right" decision. In such cases, it is sufficient if the expert's opinion at least constitutes a substantial support for the court in determining the differing specialist points of view. If it responds to the question posed, the opinion may only refer to

---

[4] Kopp, F. O., *Verwaltungsverfahrensgesetz*, München, 1996, § 86, 5, 5b.

[5] Kopp, F. O., *Verwaltungsverfahrensqesetz*, München, 1996, § 86, 9.

whether the view of the court is within the spectrum of the opinions which are considered tenable by the specialists.[6]

The involvement of specialists as a means of providing evidence comes into consideration both in the determination of general rules of experience and also for the clarification of inferences which can be drawn from the general rules of experience for a concrete set of facts and circumstances. In addition, the investigation of the facts and circumstances, i.e., of the facts necessary for the preparation of the opinion, can also be transferred to the expert. This does not apply to a case where facts are in dispute which do not fall within the expert's sphere of competence. However, it is always necessary for the court to examine or to understand the preconditions and results of the expert appraisal on its own, in order to be able to make up its own mind. The court may under no circumstances simply accept the result.

So-called "private expert opinions" - opinions which are submitted by the participants without the court requiring them to do so, in order to support their arguments - do not constitute evidence by expert opinion. However, in an administrative procedure, the public authority has the option of making such private expert opinions into officially commissioned expert opinions for the court under the terms of § 26 of the Administrative Procedure Act *(Verwaltungs-verfahrensgesetz VwVfG)*, in agreement with the relevant expert, and thus making them a form of evidence.

If defects become apparent in an expert opinion which make the opinion appear unsuitable for a determination of the facts and circumstances, it is necessary to obtain a further, so-called decisive expert opinion.[7] An expert opinion which is unsuitable because of a faulty assessment, for example, is given if the court has serious doubts about the expertise of the specialist involved or, if the expert opinion appears to the court to be flawed on the basis of the court's own considerations. The same applies to expert opinions which contradict each other. If, by contrast, the court, after examining the expert opinion itself, is convinced of the correctness of the facts forming the basis of the opinion, and of the conclusions reached, it can refuse an application to obtain a further expert opinion.

The general benefit rule, in accordance with which the party seeking to rely on a certain fact bears the burden of explanation and proof, applies in administrative proceedings, but subject to restrictions. This benefit rule has been replaced by a type of "sphere of responsibility."[8] In accordance therewith, the plaintiff must submit those facts and specify the relevant evidence which lie within his sphere of existence and which are accessible to him. Conversely, the court must aim to make

---

[6] Gerhardt, M., *Richterliche Fachkunde durch "technische Berater?,"* Bayerische Verwaltungsblätter, 1982, 489.

[7] Czajka, D., *Der Stand von Wissenschaft und Technik als Gegenstand richterlicher Sachaufklärung* Die Öffentliche Verwaltung, 1982, 106.

[8] Redeker, K., Grundgesetzliche Rechte auf Verfahrensteilhabe, *Neue Juristische Wochenschrift*, 1980, 1593, 1598.

the participating authorities reveal and prove the factual aspects which lie within their scope.

The Principle of Cooperation

The principle of cooperation refers to the structuring of the proceedings to make decisions in environmental policy by collaboration between the administrative state and society. The aim of this principle is to ease enforcement as a result of the consensus reached and to accelerate the entire proceedings. In addition, such cooperation opens up the possibility of enforcing measures of environmental protection which either could not otherwise be enforced at all or only with increased difficulty if they were based only on an order by a public authority.[9]

One facet of the principle of cooperation affects the relationship of the public authorities with economic enterprises. Another aspect aims at the inclusion of third parties in various licensing procedures. Within the scope of this inclusion, private experts acquire significant importance in the enforcement and monitoring of environmental requirements. This is intended to lead to relief for the scarce administrative resources and to the incorporation of powerful private entities in the fulfillment of tasks of environmental protection.[10] This idea is reflected in numerous statutory provisions of German environmental law (e.g., 6 14 of the Equipment Safety Act *(Gerätesicherheitsgesetz),* 66 15 et seq. of the Prevention of Cruelty to Animals Act *(Tierschutzgesetz),* 6 21 of the Circulation Economy and Waste Act *(Kreislaufwirtschafts- und Abfallgesetz -KrW-/AbfG),* 66 7, 23 to 25, 29a BImSchG, 66 4. 5 of the Atomic Energy Act *(Atomgesetz -AtomG)).* Further involvement takes place through the participation of private associations or of the technical safety standards authorities, which fulfill tasks of technical standardization.

A commission of experts is established under the name "Central Commission for Biological Safety" *(Zentrale Kommission for die Biologische Sicherheit – ZKBS)*[11] in accordance with the terms of 66 4, 5 of the Gene Technology Act *(Gentechnikgesetz - GenTG).* It is composed of experts and specialist representatives of the participating groups. The public authority must involve the Commission in all application and licensing procedures. It is responsible for the examination and assessment of questions of gene technology which are relevant to safety. While the wording of the statute does not state that the opinions of the ZKBS are binding, they have *de facto* importance for the way in which a case is decided. According to § 11 para. 8 GenTG, it is only permissible to diverge from the expert opinion with a

[9] Himmelmann, S., Pohl, A., Tünnesen-Harmes, C., *Handbuch des Umweltrechts,* München, 1996, A2, p. 28.

[10] Bohne, E., Versicherunqsmodelle zur Investitionsbeschleu-nigung und zum Abbau yon Vollzugsdefiziten im Anlaqenzulassungsrecht, *Deutsches Verwaltungsblatt,* 1994, 195, 196.

[11] Himmelmann, S., Pohl, A., Tünnesen-Harmes, C., *Handbuch des Umweltrechts,* München, 1996, B 5, p. 46.

written statement of reasons,

A typical example of the involvement of private experts is the regulation provided by the Federal Immission Control Act. § 29a BImSchG provides that the authority can order the operator of an installation requiring a license, to commission one of the experts nominated by the responsible senior state authority, to carry out certain technical safety checks and to inspect technical safety documents. This regulation serves as an example to the extent to which the examination of technical requirements lies within the public interest. The examination acquires increasing importance in proportion to the extent of the potential danger emanating from the installation. The involvement of a private expert in the first place has the effect of relieving the burden on the state in the fulfillment of public tasks. In addition, such an examination is usually quicker if carried out by private experts instead of state agencies. A factor contributing to this is that the private experts have an interest in dealing with the matter in question in a way which corresponds to the points of view of commercial efficiency; they also are subject to a certain degree of competitiveness between them.

However, in cases where – exceptionally – private parties fulfill sovereign tasks (district chimneysweeps), it must be ensured that the tasks are fulfilled in the public interest. The private expert must carry out the necessary examination as an objective instance of authority and may not, for example, be corruptible. In order to ensure that sovereign tasks are only entrusted to private parties who satisfy these requirements, the transfer of such tasks presupposes not only special knowledge and technical equipment capacity, but, in particular, a special degree of reliability. Personal independence is indispensable for this reliability. The further requirements as regards special knowledge, reliability and equipment can be specified in legal ordinances. Stipulations can also be laid down regarding the collection and evaluation of the expert's experience, as well as in relation to further training. The strictness of such requirements as to the suitability of private experts is designed to ensure that state interests are not betrayed.[12]

Participation of Witnesses and Experts in Formal Administrative Procedures

§ 65 of the Administrative Procedure Act *(Verwaltungsverfahrens-gesetz - VwVfG)* regulates the participation of witnesses and experts in a formal administrative procedure, a procedure which only takes place on the basis of a statutory order and which must fulfill special formal requirements. It differs from the simple administrative procedure in this way. In this procedure, the participants have more extensive rights. In addition, an oral hearing must be conducted. The formal administrative procedure is in some respects similar to court proceedings; it is thus particularly suitable for areas in which the rights of the parties affected and the public interest make a procedure with increased guarantees of legal protection and

---

[12] Jarass, H.D., *Bundes-lmmissionsschutzgesetz (BimSchG)*, München, 1995, § 29 a, 11.2; Martens, C.P., *§ 49 Kreislaufwirtschafts- und Abfallrecht* (Jürgen Fluck, editor), § 49, 160 et seq.

legality necessary.[13] The participation of witnesses and experts is regulated more strictly and in more detail than in the general procedure.

In contrast to the general procedure, experts are obliged to prepare opinions in the formal administrative procedure (see § 65 para. 1 sentence 1 VwVfG). The reason for this obligation is the increased interest of the general public and the participants in a thorough clarification of the facts and circumstances necessary for the decision. The scope of, and the restrictions on, this obligation are evident from the Code of Civil Procedure (Zivilprozessordnung -ZPO).

The public authority has the discretion to decide whom it wishes to hear as an expert (see § 24 para. 1 and 2, § 26 para. 1 VwVfG). The participants in the procedure only have the option of making relevant suggestions; they cannot demand or force the questioning of a certain expert.

THE EXPERT IN CIVIL PROCEEDINGS

Where there is a dispute between two private persons, the law of civil procedure is usually applicable. The most frequent cases in which it is applied are disputes over private law contracts and their consequences. An example is a claim for damages as a result of residual pollution on the basis of a purchase contract. A civil suit also has to be conducted if the owner of land wishes to defend himself against adverse effects on his property (e.g., chemicals of the neighbor are washed onto his land by rain water) (see §§ 1004 of the German Civil Code *(Bürgerliches Gesetzbuch -BGB))*.

The Principle of Party Presentation

While the court is under an obligation to investigate the facts and circumstances *ex officio* in administrative proceedings, the principle of party presentation applies in civil proceedings.[14] The parties, rather than the court, must bring into the proceedings all facts and evidence which the court is to consider. To this extent, the principle of party presentation constitutes a feature of the principle of private autonomy which applies in private law.

EXPERT EVIDENCE

The expert opinion is also a form of evidence in civil proceedings.[15] As in the case of administrative law, a so-called private expert opinion prepared by an expert for one party outside of the proceedings does not constitute an expert opinion in the official sense. In the proceedings, the private expert can be heard as an expert witness on his findings, but it is not possible, in the face of objections by one party,

---

[13] Kopp, F. O., *Verwaltungsverfahrensgesetz*, München, 1996, § 63, 2.

[14] Thomas, H., Putzo H., *Zivilprozessordnung*, München, 1995, Introduction I, 1.

[15] Thomas, H., Putzo, H., *Zivilprozessordnung*, München, 1995, vor § 402, 1 et seq.

to use his opinion by way of documentary evidence, or as an expert opinion obtained by the court.

The expert evidence can be ordered *ex officio* (§ 144 ZPO) or in response to an offer of evidence by one party (§ 403 ZPO). The decision on the involvement of an expert lies within the discretion of the court; for instance, the court can consider itself as having expert knowledge or it can consider the assessment by an expert unnecessary for other reasons. If the court has decided to consult an expert, it must select that expert (§ 404 ZPO). In addition, it also has the option of requiring that the parties name persons who would be suitable as experts. If the parties agree on a certain person as an expert, the court is bound by this (§ 404 para. 4 ZPO). However, the parties can reject an expert if they fear a lack of impartiality.

The expert's position as an assistant of the court poses difficulties if the court is dependent to a far-reaching extent on the findings of the expert. This problem arises to a more critical extent in cases in which the judges have absolutely no special knowledge in the area in question. In many cases, the court is then only in a position to check the accuracy of the factual basis and the logical homogeneity of the opinion.

As well as explaining rules of experience, the expert may also be under an obligation to investigate the facts if this presupposes particular specialist knowledge. Often, an explanation of the rules of experience is inextricably bound to the finding of certain facts. The finding of the facts of the case by the expert is permissible as expert evidence in these cases. However, further investigation of the facts and circumstances may not be transferred to the expert, because the ascertainment of the facts constitutes a task for the court.

In principle, an expert is not obliged to prepare an opinion. However, such a duty may arise if the expert has been publicly appointed for the preparation of expert opinions of the type necessary in the case, or exercises the relevant specialist knowledge publicly on a commercial basis, or has been publicly appointed to do so.

According to § 407a ZPO, the expert can enlist the participation of assistants, but the independent commissioning of another person with the evaluation is not possible.

The assessment of an expert opinion obtained by the court is governed by the principle of the free evaluation of evidence; the independent view of the trial judge alone is decisive for the assessment of the evidence.

SUMMARY

1.   Experts provide special knowledge for the assessment of facts. The function of the expert differs in administrative proceedings and civil proceedings.

2.   In administrative proceedings, the court must investigate the facts and circumstances *ex officio*. If there is no objective clarification of the facts and circumstances, there will be a procedural error.

The court must appoint an expert if it has no special knowledge of its own for the complete assessment of the case. The involvement of an expert is considered as evidence. However, so-called private expert opinions do not constitute expert evidence obtained by the court.

Private experts are particularly important in the implementation and monitoring of environmental requirements. Preconditions for the fulfillment of these tasks are special knowledge, reliability and independence.

3.   In civil proceedings, the parties must submit the relevant facts to the court and adduce evidence for them. The expert opinion is considered as evidence. Expert evidence can be ordered *ex officio* by the court or ordered at the request of one of the parties.

7 Distinguishing Good Science, Bad Science and Junk Science

Carl Meyer

CONTENTS

INTRODUCTION

This chapter explores how scientists evaluate the reliability of science, the phenomenon of "junk science," and to what extent non-scientists can test the reliability and merit of scientific conclusions and opinions. Evaluating the reliability of science in the U.S. courtroom setting presents several challenges:

- There is disagreement concerning the standards that should be applied, e.g., how much risk society should tolerate, and how the cost of adverse consequences should be distributed between the manufacturer, the victim and the public.
- The litigating party that is adversely affected by the scientific facts and interpretation has an incentive to denigrate science, distract from it, and diminish its relevance, and to accuse the expert witness of bias.

▸ In the U.S. common law system, the trier of fact depends on what the parties chose to present in court, and is not allowed to conduct an independent inquiry.

▸ Most of the litigators, who serve as ambassadors of science, lack the basic mathematical and scientific foundation necessary to fully understand the underlying scientific problems.[1]

▸ The triers of facts, including most judges, lack the basic mathematical and scientific foundation necessary to distinguish between pseudo-science and science.

▸ As used by the courts, the term "science" includes any field where knowledge is acquired through study and practice,[2] i.e., not only natural sciences, engineering and social sciences, but also clinical medicine, and other fields that use conflicting methodology and have conflicting goals.

▸ Science and the court are bound by different laws and have different goals. As the *Daubert* case states it, the judge must resolve legal disputes in a "quick, final and binding" manner.[3] His guiding principles are justice and judicial economy. The judge does not search for "cosmic understanding;"[4] he narrows the issues and rules only to those issues that are absolutely necessary to decide a case. His primary tool is the application of the rules of evidence which allow him to exclude anything that does not seem relevant and reliable to him, as outlined in the Federal Rules of Evidence and in *Joiner*. If the plaintiff does not meet all of the elements of his cause of action, the case is dismissed.

Not long ago, scientific authority, albeit resented by judges and some lawyers, ranked high in U.S. courts. A typical jury instruction would read in relevant part:

....you may not arbitrarily or unreasonably disregard the (medical, scientific, etc.) opinion testimony in this case which was not contradicted. Therefore, unless you find that it is not believable, it is conclusive and binding on you.

This is no longer so. There are now two additional choices, and the judge decides in each case which should apply:

---

[1] Litigators usually have a social science undergraduate degree; most avoided high school classes in algebra, differential calculus and statistics. A survey showed that more than fifty percent of science and math teachers in the Los Angeles public school system neither majored, nor minored, in math or natural sciences during their undergraduate studies. The percentage is not significantly different in other school systems. See, e.g., Gallegly, E., Tests Prove Needs of Classroom Teachers Overlooked, *Los Angeles Times*, Metro Section (August 8, 1998).

[2] Science is "knowledge attained through study or practice," Webster's New Collegiate Dictionary. This use is consistent with the *Reference Manual on Scientific Evidence,* Federal Judicial Center, Cecil, J.S., Drew, C.E., Cordisco, M., Miletich, D.P. Eds. (1994).

[3] *Daubert*, at 597.

[4] *Daubert*, at 597.

You are not bound by an opinion. Give each opinion the weight you find it deserves, and

An opinion is only as good as the facts and reasons on which it is based. If you find that any such fact has not been proved, or has been disproved, you must consider that in determining the value of the opinion. Likewise, you must consider the strengths and weaknesses of the reasons on which it is based.[5]

As explained in Chapter 5, in federal court and many state courts, the judge can now hold a *Daubert* hearing and exclude an expert opinion, if he finds that it is not reliable, and unless the trial judge clearly abuses his discretion, his determination cannot be appealed.[6] This development reflects a change in public attitude toward the trustworthiness of science as well as toward authority in general.

Many scientists, and most of their professional organizations, feel that disputes over scientific issues, such as the toxicology of chemicals, should be resolved by scientists themselves, by internal and self-regulation rather than by experts and lawyers in civil litigations. However, scientists are notoriously elitists; their sense of justice is not democratic.[7] Furthermore, legal disputes always include public policy and other considerations, and science cannot, alone, determine the outcome of legal disputes.

A few examples may help explain the limits of the proposal to have litigations involving scientific issues determined by scientists alone:

Example 1: While chlorocarbon fingerprinting may conclusively determine the source of a spill, the fingerprinting alone does not determine the legal ownership of the spilled liquid, or how the liability should be allocated between the manufacturer, formulator, blender or distributor.

Example 2: In a recent child custody case, a DNA test showed that a lover was the father of a child born to a married woman.[8] The lover tried to use the test to obtain custody of the child, but the law presumes that children born to married spouses are their own and assigns child custody to married couples, rather than to lovers.

---

[5] *Book of Approved Jury Instructions*, §2-40, California Judicial Council (1998).

[6] *U.S. v. Dockey,* 955 F.2d 50,54 (DC Cir. 1992), citing *Barrett v. Equitable Trust Co.,* 34 F.2d. 916, 920 (2nd Cir. 1929) *aff'd as modified* 283 U.S. 738 (1931)

[7] "Professional ethics are a scheme of law enforcement...by private policemen where privately declared laws are punished by penalties imposed by private "judges" after privately conducted trials." *Fashion Originator's Guild v. FTC,* 312 U.S. 457, 463 (1941).

[8] *Dawn D. v. Jerry K.,* 952 P.2d 1139 (1998) (Biological father's desire to establish relationship with child of married women is not a fundamental liberty interest protected by the Due Process Clause, interpreting the complicated decision in *Michael H. v. Gerald D.,* 491 U.S. 110 (1989) in which the Supreme Court was unable to achieve agreement).

Example 3: In the *Berry v. Chaplin*,[9] a child support case, a jury ordered actor Charles Chaplin to pay alimony for a child conceived after Chaplin had invited a married woman to his home and had intercourse with her during the absence of her husband, even though the blood test did not showed that he was the father. Francisco Ayala and Bert Black[10] use this case for their argument that juries are unable to understand scientific issues, while professor Jasanoff[11] suggests that the jury was motivated by public policy considerations.

Example 4: In *Flue-Cured Tobacco Cooperative Stabilization Corporation, et al. v. U.S. Environmental Protection Agency*,[12] the court granted plaintiff's motion for summary judgment and severely criticized the EPA's legal procedures and its scientific conclusions in its 1993 report on environmental tobacco smoke. Why did a scientifically untrained judge here feel compelled to criticize the scientific methodology of a Federal agency (backed by the advice of a sixteen-member advisory committee and many recognized scientists), rather than adjudicate the case on the basis of what he felt to be flawed legal procedures? Probably because the judge found procedural errors. Since procedural errors are considered harmless unless they affect material issues, and the question of whether the procedural errors affecting the EPA report were material depended on whether they were scientifically material, the scientific and legal issues could not be separated in this case.[13]

Whether good science prevails in court depends, among other things, on whether:

- The underlying scientific theory is solid,
- The theory is related to the issue before the court,
- The theory is properly applied,
- There is sufficient data to support its application,
- The expert witness understands the theory and can effectively communicate it and its application to the audience,
- The judge rules that the scientific opinion is relevant and reliable, i.e., admissible,
- The theory and the expert appear credible,
- Counsel promote the opinion correctly,
- Opposing counsel understand the theory sufficiently to bring out latent bias or error,
- It fits into the decision matrix of the trier of fact, and
- The trier of fact perceives the impact of science correctly.

[9] *Berry v. Chaplin*, 74 Cal.App.2d 652, 169 P.2d 442 (1946)

[10] Ayala, F. and Black, B., Science and the Courts, *American Scientist*, 81, 230-239 (1993).

[11] Jasanoff, S., *Science at Trial*, Harvard University Press (1996).

[12] *Flue-Cured Tobacco Cooperative Stabilization Corporation, et al. v. U.S. Environmental Protection Agency*, et al. No 6:93CV00370 (C.D..N.C., July 8, 1998).

[13] In fact, a lawyer might argue that the judge erred in granting summary judgment, because scientific facts are not questions of law and summary judgment is not an appropriate tool to adjudicate factual disputes.

▸   The trier of fact remembers the expert testimony at the time of decisionmaking.

Even if a case is scientifically strong, litigants face a mixture of other hurdles. If a plaintiff's facts do not support each of the elements of each cause of action, the case is dismissed. Furthermore, the plaintiff has to prove that it is more likely than not that the defendant is liable, i.e., the probability must be 51% or more. In a criminal trial, the State has the burden of proof to show that the defendant is guilty "beyond reasonable doubt," which is often considered to be a 95-98% probability. However, as explained in Chapter 1, the standard is more flexible than words suggest. The judge and jurors weigh the trustworthiness of evidence before they make a decision, and the U.S. courts adjudicate cases on the basis of both law and equity, and judges and jurors rely on common sense rather than on a purely rational approach, as engineers or airline pilots are required to do.

SCIENTISTS, ENGINEERS AND PHYSICIANS

Scientists, engineers and physicians use different methodologies, espouse different values and use different criteria to evaluate the trustworthiness of results in their own fields.

Scientists are fact oriented. Their goal is to enlarge the universe of knowledge and tie their findings into the web of prior existing science. Scientists use facts to derive the rules and laws that govern nature. Only a 100% accurate fit will do. If an observation conflicts with prior knowledge, the discrepancy needs to be resolved, and the theory adjusted.

There is much confusion among non-scientists, and even among undergraduate science majors, about whether scientists are allowed to make errors. Scientists are not engineers or physicians. Progress in science depends on being willing to propose and test new theories and sometimes take the risk of making an erroneous prediction. Even the most famous scientists will readily admit that they have made errors, and that they occasionally publish proposals that are later not confirmed. This does not distract from the reliability of a good scientist's statements as long as scientists clearly distinguish between confirmed facts and speculative proposals. Because scientists always keep their data and records of their observations upon which their scientific opinions are based, their accuracy and the interpretation can be verified.

Research scientists are specialists and spend most of their time communicating with peers in their own specialty or in interdisciplinary fields in which they share education, knowledge, assumptions and quality standards. Since most research requires extensive facilities and funding, researchers work in teams that share facilities, funding and responsibility for projects. These teams tend to form a world-wide family of specialists in which individual researchers can move from lab to lab, building and maintaining life-long personal ties. Furthermore, the academic and industrial world of science is characterized by a highly vertical structure in which the more senior people act as mentors for the younger, just as in medicine. The impact of this social structure is discussed below.

Engineers are licensed professionals and must work within the closed universe of currently recognized standards and conventions. We do not want engineers to make errors when they design bridges, or airline pilots to test their personally designed gadgets on an airplane full of passengers.

Health care providers include not only physicians and surgeons but a large and diverse group of other specialties, such as osteopathic surgeons and, in many states, an increasing number of alternative health care providers whose fields are not as solidly founded as medicine, but all of whom are state licensed professionals. Physicians must meet the standard of care, a sometimes elusive standard that is determined by competing factors and organizations, including medical schools, the federation of medical boards, the State board of medical examiners and the local, state and national professional and trade organizations who provide continued medical education. There are two reasons why we do not want physicians to experiment with patients. The first is concern for the safety of the patient; the second is that clinicians deal with isolated observations, i.e., most of their observations are anecdotal. In fact, conducting epidemiological studies takes detailed preparation, and the design and supervision of statistically significant experiments with humans requires governmental permission.

The Methodology of Clinical Medicine

The goal of the treating physician is to heal the patient. His approach and procedure differ from those of the natural scientist. In the majority of cases, the practicing physician does not treat causes, he treats diseases using the treatment modality that the local professional consensus considers the current "gold standard." Physicians lack the time and resources to concern themselves with scientific questions, such as causation, and most treatment modalities are based on practical experience rather than on scientific research.

A common method for diagnosing a patient's complaint is to match the subjective and objective symptoms presented by the patient against the symptoms that define known diseases:

> A disease is a pervasive, clinically significant psychological or biological syndrome or patterns of symptoms. A disease may result in present distress or disability, or may remain dormant until such time that factors within the individual or surrounding environment cause the symptoms of the disease to manifest themselves. A disease, although having a physiological origin, may manifest itself in a behavioral, psychological and/or biological manner.[14]

Diagnosing diseases is difficult, because many diseases exhibit similar, non-specific symptoms, and the accuracy of the match between the symptoms that define a given disease, and those exhibited by a patient is rarely perfect. The physician tries to find a pattern among the symptoms presented by the patient that approximates the pattern and behavior of symptoms of known diseases as a means

---

[14] *Academic Press Dictionary of Science and Technology:* a specific illness or disorder that is identified by a characteristic set of signs and symptoms, caused by such factors as infection, toxicity, genetic or developmental defects, dietary deficiency or imbalance, or environmental effects.

to find a suitable treatment plan.

A typical diagnosis is based on a combination of four elements: The patient's history, the physical exam, the diagnostic tests and the patient's response to treatment. The purpose of the first two is to discover or exclude as many symptoms and signals of diseases as possible. In selecting a diagnostics test or procedure, the physician must compare the need for accuracy, sensitivity, specificity and predictive value. The diagnostic method requires a combination of semiology,[15] clinical knowledge, prior experience and hypothesis. Finally, in choosing an appropriate treatment plan, the physicians must avoid anything that could harm the patient.

Today, as hundred years ago, physicians treat most diseases by relying on earlier local and personal experience, i.e., on precedent, combined with intuition, rather than scientific analysis.[16] A large part of their tradition is transmitted by peers and mentors to whom, according to the Hippocratic oath, physicians owe a higher duty than to patients. The tension between traditional medicine and prevailing U.S. law frequently surfaces over the question of informed consent.[17]

The misconception of medicine as an exact science distracts from the reliability of the medical art, and makes the testimony of physicians especially vulnerable to cross-examination at trial, because in the face of uncertainty, the prudent physician often needs to rely on intuition, and accept a comparatively low probability of success.

The methodology chosen by physicians depends on their specialty. Anesthesiologists and surgeons rely strongly on objective symptoms; neurologists and internists rely more strongly on what a patient reports, i.e., on subjective symptoms. Since physicians are licensed, they put much weight on complying with local practice.

How Natural Scientists Determine Facts

The method used by natural scientists to determine the reliability of new data or a new theory depends on whether the latter lies within their personal specialty or not.

Two hundred years ago, it was still possible for an educated person to gain an overview of the cultural knowledge of his own society. This is no longer possible. Furthermore, in recent years, much of the research incentive has shifted back into

---

[15] Semiology, semeiology or symptomatology, is that branch of medicine that deals with symptoms of diseases. See *Webster's Collegiate Dictionary.*

[16] For a thorough analysis of the problems that are inherent in clinical methodology see, e.g., Bleuler, E., *Das Autistisch-Undisziplinierte Denken in der Medizin und seine Überwindung,* 5th Edition, Springer Verlag, Berlin (1962). Dr. Robert Califf, Director of the Duke University Clinical Research Institute recently told Time Magazine that "only 15% of the decisions a doctor makes every day are based on evidence." Time Magazine, 68 (October 12, 1998).

[17] Determining the cause of a disease and identifying treatment options are the provinces of the medical specialist, but the selection of the choice is not a medical question, but a question that affects the autonomy of the patient, and therefore should be decided by the patient. *Cobbs v. Grant,* 104 Cal. Rptr. 505 (1981).

industry, where access is restricted for proprietary reasons.

Contrary to the belief of the public and most students, skilled researchers do not rely solely on data published in the scientific literature, but need frequent contact with their peers and mentors. A skilled researcher always wants to know the identity of the author, and his affiliation, because the performance of a scientist depends on the facilities and the peers he has available for consultation. For the same reason, young Ph.D.s still follow tradition and journey to leading foreign institutions to advance their skills.

Review Within a Scientific Specialty

In any competitive field any new discovery or report is quickly scrutinized and the experiments repeated in every competing lab by peers, even though the results of such replication are usually not publishable, because scientific journals only publish novel data. However, science has not yet reached its limits, and new results always afford an opportunity to open yet newer frontiers.

Review of Research Conducted Outside of the Scientist's Immediate Field

When it comes to scrutinizing research that lies outside of one's own speciality, scientists defer to the opinion of peers by informal or formal inquiries among recognized world-wide specialists in leading departments. It is easy to locate the leaders either by reading scientific literature or by visiting the appropriate academic or industrial department, because the science establishment is cohesive. Science is a group activity, since scientists depend on institutional and peer, graduate student and post-doctoral support to nurse and test their ideas and articulate them in a form that is useable for their intended audience. Virtually every scientist is a member of a professional organization that disseminates scientific reports by organizing annual meetings and often serves as publishers of the leading scientific journals.

The science establishment has a strong vertical structure that is based on the personal records of individual scientists, the quality of students or coworkers they attract, and the quality of the scientists that work together at the same institution. These qualities are widely monitored by annual polls among peers and by publication of statistics in the journals of the professional organizations.

Outsiders tend to underestimate the high rigor of the seemingly casual re-iterative procedures that govern the scientific exchange of information within the scientific community. All research universities, and each science department, subdivision and faculty member maintain a regular and vigorous schedule of seminars and faculty meetings with their staff and students.

HOW ANECDOTAL OBSERVATIONS DEVELOP INTO SCIENTIFIC LAW

The scientific method is based on a reiterative process. In short, it follows seven simple steps:

1. Observe some aspect of the universe.
2. Propose a tentative description, called a hypothesis, that is consistent with what you have observed.
3. Use the hypothesis to make predictions.
4. Test those predictions by experiments or further observations.
5. Modify the hypothesis in the light of your results.
6. Modify the predictions.
7. Test the modified predictions.
8. Repeat steps 5 to 7 until no discrepancies are left between theory and experiment.

When internal consistency is obtained, the hypothesis becomes a scientific theory. The theory is then a framework within which observations are explained and predictions made. When the theory is compared with other theories and fully and accurately fits into every link in the preexisting web of all prior existing theories, scientists accept it as a rule of conduct and action, i.e., as a natural law.

The tool box with which scientists measure and explain the world consists of a mixture of laws, theories and hypothesis at various stages of completion.

The beauty of natural laws is that they apply universally and eternally, and can be tested by any skilled person, any place, any time. Thus, the law of mass preservation applies in a test tube, in an automotive engine, on the moon, and in the belly of any living creature. It has universal validity within the range of its parameters.

Theories need not be universally valid. An example is the dichotomy between Condon's wave theory and Max Plank's quantum theory. Each of these theories yields powerful predictions, sometimes for the same phenomena, even though the two theories are not yet fully unified.

In chemistry and physics it is important to know the list of all parameters that define the properties of a system. The physical states of water, ice and steam are an example of widely known physical properties that have well-established limits, or "boundary conditions." The chemical reaction mechanism and kinetics have similar limits. Thus, every cook knows that turning up the heat increases the speed with which vegetables and meats cook and become tender, i.e., that the speed of chemical reactions generally increases with temperature, but we also know that there is a "border condition" above which the reaction path changes and food no longer cooks, but burns and turns into charcoal.

HOW WE KNOW WHETHER A SCIENTIST'S OPINION IS RELIABLE

Scientific activities are not driven by reason alone. As the patent literature demonstrates, the application of science is frequently based on experience rather than on a full understanding of the scientific foundation of a process. As analyzed by the California Supreme Court for DNA fingerprinting, errors can occur at every stage from data gathering to interpretation.[18]

Most instrumental analysis, such as the gas chromatography-mass spectros-

---

[18] *The People v. Venegas*, No. 48338 (Cal.Sup.Ct., filed May 11, 1998), 98 Daily Journal, D.A.R. 4901 (1998).

copy (GC/ms) analysis of gases and liquids strongly depends on the skill of the operator, and on self-discipline, i.e., quality control.[19]

Furthermore, the analysis of such spectra can sometimes yield more than one valid answer, because it involves a multi parameter analysis that may allow more than one interpretation. Thus, while GC/ms is a very powerful tool for suggesting interpretations of samples, its results usually depend on validation by different methods.[20]

While, theoretically, a scientific analysis is straightforward, the implementation is complex and requires extensive education and experience. In this respect, science and medicine are similar to law. A professional opinion can be compared to a large tower, in which the individual structural steel beams represent the elements necessary for scientific proof. If any structural element is missing, the entire tower is not reliable. A scientific opinion of someone who has not completed the appropriate formal scientific curriculum, followed by professional experience, is not worth more than a legal opinion by someone who has not completed law school.

The basic education needed to understand and analyze scientific problems starts in junior high school, when one learns to solve story problems, i.e., to use words and situations to set up and formulate a mathematical equation. In order to understand laboratory experiments, one needs basic laboratory skills in chemistry and physics. A person who does not know statistics cannot design a statistically meaningful experiment. Scientific ability and competence can be roughly divided into three progressive steps. The first step, acquired during a good lower level college education, is the acquisition of the basic knowledge, tools and skills to organize information and set up and solve problems selected by the teacher. The second step, acquired during advanced upper level courses and graduate studies, is the ability to categorize problems sufficiently to select a suitable approach and appropriate tools. The third step, for which postgraduate and postdoctoral experience is necessary, is reached when a scientist gains the ability to apply his knowledge and understanding without supervision. Even Ph.D.s rarely work alone.

INTERDISCIPLINARY DECISION MAKING

Progress in interdisciplinary areas depends on team work by people who have the requisite education and training. Difficulties arise when interdisciplinary work involves fields using conflicting methodologies. As explained above, this occurs when basic or life sciences interface with clinical medicine.

---

[19] U.S. Department of Justice; Office of Inspector General; The FBI Laboratory One year later: A Follow-up to the Inspector General's April 1997 Report on the FBI Laboratory Practices and Alleged Misconduct in Explosive-Related and Other Cases (June 1998).

[20] Bruya, J., Analysis of gas chromatography-mass spectroscopy data, National Forensic Conference, University of Wisconsin Engineering Extension Dept., R. Morrison, chair, Tucson, Arizona (August 28, 1998).

About Rats and People

A frequent issue is whether testing of chemicals on animals can be used as a surrogate for human testing. Pharmaceutical manufacturers affirm this. Manufacturers of toxic chemicals persistently deny this. Counsel and litigators accept whatever position is best for their present client.

That animals can be used as a predictor of human safety has been known for centuries, at least since miners started carrying canaries into the mine tunnels and evacuated the tunnels when the canaries stopped singing. The cosmetic industry could not function without testing new formulations on animals. Animal tests are an important and integral part of FDA and EPA and many other regulations covering hundreds of thousands of different pharmaceutical inventions and tens of thousands of toxic substances.

However, there is no simple, universal constant for translating animal data. Whether animal studies can be used to predict human behavior depends on (a) the similarity of conditions, (b) the borderline conditions within which the translation is valid, and (c) the qualifications of the person who performs the translation.

The *Joiner* decision offers a good example of how scientific and legal interpretation differ. In a nutshell, in *Joiner*, experts claimed that compound A caused cancer in rats, and that, therefore, compound B would be expected to cause cancer in humans. Chief Justice Rhenquist concluded that there was "too great an analytical gap" between the two. Whether this argument is valid, depends on whether or not compounds A and B belong to the same class of carcinogens.

Science that is settled

The natural sciences are built on a solid basis of settled laws that allow scientists and engineers to apply them reliably and reproducibly. An example of this would be the Maxwell laws of mechanics, or electro dynamics, or the law of mass preservation in chemical reactions. If the expert witnesses are competent and honest, there is no room for argument over the meaning of these laws.

In the world of science, scientific opinion is customarily expressed and discussed in the form of reports that describe the scientific findings in a standard format, including the goal, the experimental conditions, the data observed, the laws invoked, the basis for the interpretation, and firm as well as tentative conclusions. Most authors will circulate their reports informally or formally among peers, to elicit their reactions before the author proceeds with final publication.

In the natural sciences, most observations are repeated before publication. In contrast, in clinical medicine, it is common to report individual, i.e., anecdotal observations.

The problem with scientific review is that in a field where innovation has been quick, and in a world with shrinking economic resources, i.e., where time and priority is of essence, it has become tempting for scientists to publish preliminary results in form of Letters to the Editor, or Notes.

Science that is not yet settled

Disputes arise when science is not yet settled, because a link has not yet been tested, it does not fit, or something is wrong with the theory. This type of shortcoming is a natural step through which every new scientific theory has to grow before it can become accepted. Perhaps the theory is shaky because the discovery is new and rests solely on one or only a few experiments and the authors have not yet found wide support for their theory, or, perhaps, because some criticism has been raised by other groups.

When inconsistency starts popping up in a theory, scientists still may use it, but with great caution and they will always want to identify the uncertainties and warn their audience. Scientific opinions are shaky when they are based on anecdotal observations, i.e., isolated experiments or facts, because the researcher may not yet have observed all variables and contingencies. Anecdotal reports are common in the clinical literature, because the human body is complex, and epidemiological studies require much time and resources,

Science is also shaky when the researcher is sloppy; i.e., does not calibrate his equipment sufficiently, or does not measure or report critical parameters, such as sample age, temperature, history of sample and the number of samples taken or document all work and create contemporaneous laboratory records[21,22]

Invalid Science

When a link between a new theory and the prior body of science has been tested and fails, the theory is invalid and useless. In the heat of the courtroom drama, some inexperienced, or insufficiently trained experts may be seduced to exaggerate, or propose theories that are simply incorrect. Here are four different examples:

Example 1: The testimony that "all chemicals are toxic at all levels" is incorrect because whether a chemical is toxic depends on the dose. Thus, for example, selenium and arsenic are vital trace elements at low concentrations, but are highly toxic at high concentration.

Example 2: The claim that the "test of time" has proved that dental amalgam is not toxic is incorrect, because research has shown that dental amalgam releases toxic mercury at a level above the threshold level set by EPA, and poisoning by chronic exposure to low levels of mercury is difficult to distinguish. What has not been established is whether the symptoms of mercury poisoning that are found among the general population are causally connected to dental amalgam or to some other environmental vector, because the symptoms are not unique to mercury poisoning.

Example 3: It has long been established that the result of lie detector tests depends not only on the tested person but on the operator. Even though such tests

---

[21] Lederberger, J., Sloppy Research extracts a Greater Toll Than Misconduct, *The Scientists*, 9 (4) (Feb. 20, 1995).

[22] Bailar, J., The Real Threats to the Integrity of Science," The Chronicle of Higher Education, B1 (April 21, 1995).

are widely used by employers to test the reliability and loyalty of prospective employees, lie detector results are not good science and are not normally admissible evidence in U.S. courts.

Example 4: The claim that the memory of sexually molested children can be reliably refreshed when they are adults is not only not proven but is, in practice, hard to differentiate from coaching.[23]

THE ROLE OF BIAS IN SCIENCE AND IN COURT

The right to challenge a witness statement on the basis of personal or professional bias is as old as law.[24]

One frequently hears the suggestion that experts have an interest in the outcome of the litigation because some experts earn substantial fees, and that experts would be neutral if they were hired by the judge, rather than by the parties, using Federal Rule of Evidence 706. This argument misses the point.

Bias is not restricted to scientific experts. In many criminal cases the key witnesses are paid informers or convicted felons whose testimony will influence whether they will be spared incarceration.[25] Bias is not restricted to the court room. In a world that is saturated with commercial advertisement, jurors have experience with dealing with economically motivated information.

Whether bias is harmful depends on whether the nature of the bias is known to the trier of fact, or whether it remains hidden. Expert pay is regularly explored during cross-examination, and is considered by the jurors. In contrast, professional bias is harder to detect and neutralize, because it is rarely recognized by counsel, rarely explained to jurors, and sometimes the expert, himself, does not recognize it and how it affects his perspective.

Scientists and lawyers differ in their attitude towards bias. Scientists are not afraid of bias. Academic and industrial scientists are advocates, and their opinions are always based on tools that act as filters for information, and thereby introduce bias. Scientists and inventors are risk takers and are proud of being biased in favor of their work and are surprised if opposing counsel tries to see a negative side in this, even though work-related accidents reveal that scientists are notoriously overconfident in the reliability and safety of their own work.

Scientists work in small and competitive communities of specialists. They work in teams that share the same equipment, the same information and the same overall goals, and, usually, the same source of institutional support, i.e., the same professional bias. Fellow scientists and competitors know the limits of facilities and bias of their peers and competitors from their own experience and from

---

[23] *State of North Carolina vs. Walter Thomas York,* No. 550a95, (N.C. Sept. 5 1997), and *Tucker vs. State of Alaska,* No. 1404 (Alaska, April 7, 1995).

[24] A full cross-exam of a witness upon the subject of his examination in chief is the absolute right, not the mere privilege of a party and a denial of this right is a prejudicial and fatal error, *Gilmer v. Higley,* 110 U.S. 47, 50, 3 S.C. 471, 28 LED 62 (1910). *For other citations see: Lindsey v. U S,* 133 F.2d 368, (D.C. Cir. 1942), overruled on other grounds by 405 F.2d 1352, 1359 (D.C. Cir. 1968).

[25] For a discussion of the problem see, e.g., U.S. v. Posado, Ramirez and Hurtado, No. 94-20285 (5th cir. June 20, 1995)

contacts with their competitors, and this helps them to determine what type of findings are reliable and to what degree.

The impact of an expert witness' bias is more difficult to evaluate, because the litigator who mediates between the expert and the court, and the trier of facts are not professional peers and are not familiar with the nature and source of the expert's bias, unless the expert represents a special interest group.

Modern science depends on large institutional facilities and financial support. Virtually all progress that can be made in chemistry, physics, biochemistry, and biotechnology is directly applicable and, therefore, has potential economic value to the researcher or his sponsoring institution. Rare is the outstanding scientist who does not hold patents covering some of his inventions. The post-world war II period, when much of the government sponsored research was quickly published and widely shared, is long over. Much of the best current research has direct economic value for its author, either in the form of continued research sponsorship, in the form of consultancies or royalties from industries that develop and implement the research, or in the form of personal rank within the scientific community. Furthermore, physicians as well as scientists are strong advocates of those procedures and of that type of machinery that is connected to their daily expertise. Another form of professional bias that is harder to identify for outsiders is the intense rivalry for funds and fame that dominates all fields of competitive science.

Another example of bias that judges and jurors tend to underestimate is the professional and institutional bias of scientists that is implicit in their skills or training. While judges know that physicians tend to stigmatize colleagues who break rank with majority positions, they usually underestimate how strongly a technical expert's career may depend on compliance with peer pressures.

The objectivity of professional licensing boards is a complex issue, because these boards must represent – and should balance – the conflicting interest of the public and those of their own profession, but as many of the disciplinary actions show, the board members usually lack the professional training to insure that procedures are fair enough to yield unbiased decision.[26]

Similar, and even more complex, problems affect professional organizations, because these organizations need to serve constituencies with diverse goals. The goals usually include the pursuit of high professional standards, public service, advancement of the economic interest of their members, legislation to protect against competition by other professions, protection against unwanted governmental regulation, and protection of their own interest in encouraging – or forcing – professionals to become and remain members of the organized profession. In this competition,[27] the goal of influencing public policy tends to overshadow that of

---

[26] See, e.g., Felmeth, R. C. and D'Angelo, L., Physician Discipline in California, A Code Blue Emergency 9(2) *Cal. Reg. L. Rptr.* 1-192 (1987).

[27] The problems can range from the promotion of remunerative standards of care, that result in over-treatment to price fixing. See e.g., *Federal Trade Commission v. California Dental Association*, No. 9259, Final Order (March 26, 1996), in which the FTC found that "The CDA is at the hub of an agreement among its members to restrict competition in the market for dental services;" see also *Wilk v. American Medical Association*, 895 F.2d 352 (7th Cir.) *cert. den.* 496 U.S. 927 (1990) where the court found that the AMA waged "a war to contain and

public service,[28] especially when the interests are linked with industrial goals.[29]

In recent years, professional bias has also become visible in some of the articles published in scientific publications that have traditionally been proud of being neutral. Thus, the editors of *Science* and the *New England Journal of Medicine* have recently favored articles that belittle the risk of toxic products, and support the transfer of control of toxic injury issues from the courts to the organized professions,[30] without providing the balanced picture that professionals and the public would need to form fully informed opinions. Other examples of professional bias are listed on several Internet sites.[31]

Fraud

Scientific testing can become tedious, especially when the tasks are repetitive. Outright fraud is a relatively rare event, because sloppy scientists lack the intent necessary for fraud,[32] but actual fraud is as old as science, and neither competence nor public recognition seems to prevent some overeager or corrupt scientists from ruining their careers by engaging in it. It is an unfortunate fact that technicians in government and private contract crime labs can become complacent, if the opposing party does not understand or carefully verify the data underlying an expert's testimony.[33] However, since one cannot cheat nature, such fraud is

---

eliminate" the chiropractic profession; see also Friedman, J.W., and Atchison, K.A., The Standard of Care: An Ethical Responsibility of Public Health Dentistry, 53 *J. Pub. Health Dent.* 165-169 (1993).

[28] By way of example, the AMA long ignored the dangers of tobacco smoking, and the toxic propensities of formaldehyde. Furthermore, in 1998 the AMA passed a resolution that asks for the establishment of a disciplinary body for reviewing expert testimony by association members whose expert opinions do not comply with mainstream medicine.

[29] An example is the product certification and approval program of the American Dental Association. The AMA recently experimented with a similar program, but abandoned it after a year.

[30] See, e.g., Angell, M., *Science at Trial, the Clash of Medical Evidence and the Law in Breast Implant Cases*, Norton (1996), and the *Amicus Curiae* brief of the *New England Journal of Medicine* and Marcia Angell, M.D., in Support of Neither Petitioners Nor Respondents, submitted in the *General Electric v. Joiner* case, 1997 WL 304759.

[31] See the Internet site <http://www junkscience.com>, operated by Steven J. Milloy for The Advancement of Sound Science Coalition (TASSC).

[32] The definitions of criminal and civil fraud differ. Civil fraud requires a showing that the defendant misrepresented a material fact, that he knew that his statement was false, that he intended to induce plaintiff's reliance, that the plaintiff justifiably relied on the misrepresentation, that plaintiff suffered damages, and that the misrepresentation is the cause of the damages.

[33] U.S. Department of Justice, The FBI Lab One Year Later: A Follow-up to the Inspector General's April 1997 Report on the FBI Lab. Practices and Alleged Misconduct in Explosive Related and Other Cases (June 1998). Available on the

invariably detected and usually promptly.

Competent scientific experts rarely lie in court, because the risk of being exposed is great and the expert's professional career and reputation would be ruined, since the scientific community is small and competitive, and the professional peers and competitors are not forgiving. Experts tend to lie more frequently when their testimony is outside of their own area of professional competence. Among the most frequent misrepresentations by experts is that he does not believe the opponent's theory, when, in reality, he does not understand it.

Another example is the physician who denies a causal link between an incident of poisoning and the manifestation of a matching pattern of symptoms, because he had no training in toxicology and was trained to deny any links that he does not understand.

Misinformation and fraud occasionally occur among researchers who work without adequate supervision. There is a continuum stretching from inadvertent error, to puffery, bias and excessive advocacy until it eventually reaches legally actionable fraud.

Since scientists are advocates of natural laws and theories, most scientific papers contain some recommendations that are as yet unproven hypotheses. There is nothing wrong with this as long as the author clearly distinguishes between his scientific conclusions, which must be solidly backed by falsifiable data, and his hypotheses which are traditionally contained in a separate section. Problems arise when the author is sloppy or over enthusiastic and confuses firm conclusions and hypotheses, or when a reader is insufficiently familiar with the subject matter to recognize the difference. A more serious problem arises when researchers are engaged in high stakes competition for fame or the priority of patentable work.

The legal and the popular definitions of the term fraud are different. The main difference is that to prove legal fraud, one has to demonstrate that the actor made the misrepresentation with the knowledge that it was wrong, that he intentionally misled the victim to induce the victim to rely on the misrepresentation, that the victim reasonable relied on the misrepresentation, and that the damages suffered by the victim were directly due to the misrepresentation.

The legal proof that scientific fraud, or any fraud, has been committed is difficult for several reasons. The plaintiff has to prove intent to deceive, called "scienter." It is hard to differentiate between intentional misinformation and mere "puffery," and in the age of hard ball commercial advertisement and infomercials, the public and the courts have been desensitized and often find it difficult to differentiate between negligent and intentional misinformation.

When scientists accuse each other of fraud, the underlying problem is usually not fraud but the theft or insufficiently authorized use of intellectual property, or of laboratory samples, or merely rivalry among long-term rivals. The analysis and resolution of such disputes can be difficult, because in the competitive world of science it is difficult to differentiate between simultaneous discoveries, espionage and inadvertent exchange of valuable information.

This type of rivalry is fairly common[34] among academic as well as industrial

---

Internet at <http://www.usdoj.gov/oig/fbi1yr.htm>.

[34] Sharon Begley and Adams Rogers, War of the Worlds, *Newsweek*, February 10, 55-58 (1997).

labs that compete in the race for a Nobel Price, or for commercialization of new invention, because competitive science always involves high personal and financial stakes. A well-known example was the rivalry between Robert Gallo of the NIH and Luc Montagnier and his colleagues at the Institute Pasteur in Paris over the discovery and patent rights of the HIV virus. This dispute was eventually resolved by personal intervention of the Presidents of France and the United States.[35] Science and research fraud can involve plagiarism, falsification or fabrication of data. The motivation covers the entire gamut from purely economic considerations.[36]

An example of economically motivated fraud led to the recent criminal conviction of the director of a test laboratory who accepted payment for fabricated data for testing and research that was never performed.[37] More complex motivation lies behind cases that have been ferreted out by the Office of Scientific Integrity, a Division of the National Institute of Health. In one case, university researchers misrepresented multiple blood samples from a patient as samples from different patients, and interpreted some of their data by incorrect averaging methods.[38] In another case, a researcher compromised a long-term study of patients conducted by a large group of universities by substituting new patients for old ones that left the program.[39,40]

A different problem is the unauthorized use of research data by fellow researchers. Such fraud occasionally occurs in highly competitive research labs that are headed by widely respected scientists who attract a large number of visiting scientists. This type of problem tends to fester for years and can delay or damage the careers of coworkers, because the scientist's supervisors and their institutions are usually reluctant to admit the fraud of their employees for fear of losing financial sponsorship, and because this type of fraud is frequently associated with negligent supervision of the employee. Both the science establishment and the courts are notoriously hesitant to get involved in these type of cases.[41]

---

[35] Gallo and Montagnier, 8 *The Scientist* No.6 (March 21 1994).

[36] William Broad, Nicholas Wade, *Betrayers of the Truth, Fraud and Deceit in Science*, Oxford Press (1982).

[37] *U.S. v. Hess Environmental Labs*, No. 97-531 (DC EPA Nov. 11, 1997); *U.S. v. Klusaritz*, (DC EPA Nov. 11, 1997).

[38] *U.S. ex rel. Condie v. Regents of the University of California*, University of Utah, and John L. Ninnemann, No. 89-3550 (N.D. Cal. 1989).

[39] Joshua Lederberger, Sloppy Research Extracts a Greater Toll Than Misconduct, *The Scientists*, 9 (4) Feb. 20, 1995).

[40] John C. Bailar III, The Real Threats to the Integrity of Science *The Chronicle of Higher Education*, April 21, B1 (1995).

[41] *U.S. ex rel. Pamela A. Berge, U.S. v. Board of Trustees of University of Alabama*, Robert F. Pass, Professor of Pediatrics, Sergio B. Stagno, Professor and Chairman, Department of Pediatrics, Charles A. Alford, Professor of Pediatrics, Karen B. Fowler, American Council on Education, American Association of State Colleges & Universities, National Association of State Universities and Land-Grant Colleges, American Association of Community Colleges, Council of Graduate, 104 F.3d 1453 (4th Cir. 1997).

Fraud can infiltrate court proceedings in the form of testimony of experts or in the form of fraudulent data that is intentionally or inadvertently underlying an expert's opinion.

In court, scientific fraud and perjury by witnesses are closely related. Both are hard to prosecute because of the so-called "litigation privilege" which protects the statements of witnesses and lawyers who testify in court. The purpose of the litigation privilege is to encourage witnesses to freely testify without fear of repercussions.

Unfortunately, laboratory misrepresentation and fraud have been persistent problems in programs in which federal law assigns the responsibility for toxic testing to a contractor for the regulated party. A study performed for the U.S. EPA has shown that 11% of 2,000 reports showed "serious deficiencies." [42] Testing of pesticides has been an especially sore area.

JUNK SCIENCE

This term was popularized by Peter Huber's 1991 book "Galileo's Revenge." Junk Science is an emotional term intended to stigmatize the messenger and his message. The term is used by legal and political advocates when they wish to move scientific issues from a rational into an emotional arena, or when they feel threatened by a scientific opinion and are not capable of explaining their criticism in rational terms. The Advancement of Sound Science Coalition (TASSE), a group that includes a former president of the National Academy of Sciences, a Harvard University chairman and a former U.S. Congressman defines junk science as follows:

"Junk science" is bad science used by: personal injury lawyers to shakedown deep pocket businesses; the "food police" and environmental Chicken Littles to fuel wacky social agendas; power-drunk regulators; cut-throat businesses to attack competitors; and slick politicians and overly ambitious scientists to gain personal fame and fortune.[43]

The definition used by the Union of Concerned Scientists, which includes several distinguished scientists, including a Nobel Price winner, is:

Junk science is work presented as valid science that falls outside the rigors of the scientific method and the peer review process. It can take the form of presentation of selective results, politically motivated distortions of scientifically sound papers, or the publishing of quasi scientific non-reviewed journals. At its worst, it is opinions and speculation of scientists financially supported by self-interested lobby groups trying to confound the real scientific debate on important policy decisions.[44]

---

[42] Deficiencies in EPA's FIFRA Program, *JAMA*, 2505 (May .5, 1989).

[43] The Advancement of Sound Science Coalition (TASSE), Internet: <http://www.junkscience.com> Milloy, S. Webmaster.

[44] Union of Concerned Scientists, Internet <http://www.ucsusa.org/junkscience/whatisjunk.html>

The meaning of the term has been substantially broadened, and now includes any type of science that the speaker perceives to be unfavorable to his own cause. The popularity of this term among non-scientists reflects a reaction to the role which science has assumed in our society. As Ann Lennarson Greer describes the latter:

> Science itself occupies a unique position in modern society in that it is embraced as a point of reference in many arenas of activity which are not themselves scientific. Science may perhaps be compared to the medieval church in the pervasive role it has achieved as a point of reference for other activities. The impressive success of science in establishing its authority has depended upon the distinct commitment of scientists to the goals and procedures of science. Most users of science, however, seek scientific input as a means to their own quite different purposes. Thus, scientists are called to contribute to decisional areas, including the judicial system, which in turn must struggle to incorporate science into their own distinct systems of thinking and acting. If scientists want scientific laws to be respected in the legal forum, they need to explain the applicable laws in terms that non-scientists can understand.[45]

An example of the use of the term is the battle cry of a former president of Olin Chemical Company against federal regulation.[46] Professor Nicholas Ashford analyzed the accusations and explained in rational terms why this attack is unfortunate.[47]

Another example is the current political drive to discredit the scientific basis of the basic research work which earned Mario Molina, Sherwood Rowland and Paul Crutzen the chemistry Nobel price in 1995, in order to block a U.S. Senate vote on the ratification of the Kyoto Protocol to the 1992 Climate Change Treaty that would require the U.S. and thirty-eight industrialized nations to reduce their "greenhouse" gas emissions from 1990 levels between 2008 and 2012 by an average of 8 percent. Some members of the chemical industry claim that the treaty would cost more than 2 million jobs and $300 billion a year.

The overwhelming majority of claims of junk science involve the scientific basis for health claims or health risk, an area where experimental research is difficult, time consuming and expensive, where science and medicine apply incompatible methodologies, and where the battle between scientific and clinical values overlaps with the political and economic agendas of the litigating parties or of third parties.

---

[45] Greer, A.L. and Meyer, C., Explaining Science to Judges and Jurors, *The Chemist*, 19, 35-44 (Spring 1998).

[46] Johnstone, J.W., Jr., Combating Junk Science. Guest Editorial in *Chemical and Engineering News*, 5 (April 28, 1997).

[47] Ashford, N., Letter to the Editor, *C&E News*, 8 and 71 (May 19, 1997). See also, Ashford, N.A. and Miller, S.C., *Chemical Exposures: Low Levels and High Stakes*, Second Ed., John Wiley, N.Y. (1998).

EVALUATING THE TRUSTWORTHINESS OF SCIENTIFIC EXPERT OPINIONS

The National Conference of Commissioners on Uniform State Laws (NCCUSL) has submitted a proposed, revised version of Federal Rule of Evidence 702 to the federal judicial council,[48] that lists some of the criteria that help determine the validity of a scientific expert opinion. Scientists test the validity of an opinion by an expert applying a five-step analysis:

▸   Is the theory applicable to the problem and is it sufficiently reliable to obtain the proposed result?
▸   Is the equipment or method used to apply the theory suitable for the intended purpose and reliable enough?
▸   Is the data proffered adequate and of sufficient quality to be reliable?
▸   Is the expert who proffers an opinion sufficiently qualified to understand the strength and limits of the theory, experiment and data to apply it to the present case in such a manner that his opinion is relevant and reliable?
▸   Can the expert validate his assumptions, and
▸   Has the expert considered whether there are equally likely alternate explanations?

Each of the above steps might require a separate expert. However, in litigations involving smaller damages, it is common for counsel to stipulate to a part or subpart of the above steps. By way of example, in drunk driving cases, the parties usually stipulate that the Breathalyzer is correct and that the chain of evidence was proper. In each case, counsel and experts need to work closely together to determine whether such a stipulation is warranted.

Evaluation of Training

Any meaningful evaluation of a scientific statement requires an evaluation of the quality of the expert's training. Unfortunately, a large number of expert witnesses act merely as messengers of opinions prepared by others and propound opinions that they, themselves, do not fully understand. This is especially frequent in chemistry and other fields that do not require professional licensing.

This situation is due to the failure of opposing counsel to test the expert's qualifications. Scientific education and understanding include well-defined skills that are recognized internationally and are acquired in courses with a well-established syllabus. An expert's level of competence can usually be tested by reviewing the courses he has completed.[49] High school education can provide some of the basic mathematical tools and, perhaps, some broad overview of some basic sciences. Undergraduate courses provide textbook knowledge, i.e., science students

---

[48] National Conference of Commissioners on Uniform State Laws (NCCUSL), *Federal Rule of Evidence 702* (rev. August 8, 1998).

[49] Examination of the educational record of a treating physician acting as toxicological expert will frequently reveal that the physician did not attend a single course in toxicology, and that his testimony in this area is based on lay opinions.

acquire select basic knowledge and learn to regurgitate it in the context of their course program. Graduate students share a certain basic set of scientific tools. Their admission to graduate school is not only based on undergraduate grades, but by a standardized admission test which in chemistry, for example, is sponsored by the American Chemical Society and used almost world wide. While a science bachelors degree is based on textbook, i.e., second-hand knowledge, a scientist with a master's degree is expected to be able to use the scientific literature, find relevant information in the basic research literature and know how to use it. A Ph.D. scientist has completed an advanced course of study in his specialized field and has successfully completed an apprenticeship under the supervision of a skilled research professor acting as a mentor. A Ph.D. scientist has learned to formulate a research project, become familiar with the state of the art in his chosen specialty, reconcile his own work with that of others, and, hopefully, contribute some new knowledge to the body of science. However, it has been long recognized in industry as well as in academe that a scientist with a fresh Ph.D. requires up to ten years of additional study and practical experience before he is able to work independently on a project. Thus, in chemistry, Ph.D.s either work under the direction of others, or they shift with increasing experience into management positions, or they continue their studies as postdoctoral fellows in academe, government, nonprofit or industrial research and development labs.

While education alone does not show whether an author's scientific opinion is correct, a person's lack of training in a basic field such as statistics, by itself, is sufficient to make it unlikely, if not impossible, for him to voice a reasoned opinion that depends on that specialty.

Did the Researcher have the Necessary Facilities and Adequate Data?

Research errors, negligence and fraud result when a researcher ventures beyond the limits of his competence or resources.[50] The unfortunate fact about the Ninnemann case is that his faculty colleagues at two major universities failed to recognize and face the festering problems.

Have All Standards been Observed, and All Required Steps Performed?

While a complete evaluation of a scientific opinion requires an analysis by an equally competent peer, a large part of the reliability of an opinion can be determined with the help of a check list of the factors that much scientific work entails. The most common procedure is to rely on standards. While individual research scientists and groups usually develop their own quality control documents, some common scientific activities, especially laboratory activities, follow standard-

---

[50] An example is the case of Ninnemann, a biologist who conducted research in the field of immunology, established a prolific publication records, and became a surgery professor, until it was discovered that his statistical methods were badly flawed, that he did not have enough patients for some of his studies, and that he used multiple blood samples from some patients as surrogates for samples from different patients *U.S. ex rel. Condie v. Regents of the University of California, University of Utah, and John L. Ninnemann*, No. 89-3550 (N.D. Cal. 1989).

ized procedures established by voluntary consensus organizations such as the American Society for Testing and Materials (ASTM). These follow rigid protocols requiring participation of government, industry and consumer representatives, and round robin validation of procedures by the circulation of samples among participating laboratories.

The U.S. Environmental Protection Agency is currently preparing to phase in a new methodology for quality assurance that validates scientific work on the basis of performance rather than procedures. Performance-based codes and standards are documents that state goals and objectives, together with rules and procedures, usually involving testing and modeling, for determining when performance is achieved. Performance based standards allow designers greater flexibility, which can be use to achieve cost savings, greater safety, or greater quality, and allow laboratories to reach defined regulatory goals by using methods that are more appropriate for their facilities.

CONCLUSIONS

The term "junk science" is not used in the scientific community. It is used by, or for the benefit of, lay people who cannot distinguish between science and pseudo-science, in order to denigrate any scientific evidence that is adverse to the speaker's interest.

Each science and each observation and expert opinion has its own strengths and weaknesses. By necessity, medical diagnosis is based on a combination of experience and scientific reasoning, and physicians must deal with incomplete information. Findings in some areas of the social sciences also tend to remain tentative because social systems are complex and difficult to test. In contrast, in the traditional natural sciences, facts and laws have universal validity and can be verified anytime, anywhere, by anyone who has adequate facilities and skills. Furthermore, in chemistry and in engineering, a large number of methods and procedures have been standardized by consensus organizations, such as the American Society for Testing and Materials (ASTM). These standards are prepared by panels including representatives of industry, government and consumer groups. During the past decades, the U.S. EPA and several other federal agencies have developed quality control and validation schemes that help non-specialists to evaluate results. However, where a thorough review of data is necessary, there is no substitution for professional training and experience, including laboratory work.

One problem with experts is the natural tendency of those who possess superior knowledge in one field to over-reach and make claims that are outside their professional competence or authority. It is the responsibility of the litigators to help the trier of fact recognize the basis and reliability of the experts' opinions.

A difficulty, specific to the U.S. common law system, is that scientific opinions are evaluated and filtered by attorneys before they reach the trier of fact. The evaluation of scientific opinions could be greatly facilitated if scientific expert reports would be circulated among scientific peers – preferably, working scientists – and if the peer reviews, and the experts reply, would be made available to the trier of fact in their entirety, as is the case in certain administrative procedures, and in the civil law system of continental Europe.

8 The Five Dimensions of Scientific Testimony

Kathey M. Verdeal

CONTENTS

INTRODUCTION

I received my doctorate in the field of Environmental Toxicology in 1982 from the University of Wisconsin-Madison. A few years later I had a rather unique opportunity to take over the operation of a laboratory with an established clientele. The majority of the analytical applications involved forensics. As a consequence, I was launched head first into the legal system and began my career as an expert witness.

While it must be nearly a thousand, I have years ago lost track of the number of times I have testified. More honestly, I have never put feathers in my cap, notches on my belt, nor blown the smoke from the tip of a .45 before putting it into my holster. The time of the scientist as an expert is best spent focused on scientific evaluation and the dimensions of effective communication in the courtroom, rather than on keeping tedious lists of past case information, as is currently required by both Federal and Colorado rules. But alas, I find that respectful compliance with the rules demonstrates sincerity and the desire to be the best professional one can be. So here one finds oneself in the type of predicament which becomes familiar when working as a scientist in our adversarial legal system.

Litigators will seek to hire the expert based largely on the expert's familiarity with, and success in the courtroom. The presentation to the jury of their experienced expert then becomes a challenge to the litigator. The appearance of naiveté takes on a life of its own. Attempts to mask experience through well chosen words, are countered by theatrical intimations. Somehow the value of experience is made to be a thing of disrepute.

I used to wonder how the jury could ever make sense of what was occurring before their eyes, and how they could reach a decision with confidence, seeing through some of the confusion and contradiction in the courtroom. I now wonder about this less, as my goals in the courtroom have developed. The goal is focus and presentation of the scientific issues with the honest simplicity of common sense whenever possible. While the jurors may not have knowledge of the science, or ability to follow analytical detail, they do appreciate respect and common sense.

I share with you some of the knowledge I have gained through excitement, fatigue, and the stress of success as a scientific expert in the court room.

One measure of success is if, in fact, you the expert continue to get hired. I have inquired of litigators what they believe is important in an expert, and why. The answer is simply, where the rubber meets the road. All the brilliant analysis and the application of science to real life problems comes to a screeching halt if it remains stuck in the mind of the scientist, or flies over the heads of the judge and jury. Virtually any scientist can analyze a case and write a report. Very few are good in the courtroom. In a matter of an hour or two, while publicly under fire, the knowledge of a career and the essence of an analysis must somehow be stated, supported, and defended by the expert. All of this must be done under the constraints of courtroom protocol and the watchful control of the judge. The cost of expert failure in the final phase, in the courtroom, is far more than the cost of the expert's time.

Most cases settle and the trial never materializes. An agreement is reached. The costs are controlled by the consensus of the litigators and the clients they represent. On the other hand, if a case reaches the trial phase, the stakes are high: a win or loss, monetary gain or debt, a precedent being set. The cost of trial preparation and case presentation is high. Concentrated effort results in escalating costs. The verdict and monetary award is then beyond the litigators, and in the hands of the judge and jury.

THE FIRST DIMENSION: INDIVIDUAL PRESENTATION

The first dimension of Scientific Testimony is that which is uniquely you. It is the combination of your appearance, words, demeanor, confidence, and style. It is that of your unique presentation. Awareness of one's individual characteristics and limitations is essential. Everyone has something that can work against them, or they can work with it to minimize its negative aspect.

A little bitsy head sitting on a gigantic box, with no neck. A bobbling head, that "walks like an Egytpian." From the mouth comes science. Very impressive indeed!

Myself, for example, I'm small. I realized long ago that I have a problem giving a presentation while standing behind a podium. A little bitsy head, sitting on a gigantic box, with no neck. A bobbling head, that "walks like an Egyptian." From the mouth comes science. Very impressive indeed!

The witness stand offers a similarly impressive sight. The wooden box, chairs so deep that I often think of a child looking over the top of a steering wheel while sitting in the driver's seat of a large motor home. So the thing I do is sit tall, stand tall and wear high heels. If I get the opportunity, I will walk purposefully over to the jury, and draw a diagram in front of them. Then I become a person. I may be a short person, but I am a person, no longer just a head sitting on a box.

The presentation of the unique package, you the expert, is an important aspect in the courtroom. Some individuals use highly technical terms, others may speak with simple words using comparisons between the scientific issue and common life experiences. Questions may be answered by some individuals with short simple statements. Others may answer questions with paragraphs of condescending professorial flower, with theory of basic science failing where scientific application could succeed. Adversity can create embarrassment, sweat, flaring tempers, confusion, and fast, fiery verbiage. Or, adversity may be handled with the control of a deep breath, a smile, and the calm of confidence.

Individual communication styles vary as does one's comfort level with their style. To thine own self be true, but not at the cost of becoming offensive or rude to the judge and the jury. There is confidence versus arrogance, control versus unresponsiveness, and clearness versus confusion. Then there is the KISS theory (Keep It Simple Stupid). The reality of the communication problem is: complex scientific issues, technical terminology, a limited time to testify, and the short attention span of the jury. Hopefully, testimony may take an hour or two, rather than all day. The jury attention span is even shorter than that, generally twenty minutes or so.

One problem all scientists have is that our technical words have special meanings. We find the technical aspects easier to communicate with our very specific technical terms, so we tend to use them. One's use of words in the courtroom is very important, because you can completely lose the listener. They simply don't understand the words. It took us, the scientists, years of advanced education to learn those words, their meanings, and how to use them. Some of the jury members may not have a high school education. Certainly, most will not be able to understand a technical term with inadequate time or explanation. It is not just a single term that is the reality of the problem. The combination of several technical terms in a sentence, or worse, stated in a long sequence, may appear as if you are speaking a foreign language. The jury responds with a puzzled look, or worse, with a smirk on their faces that says .... "You must be joking!" Simplicity of words, sentences and concepts is part of the art of the scientific expert.

The jury may not understand the words, but they can feel confidence or arrogance. It is not just the words you say, it is the way you use them. If the expert wants to draw a diagram during testimony, you can say " I want to draw a diagram because there is *no way you can understand* this concept without me drawing it for you." Or you can say, "It would be easier for me, and *it would help me a lot* if I could draw a diagram for you." You have expressed a desire to do the same thing in both approaches, but communicated two different things. Courtroom courtesy dictates that the expert makes himself/herself understandable to the judge, jury, and litigators. This has to be accomplished, of course, within the limitations of: the abilities or inabilities of the expert to communicate what is important; the attention span of the jury; the questions from the litigators; and the control of the judge over the courtroom. The expert, the lawyers, members of the jury, and the judge all have their own intelligence and importance in the trial.

The judge has a high degree of importance to the expert, since they may rule on objections from the litigators during the testimony of the expert. This act either allows the expert to continue, or stops him/her from further discussion and opinion on the issue at hand. In essence, this controls what information and opinions get to the jury. The judge can essentially stop an expert from testifying on a point or in an area which may be deemed important to either the plaintiff's or the defendant's side of the case. The more understandable that the expert is, the better their rapport with the judge will be. This will create an interest in the judge and a desire to hear what the expert has to say. The result is that the expert will be allowed to continue, because the judge understands that there is a point to what the expert is attempting to say.

The jury has an intelligence of their own. The majority of the technical aspects may not be understood by the jury, but they pick up on other levels of communication. Confidence can be projected. Body language, vocal tone, and the attitude of the expert and litigators are noticed by the jury members. Tension may be sensed. An insult may be felt. All of these factors are part of the ultimate decision of the jury.

The intelligence of experts lies in their ability to communicate on multiple levels, and weave a thread through their testimony to make a point to the jury and focus on what is ultimately important for the case.

THE SECOND DIMENSION: CURRENT SCIENTIFIC KNOWLEDGE

The second dimension is an area that has to do specifically with you as the expert. As a scientist you must be prepared and have current knowledge in your field. This can be difficult in relation to current technology, since it advances so rapidly. Often when one finishes with their formal education, their development in the field slows drastically, as they begin to apply what they have previously learned. This can be a big risk for the educated professional who becomes an expert witness. Sometimes the expert can get away with it. The time when you don't, and get caught with dated knowledge, can be both embarrassing and damaging to your career.

To be good as an expert witness constantly challenged in the adversarial system, it is important to stay abreast of the new information. This is sometimes where we have to check our egos. We have gone to school for so long, and we are experts in our area. It is so easy to fall into thinking that we already know. There are changes out there rapidly driven by numerous factors such a young creative minds, the challenge of success, and money. Another complication which makes it difficult is that publishing one's work takes time. By the time the published work is accessed by the reader, it may already be dated. Others are ahead of you. The authors have developed and published the work before you locate and review it. They have moved forward. You are trying to catch up to them, and you may meet them as opponents in the court room.

Breaking down the ego and being realistic about one's aging knowledge is not the only problem; it's a matter of time. Advancements occur not only in our own area of expertise, but develop in related areas as well. Even with serious attempts to stay abreast of your field, your time is very limited. A litigator who has a consultant or expert who is coming at the same issue from a slightly different angle may cross examine you. That expert's literature and awareness of the changes in technology is different, although it interfaces. If you are examined on that literature you are less likely to be familiar with it. Clearly, it is not possible to read up on your speciality and every potential interface. So be smart. Stay educated in your area. Inquire as to the opposing expert's background. Identify similarities and differences. Be ahead of the game before you're on the witness stand. Stay strong within your expertise. An educated suspicion about where the cross-examining attorney may be leading you could prove to be very helpful. Avoid the trap of going beyond your expertise, into areas where you are weak. It will become a matter of your credibility, which can be an essential element of your involvement in the case.

Monetary constraints may be a problem in case preparation. The cost of not being prepared may be greater than any pro bono preparation you do. The loss of credibility and poor testimony that becomes public record is a cost you as an expert can't afford. Advances in computerized technology make accessing your bad testimony as easy as accessing your good testimony.

It is in this dimension that you have to start thinking about focus. Your focus will be different from the opposition. The issue may be the same, but presented from the opposite point of view. Alternatively, your issue may be ignored or downplayed by the other side of the case, while another more favorable issue is stressed by them.

THE THIRD DIMENSION: THE LAWYER'S UNDERSTANDING OF THE SCIENTIFIC ISSUES

The third dimension is a place where the expert can be an aid to themselves and the attorney that has hired you. It is essential to have a communication and understanding between the two of you regarding the scientific issues. In the event that you fail to accomplish this, what should be smooth sailing on direct examination may become a troubled exchange. Preparation has to be not only on your own level, but with the attorney that is going to exam you. It's a teamwork issue.

Some attorneys don't take the time to adequately prepare with the expert. When you run into this situation, following your testimony, you will leave the courtroom wondering what it was that you said. If you as the expert feel that way, so will the jury. I have had this disturbing experience before. My job was not accomplished because I could not get the information out to the jury and the judge. The right questions were not asked. There was no plan. I knew that the testimony was going nowhere. Attempting to direct the testimony in a productive direction is risky. The judge can stop you dead in your tracks, because you are not being responsive to the question that is being asked.

In addition to the problem with lack of preparation, there can be a lack of understanding or a lack of accuracy regarding the scientific issues by the attorney. It is essential to make sure that you are both on the same page with the interpretation of the science. I will give you an example. The concept of Divided Attention is an element common to both criminal and civil litigation where an individual is impaired by alcohol. Reduced Divided Attention means that instead of being able to pay attention to many pieces of incoming information, that is, perform multiple tasks at once, a person who is impaired by alcohol will miss a lot of the information. Their mind is impaired and they can only handle a few pieces of information at once, instead of many. One attorney that deposed me thought that Divided Attention meant shifting attention from a single issue to another single issue. In other words, his understanding was a misunderstanding. Hours of deposition time were wasted not being able to understand each other's point of view or questions and answers, because we were not on the same page. Eventually, I figured out that he did not know what Divided Attention was. I addressed the issue with a definition, and we were able to get past it.

Under direct examination, your attorney may repeat a question when he does not get the answer that he expects. If his expectation is based upon a misunderstanding, he may continue to try to elicit the response that he expects, and he is not getting it from you. If the issues haven't been worked out before hand, and he is trying to get an answer that you can't give, you may have to do some side stepping around the question. So there you are, doing a verbal dance around each other. It ends up looking like you're adverse to the person you are working for. Not a pretty sight! Then you may appear adverse on both direct and cross examination. That is what it will feel like, and that is what it will look like to the jury.

It is an essential part of preparation to make sure that the attorney's understanding of the science is consistent with that of the scientist who is their expert. The goal is to avoid being under "friendly fire" during direct examination.

THE FOURTH DIMENSION: DEFINING THE FOCUS AND DIRECT EXAMINATION

Preparation with the attorney goes beyond having a common understanding about the scientific matters. The issue of *focus* has become one of the most valuable approaches that I have developed through experience. I will consult with the attorney in a way which attempts to get him to focus on the important areas of my testimony. It is amazing how many attorneys have not really defined what the scientific point is that they want to make. Sometimes they have a general idea, but there is really no specific definition or plan. The general nonspecific approach with the science may not help them achieve their goal on the legal end.

I will ask the attorney to tell me what the three most important points are that he wants my testimony to get across. We define the three major concepts in order of importance. I inquire as to how the concept or point helps him achieve his legal goal. This exercise is a tremendous benefit to the attorney because it helps define both the science and what legal aspect of his case the science benefits. Not only does it help him, but it does something for both of you. The way in which the science helps achieve the legal end is something that the expert may not understand or may misunderstand. What is the legal issue that the litigator is trying to accomplish and how is it that the science can help accomplish it? The laws change. The litigator will probably be aware of current law as well as the specific legal angle that he is using in his case. The scientific expert and consultant must focus on which scientific points will aid the litigator in accomplishing his goal.

Communication on direct examination is absolutely critical. I think it is even more critical than what happens during cross examination, because by the time you get to cross examination, the jury is fatigued. That is not to imply that cross examination has little importance. The major opportunity to clearly focus and communicate the major scientific points occurs during direct examination. A smooth presentation, being able to understand the questions being asked, and being able to answer those questions in a helpful way requires that you get it worked out with the attorney before you testify. You both know where you want to get with the testimony. When the attorney asks you a question, you can answer it in a way that keeps the focus, since it has previously been defined by both of you.

The goal is to avoid being under "friendly fire" during direct examination

The main point that the attorney wants to communicate may be related to several other important scientific points. Once these major points are defined, the expert will be better able to answer the questions in a way that identifies or relates to one or several of the points. That's what I mean by focus. It is important that the focus does not become lost during the expert's testimony. Throughout your expert testimony, you want to develop a thread of consistency and support for the main scientific point. If the jury doesn't understand anything else but the major point, and that point supports the underlying legal theory, then you have been successful. Repeated exposure to the jury of the major point and related issues increases your chance of success. This requires a degree of skill on the part of the expert, since repetitious testimony can be stopped by the judge.

It is very difficult to achieve the desired focus by the expert alone. If the focus can be maintained by you the expert without the aid of the attorney, that is when the you will appear to be fighting your own side all the way through direct testimony. That doesn't work well, and your chances of success are minimized. The loss of focus can easily happen due to lack of understanding and preparation, although sometimes, with much understanding and preparation, a lack of focus may still occur.

Some bright attorneys will really want to learn the scientific material. They learn so much, and are excited about the science. The little details are seen by the attorney as being important to really understand the technical information. The attorney wants to share this opportunity to understand the science with the jury. Questions on the details are asked of the expert by the attorney. The testimony will become a blur of details with nothing to connect them to, and the point is lost or never reached. Time runs out. The jury is put to sleep. The judge is getting upset because it appears to be getting nowhere. You have lost the focus and never get to the main scientific point. While this may be great fun for the scientist and the knowledgeable attorney, it defeated what you were trying accomplish.

This gets back to two points that I mentioned earlier: the jury has a very short attention span, and KISS, Keep It Simple Stupid. Simple to the jury is a few identified points with some repetition. If you try to give the jury all the underlying scientific details so they can really experience understanding, you are probably going to fail. It took years for the scientist to really achieve understanding. The jury can't do it in 20 minutes, two hours or even a couple of days. During a trial, there is a limited attention, limited time, and variability in human intellect.

It is in direct examination that the expert can develop and demonstrate their intellect through verbal art. Mental analysis occurs and interpretation of what is happening on different levels in the courtroom goes on by the expert at the same time as a question is being asked of the expert. A decision is made regarding how to answer the question at the same time the expert is setting the stage to reinforcing the main point. The expert must answer the little questions responsively while keeping the big focus in mind so that your answer supports the main points you're trying to get across.

THE FIFTH DIMENSION: THINKING ON YOUR FEET WHILE SITTING IN THE HOT SEAT

It is in this dimension that testifying can become a lot of "fun." Direct examination is where the most can be done in terms of getting the judge and jury to grasp the main points. But beware, cross examination is nothing to be taken lightly. It is during cross examination that thinking on your feet becomes a significant element of testifying. It is mental gymnastics. With the aid of your attorney, some preparation can be done before the trial to get the expert prepared. Although cross examination may be full of surprises, it is during cross where you, the expert have to keep yourself emotionally under control, maintain your professionalism, and stand up for yourself and your opinions. This is the adversarial system. Your words will be twisted, taken out of context, and frequently misrepresented. Intimations, intonations and sometimes direct accusations of dishonesty as a hired gun may be used in an attempt to upset or rattle the expert, and discredit you in the eyes of the jury. I have been asked before how it is that an expert can remain confident and withstand this on cross examination. My answer is simple. The strength comes from one's honesty and integrity.

Cross examination and being publicly under fire are where one's skill as an expert really develops. This is where one integrates the various aspects of the other four dimensions. The *First Dimension*, keeping your cool, the manner in which you speak, confidence rather than arrogance, may be the only aspects of testimony that the jury will remember during deliberation, because they didn't understand the technical testimony. The *Second Dimension*, the knowledge and memory of the scientific literature is the expert's reservoir. The ability to access this knowledge quickly under fire is difficult when the cross examining attorney is trying to cause emotional noise and intimidation in the expert. The *Third Dimension* is where a common understanding of the science between the attorney doing direct examination and the expert can really pay off. The expert's answers to the cross examination questions can cue the attorney who conducts the direct examination. The direct attorney should be able to pick up the hint regarding the questions they should ask on *redirect examination,* which will follow cross examination. Redirect can then recapture the focus or the main points that cross examination was designed to diffuse or confuse. A focused redirect is facilitated because you have previously clarified the understanding of the scientific issues with the direct attorney and you both know where you are going. The *Fourth Dimension* is having made the main points without losing the focus of the testimony on direct examination. If this has been accomplished on direct, it then becomes a matter of support during cross examination.

Adversity may be handled with the control of a deep breath,
a smile, and the calm of confidence.

Creating or recognizing an opportunity to support the main points during cross examination is a powerful tool. It is in the *Fifth Dimension*. It is artfully changing a direction, creating an inversion, refocusing scattered particles of information. If during cross examination the expert can accomplish this, even just once, they have not lost or have perhaps even controlled the focus. The cross examining attorney may be asking questions that require negative responses, which make it appear that the expert knows absolutely nothing. There is nothing wrong with admitting that there are things that you as the expert don't know. A series of these types of admissions can be quite disturbing to the expert, although it is an opportunity to refocus and subtly gain control. The skill here is the ability of the expert to answer that type of question with a " no, but in fact, there is related information which supports my earlier point ....." Another opportunity may be if, upon being asked the right question, the expert can turn to the jury and say, " But that's exactly my point! How I see that issue is...." You have accomplished a change in direction by ending with the use of a positive phrase. Your point has been supported, and you have done so with dramatic emphasis because you have turned your face, head and body to the jury, thereby opening yourself to them. You have refocused.

Accomplishing this during cross examination probably means that the jury is going to understand what your point is because you made it on direct and you maintained it on cross, and opened the door for further support during redirect examination if necessary. The points will be solid, the focus maintained, and success achieved.

Your heart sinks to the floor. You look at him with down turned eyebrows and
disappointed puppy dog eyes that beg, "Oh, no... please don't go away... oh,
couldn't you just ask me a few questions ... oh, please ... just
one little question ... oh no...."

You know that you have truly transformed into being an "expert" when you look forward to cross examination: adrenal glands pump, hands sweat, you eagerly anticipate and listen for the first of a series of difficult questions. The attorney stands and utters those dreadful words, " I have no questions your honor."

ACKNOWLEDGMENTS

Thanks to Dan Victor Chavez for the cartoons. Dan is a senior at North High School in Denver, Colorado. Also thanks to my brother, Victor Verdeal, who dedicates his life to his art students at North.

RECOMMENDED READING

Bronstein, D. A., *Law for the Expert Witness*, Lewis Publishers, Boca Raton (1993).

Matson, J. V., *Effective Expert Witnessing* (second ed.), Lewis Publishers, Boca Raton (1994).

Loftus, E. and Ketchum, K. *Witnesses for the Defense.* St. Martin's Press, New York (1991).

9 Presenting Sophisticated Evidence Persuasively: The Role of the Scientific Expert and the Attorney at Trial

Patricia M. Ayd and Merle M. Troeger

CONTENTS

THE TASKS OF A JUROR

During a trial and the deliberations that follow it, jurors have only two tasks: to understand and to evaluate the evidence. Most jurors find these tasks very challenging.

> Being a juror was a terrible thing. I'm not smart and I'm not educated, and I don't know if it's right to put a person like me in that position of being a judge. It was awful. I had to think like I've never thought before. I had to try to understand words like justice and truth. . .[1]

The ability of jurors to assimilate scientific information and reach a reasonable verdict is usually greater than many people, including jurors themselves, believe. This is particularly true when the evidence is presented

by credible experts
using comprehensible language
in vivid form.

---

[1] Villasenor, Jury: *The People v. Juan Carona*, quoted in *Jury Comprehension in Complex Cases*, Report of the Special Committee on Jury Comprehension of the ABA Section of Litigation (1989).

The burden of understanding and evaluating scientific evidence is often heavier than a jury is initially prepared to accept. It is the job of the judge, trial attorneys, and the expert witness to provide the jurors with the tools to undertake this burden. The scientist-witness, with the help of the attorney, must instill confidence in the members of the jury that they can understand and evaluate the scientific evidence presented. This will require advance planning and careful preparation. If the attorney and expert do not provide the proper tools, the jury will be left with no choice but to rely on decision making criteria that do not relate to the evidence presented or the merits of the case.

THE CHALLENGES

The general level of scientific knowledge in the U.S. population is low. A juror walking into the courtroom to hear a case involving scientific evidence may have a very limited exposure to scientific ideas. Unfortunately, the courtroom environment is totally unlike the laboratory or classroom environment as a place for learning. The members of the jury lose their personal autonomy: they cannot go to the restroom, drink a cup of coffee or eat a meal on their own schedule. The environment is unfamiliar and the person sitting on either side is a stranger. The chairs are usually uncomfortable, the lighting is terrible, and the acoustics are poor.

The jurors are expected to learn new information under these adverse conditions in a limited amount of time. The information is presented in a question and answer format between the attorney and witness, and the jurors are only observers of the interchange. They are not allowed to ask questions and may not be allowed to take notes. If a juror does not understand the information, did not hear something, or lost the train of thought, there is no opportunity to let the witness or lawyer know. The information will be lost unless it is repeated later. Because they cannot discuss the evidence until deliberations begin, the jurors cannot even seek clarification from their fellow jurors.

The scientific expert and the trial attorney must remember that each of the individual jurors has a different ability to acquire and understand new information. Each juror also has a different style of learning. Furthermore, each juror has a different life perspective that serves as a filter through which to view the world, authority, law, justice, and "truth."[2]

Not only must jurors learn new scientific information, they must learn how to evaluate the information. Depending upon their individual analytical skills and exposure to scientific ideas, jurors will evaluate scientific evidence in various ways. They may use rational scientific standards, or they may use their own evaluative criteria. Neither the scientist expert nor the lawyer may ever know the criteria the jury actually employed to arrive at a verdict.

---

[2] Shuman, D.W., Champagne, A., and Whitaker, E., Assessing the Believability of Expert Witnesses: Science in the Jurybox, 37 *Jurimetrics* 23 (1997).

The courtroom is also far different from the laboratory or the classroom as an environment for evaluating scientific information. In the courtroom, jurors are frequently asked to render verdicts based on imperfect or incomplete information. In the laboratory, the scientist might design another test protocol, conduct another study, or bring in collaborators. The scientist may even defer decision making altogether if he has insufficient data. None of these alternatives is available to a jury. The jury must reach a verdict based on the information at hand, well or poorly presented, well or poorly understood and evaluated.

In addition to being asked to acquire, assimilate, and evaluate information in an unfamiliar and sometimes unfriendly environment, jurors are also asked to perform these functions in an adversarial context. A civil or criminal trial is set up to present the competing sides of any controversy. A trial is, in essence, a contest. The jury's job is to declare a winner. Most people do not want to live with ambiguity, and this polarizing approach to decision making may leave some members of a jury confused and uncomfortable.

The expert scientist can help relieve some of the jurors' discomfort by serving, not as an advocate for a party, but as an independent witness and credible guide through the thicket of scientific evidence.

MEETING THE CHALLENGES

By understanding jurors' learning styles and life perspectives, and creating a trial presentation that accommodates the jury, the scientific expert and the attorney form a team to meet the challenges.

Learning Styles

To communicate effectively to the members of the jury panel, the attorney and the scientist must remember that not everyone learns in the same manner. The learning style that made the scientist successful in the academic setting and in the laboratory is not the learning style that predominates in the jury box. While educators may categorize learning styles in different ways, there are generally four learning styles: visual, kinesthetic, auditory and ideational.[3]

The ideational learner is one who is interested in concepts and appeals to logic. Many scientists and attorneys learn this way. Most jurors do not. Their predominant learning style is visual. We normally consider this a good thing, as reflected in a favorite saying, "Seeing is believing."

---

[3] In conversation with professor H. Edward Everding, summarizing the work of many scholars. See George Isaac Brown, Ed., *The Live Classroom: Innovation through Confluent Education and Gestalt*, New York, Viking Press (1975). For further reading, see Malcolm S. Knowles, *The Modern Practice of Adult Education: from Pedagogy to Adragogy*, Chicago, Association Press Follet Publishing Company (1980).

The kinesthetic learner learns by doing and experiencing the new material. This is the person who never looks at the owner's manual but starts turning knobs and pushing buttons.

Despite the fact that it has been estimated that only 30% of the population are auditory learners, most of the information that a jury is expected to master is presented by the spoken word alone. Hearing is one of the least effective learning tools, yet we use it constantly in the courtroom.

In light of the fact that people learn in so many different ways, the attorney and the scientific expert must tailor their presentation for all learners. Jurors are most persuaded by what they comprehend best. In a simple example, the scientist must explain a human cell in four ways. Visual learners need to see a picture of a cell. Kinesthetic learners need to build the cell with its component parts. Auditory learners need to hear a description of the cell. Ideational learners need to study the cell's functions.

The particular learning style that will predominate in any jury panel is never known. However, it can be assumed that if the evidence is not presented in a manner which considers all learning styles, the likelihood of an informed jury verdict is reduced.

Life Perspectives

Jurors also have varying levels of sophistication in life perspectives which affect how their view of the world, authority, the law, justice and truth, and, for our purposes, how they evaluate scientific evidence. These levels of sophistication have been described as six developmental levels in which the person builds on the preceding level as he matures.[4]

1. Magical (pre-school).
2. Literal, centered on own wants (elementary).
3. Centered on personal relationships, stereotypes (junior and senior high, adult).
4. Centered on personal relationships, diversity (junior and senior high, adult).
5. Centered on rationality, systems (senior high, adult).
6. Centered on vision, complexity (adult).

When the scientist is researching, writing, and teaching chemistry majors, he is engaged with a world view at Level 6. When teaching in the courtroom, he is perhaps operating at Level 5. Some of the jurors may have a world view at Level 5 or 6 as well. However, there will be jurors whose world view corresponds to Levels 4 and 3, and maybe even Level 2.

---

[4] This information is based on the research of Professors H. Edward Everding, Jr., Clarence H. Snelling, Jr. and their colleague, Mary M. Wilcox, who have done a cross-generational study of the stages of cognitive development. See also, Wilcox, Mary M., *Developmental Journey,* Abingdon Press (1978).

This abbreviated model is useful for looking at how individual jurors may be reasoning and evaluating information:

1. Magical, not logical.
2. Logical, concrete.
3. Abstract, not separated from feelings.
4. Abstract, not separated from feelings, imitates analytical process.
5. Abstract, analytical, searches for rationality, consistency, coherence.
6. Abstract, dialogical, critical self-awareness.

While some jurors may be reasoning at Level 5, some will be reasoning at Level 4. That is, their reasoning is not separated from their feelings: "I like the plaintiff, I want to reason so that I find in her favor." This imitates the analytical process, but is not separated from the jurors' feelings about the proof or the parties. Some jurors may be reasoning at Level 3. Again, their reasoning ability is not separated from their feelings, but they make no attempt to mask this with a veneer of the analytical process. The scientific expert could carefully teach information, data and scientific principles, and still not persuade a particular juror because that juror does not reason beyond Level 3. Thus, the scientific expert and the trial attorney must consider carefully how to engage not only the analytical thinker, but also the "feeling" thinker. From a practical standpoint, it is important that the feeling jurors like the witnesses and the attorneys as well as understand the evidence.

It is useful to remember, that jurors teach each other and engage each other in evaluating testimony during their deliberations. However, it is unwise to assume that a trial presentation can be geared only to certain types of learners and thinkers because they will convince the others. The result may simply be compromise between the jury members which leads to a less than desirable verdict.

Educating the Attorney

Although this chapter focuses on the role of the expert at trial, the expert will have many roles before the trial begins, or even before the suit is filed. The wise attorney will ask the expert to help decide whether a particular claim or defense is meritorious before filing suit. Generally, attorneys and their clients are not scientists and do not recognize the scientific issues in the case. Most lawyers went to law school because they were "scared of science."[5] The expert can identify and analyze scientific issues for the client and attorney. She can provide a primer on the science and identify literature that will help the attorney understand the scientific issues.

As the case progresses, the expert can also identify and analyze documents, help prepare interrogatories and deposition questions and evaluate the answers

---

[5] Wall Street Journal, "Scared of Science," (July 22, 1997).

given by opposing witnesses in their discovery materials. The expert will serve as a sounding board for critiquing and challenging the opposing party's theories. She can identify weaknesses in the opposing case, such as poor test data, inadequate documentation, or reliance on "junk science."

One of the most important pre-trial functions of the expert is to participate in decisions regarding *Daubert* hearings.[6] The *Daubert* case established that trial judges in federal courts must evaluate scientific testimony before trial and focus on whether the testimony is "scientific knowledge" and will "assist the trier of fact to understand or determine a fact in issue." Such a hearing provides an opportunity for the judge to decide whether the jury should hear the proposed scientific evidence. The expert's role is to identify "junk science" offered by the opposition, help the attorney prepare for the hearing to challenge it, and, in all likelihood, testify at the hearing.

The *Daubert* hearing will be the first opportunity to present sophisticated scientific evidence persuasively. All of the ideas presented here in relation to jury presentations are applicable to the *Daubert* hearing before a judge. The judge may be no better prepared to understand and evaluate conflicting testimony on scientific subjects than a juror. The expert and attorney must exercise the same care in preparing for the *Daubert* hearing as they will for the trial. In fact, since it is possible to eliminate the heart of the opposing party's scientific case at a hearing (or even suffer preclusion of the retained expert's own scientific testimony), it is crucial to prepare carefully and thoroughly.

By the time they try the case to a jury, the attorney and expert should be well prepared to work as a team to create an underlying theme for the case, design the most effective trial plan and prepare persuasive exhibits.

EDUCATING THE JURY

As a teacher, the scientific expert serves as the jury's tutor, providing individualized instruction for the visual, auditory, kinesthetic, and ideational learners in the jury box. At every stage in the presentation, the expert must provide diagrams, photographs, demonstrations, constructions, concepts, and explanations

---

[6] *Daubert v. Merrill-Dow Pharmaceuticals, Inc.*, 113 S.Ct. 2786 (1993), established that trial judges in federal courts must serve as "gatekeepers" and evaluate expert scientific testimony at the outset of trial. The Supreme Court provided some general guidelines: whether the theory can be or has been tested; the known or potential error rate associated with application of the theory; whether the findings have been subjected to peer review and publication; the existence and maintenance of standards and controls; and the degree to which the "science" has received "general acceptance" in the scientific community. On remand, (43 F.3d 1311 [9th Cir. 1995]), the Ninth Circuit added another guideline: if the expert's research was prepared in anticipation of the litigation, rather than independent from it, the testimony is presumptively unreliable.

that will serve the learning styles of all the jurors.

As a guide, the expert must take the jurors through the scientific portions of the case and demonstrate the evaluative techniques that will persuade each life perspective represented on the jury. The scientific expert must also help the jurors understand how her analysis takes into account opposing viewpoints and seemingly contradictory evidence to arrive at an opinion that is more credible than that of the other experts.

TEACHING THE JURY

Identify the Issues
Provide Relevant Scientific Information
Identify the Relevant Facts for the Jury
Provide Opinions
Explain the Basis of the Opinions
Identify Disagreements with the Opposing Opinions
Maintain Credibility

PERSUASIVE PRESENTATION STRATEGIES

Some strategies for helping jurors understand and evaluate scientific information include:

1. *Clearly identify the issues that must be resolved.* Nothing is harder to decide than a case that contains an unclear definition of the issues. It is the job of the attorney to define the issues clearly and precisely in the opening statement. Both attorney and expert must highlight those issues throughout the trial so the jury has a framework for understanding the scientific evidence.

2. *Experts should testify both early and late in the case.* Jury studies conducted in 1988[7] found that expert testimony was more influential when it was presented early in the trial. Under these circumstances, the expert "acts as a filter" through which jurors interpret the rest of the testimony. If the expert testimony comes too late, jurors may have interpreted the facts and evaluated the evidence using their own preconceptions and biases.

Toward the end of the trial, expert witnesses should summarize the evidence

---

[7] Brekke, N. and Borgida, E., Expert Psychological Testimony in Rape Trials: A Social-Cognitive Analysis. *Journal of Personality and Social Psychology, 5,* 372-386 (1988).

so that the jury has a reminder of the important points just before they begin their deliberations.

3. *Use everyday language.* It is important not to use any scientific language without defining it. Recall that most Americans read at a fourth grade level and our newspapers are pitched to this level. One of the best ways to make sure you pitch your presentation at the correct level is to find a fourth grader and explain the scientific testimony to her. Failing this, find a lawyer, perhaps the lawyer who has retained you. This is the second best choice, however, because the lawyer will pretend she understands, even when she does not. The fourth grader will be more honest and give you a quizzical look or walk away if the information is not understandable.

4. *Define all technical terms.* Explain the terms, make poster boards with the terms and, where possible, use non-technical language. If the jurors are focused on trying to figure out the meaning of the words, they lose the content of the presentation.

5. *Use vivid language.* Remember the number of visual learners that are probably in the courtroom. What pictures does your science paint? What pictures, graphs, charts or images you would prepare if you were illustrating a chemistry text for fourth graders?

6. *Provide concepts and descriptions in addition to images.* Not everyone in the courtroom is a visual learner. Some jury leaders may be the auditory and ideational learners. If they are going to direct the discussion and educate the others, the expert must teach them in a way that appeals to their learning style.

7. *Use analogies for everybody.* Analogies are very useful for describing scientific concepts and explaining their significance. A series of studies in 1988[8] found that jurors were more likely to rely on expert testimony if it contained examples directly related to the case. Abstract testimony was less useful in their decision making. Analogies also set the stage for the theme of the case and suggest concepts the expert wants to communicate. Thus, it is important to spend as much time as necessary to develop solid analogies to explain scientific principles. For instance, I heard an inventive non-scientist compare DNA to a refrigerator: When one person goes to his refrigerator, the milk bottle is on one shelf, the jar of mayonnaise is on another, the bottle of catsup is on the door shelf, etc. Another person goes to her refrigerator, and a bunch of grapes is on the middle shelf, a wedge of cheese is in a drawer, the butter is on the bottom shelf. This analogy suggests that everyone has a refrigerator (DNA), that each refrigerator is unique, but that there are an infinite variety of refrigerators, all of which can be visualized and are

---

[8] Brekke N. and Borgida, E., *supra,* footnote 7.

measurable in some way. The appeal of this analogy is that it explains DNA in everyday terms and illustrates some concepts related to DNA which jurors may find helpful in understanding the case.[9] Similarly, I once heard a medical expert describe the blood supply to the uterus: "It's like that white stuff all around the orange after you peel it." This striking analogy gave visual learners an idea of the organ surrounded by its blood supply. It also suggested the delicacy of the vascular system and how easily careless surgery might disrupt it. It is worth taking as much time as necessary to think about good analogies as it is to arrive at the scientific opinions. A credible expert can build into an analogy much of what she must accomplish in the courtroom: explain the science, establish the reliability of the science ("yes, that's the way an orange really is"), model the reasoning process ("the blood supply is really delicate") and plant the seeds of her conclusion ("you really have to be careful when you perform surgery near the uterus").

8. *Provide internal summaries.* Before moving onto a new topic, concept or idea, pause to repeat what went before. Once a particular portion of the topic is explained or discussed, go back to summarize it again. After summarizing the material, make a transition to new material by telling the jury what the next topic will be. The trial attorney who is questioning the expert should use this technique in eliciting scientific testimony.

9. *Use demonstrative exhibits.* Visual aids can be anything from Legos to the most sophisticated computerized graphics. Generally, the simpler the visual aid, the better. Most jurors have Legos at home but not a sophisticated computer graphics program. Don't forget that Legos are great for the kinesthetic learners. If you play with Legos on the witness stand, you may get at least one juror to go home and pull out the Legos that night as he experiments with new information. The scientific expert and the trial attorney should spend time developing exhibits that are comprehensible and persuasive and well suited to all learning styles.

10. *Illustrate only one concept at a time.* Most people can acquire new information if it is presented in small, palatable pieces. No matter how sophisticated or simple the visual aid, illustrate only one concept at a time. Try out those illustrations, visuals, and programs on an uninformed layperson or the trial lawyer. The trial team may find that the lawyer understood less than was originally assumed.

11. *Simplify.* The volume of evidence has a direct impact on the degree and quality of juror comprehension.[10] Identify the scientific facts the jury must understand.

---

[9] Mooy, J., John Mooy Communications, Des Moines, IA.

[10] Jury Comprehension in Complex Cases, *supra,* p. 25.

Spend sufficient time preparing the case to remove distracting and unnecessary information and thus focus attention on the pertinent data. Present only the information, data, and opinions that bear directly on the decision the jurors must make.

12. *Start with the basics.* Give the jury the basic building blocks of information before moving on to the next level of complexity.

13. *Use a logical order of presentation.* Our trial procedures do not make it easy to present evidence in an orderly way. Evidence is presented through a variety of witnesses who may testify when they are available, not when their testimony fits the presentation best. It is the job of the attorney to work with the witnesses to make sure that the presentation is in the most logical order.

14. *Enumerate.* Let the jury know how many points you will be making under each topic and subtopic. Enumerate those points, then describe each point. Remind the jurors what each point was by providing a single word or phrase description for each point.

15. *Develop a Theme.* Work together to develop a theme for the case, expressed in non-technical language. This should be a theme that you can be committed to scientifically, that does not go beyond the scientific facts, and that you can refer to frequently throughout your testimony.

16. *Experiment.* Conduct tutorials before the opening statements, giving jurors the opportunity for hands on experience of the scientific information. Permit the jurors to ask questions after direct and cross examination is concluded.[11] It would be useful if jurors were permitted to discuss certain aspects of the case before their deliberations, with the court's permission and appropriate monitoring. Juror notebooks are quite commonly used with a stipulated summary of the case, a witness list including brief biographies of the experts, a glossary of legal and technical terms, and copies of exhibits.

17. *Give a reason for providing the expert testimony unrelated to the outcome.* The jurors' perception of an expert's credibility is closely related to their perception of why he is in the courtroom. Describe the scientific motivation for the expert's interest, research in the field, and willingness to testify.

18. *Provide a step-by-step roadmap of the expert analysis.* Describe precisely the scientific assumptions upon which the expert opinion is based. Connect the assumptions to the facts of the case and show the jurors how the facts support

---

[11] Richard H. Abramson, Presenting Technologically Complex Cases to Lay Judges and Juries, *Hastings Communications and Entertainment Law Journal*, 14, No. 2, (1992).

the opinion. Do not leave the jurors out of any step, no matter how small, in the analytical process.

19. *Provide an emotional anchor for the expert opinion.* If the expert can tap into the life experiences and beliefs of the jurors, the scientific testimony will ring true. If they perceive that they have some personal involvement with the issues in the case, they will have a greater motivation to learn, understand and evaluate.[12] Furnish a context for evaluating data that is consistent with the jury's life experiences by asking how the science involved in the case may relate to their perceptions about safety, health, or scientific progress.

20. *Thoroughly explore contrary opinions.* Part of the teaching function is to explore contrary opinions. The expert must explain why the scientific evidence does not support the contrary opinion of the other party's expert. She should anticipate questions, acknowledge the disagreement between the parties and explain why her opinion is more sensible than the other expert's opinion. The total presentation should be designed to make the jury feel comfortable with the conclusion they are being asked to reach.

PERSUASIVE ATTITUDES

FACTORS THAT INTERFERE WITH JURY COMPREHENSION

Overly Sophisticated Presentation
Complex Language
Undefined Technical Terms
Complicated and Unclear Exhibits
Illogical Presentation of Evidence
Spoken Testimony Only
Cluttered Presentation
Demeaning Attitude
Arrogant Attitude
Pontificating Versus Explaining
Conclusions without Explanations
Talking with the Attorney, not the Jury

---

[12] Rodney Jew, *Motivating Jurors - from Skepticism to Advocacy: How Juries Learn,* paper presented at Primerus National Conference, Kiawah Island, South Carolina (1997).

Explaining scientific principles to a jury and asking them to make a decision based upon those principles requires that the expert witness and trial attorney adopt attitudes that convey their respect for the jurors and confidence in their ability to perform their tasks.

1. *Expect the jury to learn, and convey that expectation to the jury.* If a teacher assumes that the class is incapable of understanding scientific principles, the class will generally live up to that expectation. Witnesses and attorneys who have confidence in jurors' abilities are effective teachers.

2. *Express confidence in the jurors' ability to decide the case.* The role of the expert is to provide information to the jury that empowers it to decide the case. The expert's demeanor should say to the jury, "I am giving you the tools to understand the facts and evaluate the opinions in this case so you can apply the law and come to a decision." Empowered jurors make reasoned decisions.

3. *Treat the jurors as adults.* Jurors do not want to be told what the conclusion is. They need assistance in working through the process of arriving at their own conclusion. If they feel they have been treated as children or demeaned in the trial process, they have the ultimate weapon of retaliation in their collective hands: an adverse verdict.

4. *Develop a genuine rapport with the jury.* The expert teaches the jury at trial, not the attorney. If he watches the jurors, he will see whether they are following the testimony, when another example is necessary, when a connection is missing, when to repeat an idea, and when to summarize again.

5. *Appreciate that jurors sincerely want to do their job well.* Jurors are thankful for the expert who is concerned about their need to understand the science of the case. They will be more likely to adopt the science and the reasoning of the expert who makes their job easier.

CONCLUSION

It is not the science of a case alone that persuades jurors. Persuasion is a composite of factors that includes the jurors' conviction that they have understood and properly evaluated the applicable science. When the expert scientific witness recognizes the various learning styles and reasoning levels represented in the jury box, and designs a vivid, comprehensible presentation that addresses everyone, the jurors will have the tools to render a sensible and reasonable verdict.

10 Forensic Techniques for Establishing the Origin and Timing of a Contaminant Release

Robert D. Morrison

CONTENTS

INTRODUCTION

Common issues in environmental coverage cases include determination of the origin of the contaminant release, the timing of the release, the distribution of the contamination in the subsurface and the reasonableness of the alleged remediation costs. Of these issues, the origin and timing of a release is pivotal and frequently the most difficult to resolve. The timing of a release and whether it is sudden and accidental is especially relevant given that it is foundational as to when a particular insurance policy is "triggered."[1,2] The selection of triggering theories such as "exposure" (or when the property was exposed to hazardous waste), "manifesta-

---

[1] *Shell Oil Company v. Winterthur Swiss Company*, 12. Calif. App. 4th 715 (1993).
[2] *Service Control Corporation v. Liberty Mutual Insurance Company*, Cal. App. 4th, D.A.R. 7748 (1996).

tion" (or discovery of the contamination),[3,4,5,6,7] "injury in fact" (or the date on which the property damage occurred),[8,9] and "continuous trigger" (or the continuous damage to property throughout all policy periods) are all influenced by the ability to identify the timing of a release.

In instances where conclusive evidence is lacking to identify the timing or origin of a release, a forensic review of the environmental data may provide this information. Techniques available include aerial photography interpretation, identifying the date when a chemical was commercially available, association of a particular chemical with a manufacturing process, chemical profiling, chemical degradation models and groundwater modeling. These techniques individually, or in concert with other information, can provide the evidence to identify the timing and origin of a release. Acquire stereo pairs whenever possible, so that three-dimensional analysis of relevant features can be performed.

AERIAL PHOTOGRAPHY INTERPRETATION

Interpretation of aerial photographs can provide convincing evidence in establishing the timing of a hydrocarbon release and represents an established application of identifying historical information concerning the site's waste history.[10,11] The successful use of this technique is dependent on acquiring a complete list of coverage dates and retaining an individual who is truly an expert in aerial photographic interpretation. The individual's expertise is important, as the interpretation of aerial photographs is dependent on both the sophistication of the diagnostic equipment as well as the experience of the interpreter.

Acquisition of a complete list of aerial photographs requires using a firm that specializes in this service. These firms can access private collections and aerial photo brokers (for example, Chinese and Russian satellite imagery) that can

[3] *Sphinx Oil, Inc. v. Federated Mutual Insurance Company,* 427 S.E. 2d 649 (1993).

[4] *West American Insurance Co., v. Tufco Flooring East, Inc.,* 104 N.C. App. 312, 409 S.E. 2d 692 (1991).

[5] *Mraz v. Canadian Universal Insurance Company,* 804 F. 2d 1325, 1328 (1st Cir. 1987).

[6] *Eagle-Picher Industries, Inc. v. Liberty Mutual Insurance Company,* 682 F. 2d 12 (1sr Cir. 1982).

[7] *Aetna Casualty & Surety Company v. Gulf Resources Company,* 948 F 2d 1507 (9th Cir. 1991).

[8] *Village or Morrisville Water and Light Department v. USF&G,* 775 F. Supp. 718 (D.C. Vt. 1991).

[9] *Savoy Medical Supply Company, Inc., v. F&H Manufacturing Corporation,* 776 F. Supp. 703 (E.D.NY 1991).

[10] Pope, P., Eeckhour, E., and C. Rofer, Waste site characterization through digital analysis of historical aerial photographs. *Photogrammetric Engineering and Remote Sensing.* Volume 62, No. 12, pp. 1387-1394 (1996).

[11] Weil, G., Graf, R. and Forister, L., Investigations of hazardous waste sites using thermal IR and ground penetrating radar. *Photogrammetric Engineering and Remote Sensing* Vol. 60, No. 8, pp. 999-1005 (1994).

provide the crucial evidence for identifying a surface feature or activity consistent with a release.

While an aerial photograph can identify a dark "stain" or other evidence of surface contamination, it is two-dimensional and does not provide information regarding the depth of contamination. As such, it must be combined with other causal information (historical, chemical, deposition testimony) to develop a direct link between the aerial photograph and subsurface contamination. The following is an aerial photograph of the Richmond Shipyards near Oakland, California in 1943; this type of photo interpretation of surface staining in conjunction with hydrocarbon fingerprinting information can provide this kind of causal relationship.

While aerial photography is useful for identifying potential source areas indicative of a contaminant release (drum storage areas, standing liquid, landfills, stains, etc.), it can be combined with soil chemistry results to associate the release of specific contaminants with a particular time frame. The technique combines identifying a unique chemical associated with a discrete soil horizon and combing aerial photos to bracket when the contaminant was released. The concept is similar to dating an archaeological dig except that chemistry and photos are used in place of artifacts and dating techniques such as carbon 14.

Figure 1. Aerial Photo of Richmond Harbor

For example, assume that an asphalt emulsion plant and associated contaminants are identified by aerial photographs to be operational between 1960 and 1969. Excavations in the area reveal discrete soil horizons contaminated with asphalt and related compounds indicative of an asphalt emulsion plant overlain by several feet of uncontaminated soil and asphalt/concrete road bases. The various road bases and filling activities are identified in aerial photographs and thereby bracket a time when the release occurred. Given this information, the release of hydrocarbon contaminant into a discrete soil horizon is associated with a particular activity, a responsible party, and time period.

Figure 2 shows the sidewall of a trench with two layers of concrete and a clean layer between the two concrete pavement layers. The clean fill layers, in turn, are associated with a nearby quarry that allowed dating of the fill excavation and placement to complement the aerial photography information. The oil-saturated layer is underlain by clean fill. Tenants and/or operators of the property for discrete time periods can therefore be identified, and cost allocation schemes developed based on this analysis.

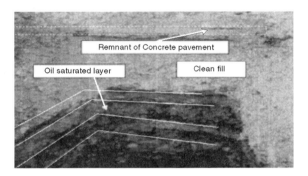

Figure 2 Sidewall of trench showing sequence of fill

COMMERCIAL AVAILABILITY OF A CHEMICAL

If the chemical of concern is known, the date that it became commercially available can bracket the earliest time period that it may have been present at a site. Chlorinated hydrocarbons, chemicals associated with fuel additives, pesticides, herbicides, fungicides and insecticides are especially amenable to this dating analysis. Knowledge of the synonyms and trade names of the chemical is necessary to perform this analysis as a chemical can have numerous trade names with no similarity to the chemical name. Numerous texts are available for this examination.[12,13,14]

The following table provides such information for various contaminants. Similar lists that specify the date that a chemical was first available can be obtained for other groups of chemicals.

---

[12] IARC Monographs on the Evaluation of the Carcinogenic Risk of Chemicals to Humans, *Halogenated Hydrocarbons*. Volume 20. International Agency for Research on Cancer, Geneva, Switzerland (Oct. 1979).

[13] United States Environmental Protection Agency, *EPA Compendium of Registered Pesticides*. Volume III. Washington, D.C., United States Government Printing Office, PP. III-C-16.1-III-C-16.10 (1971).

[14] Montgomery, J., *Groundwater Chemicals Field Guide*, Lewis Publishers, Chelsea, MI, p. 275 (1995).

Table 1. Commercial Availability of a Compound

CHEMICAL	DATE
Dibromochloropropane	1955
DDT	1942
Aldrin	1948
Bromacil	1963
Dieldrin	1948
Dinoseb	1945
Parathion	1947
Phorate	1954
Trifluralin	1960
Carbon tetrachloride	1907
Trichloroethylene (TCE)	1908
Perchloroethylene (PCE)	1925
Chlordane	1947
Toxaphene	1947
Chloroform	1922
1,2 dichloroethane	1922
1,1,1 trichloroethane (1,1,1 TCA)	1946
1,1,2 trichloroethane	1941-3
1,2 -dibromo-3-chloropropane	1955

CHEMICALS UNIQUE TO A MANUFACTURING PROCESS

An understanding of a site's manufacturing processes and material handling systems can provide insight regarding probable locations of a release. For a semiconductor manufacturing site, likely locations where chlorinated solvents can enter the subsurface include neutralization sumps, corroded sewer and transfer piping, and chemical storage areas. The chemical distribution of chlorinated solvents in the subsurface in relation to these features can then assist in developing a causal relationship between these features and the observed contamination.

The spatial association of a particular chemical with various unit processes at the facility is used to further define the origin of the release. Chemicals, such as chlorinated solvents that are uniquely associated with particular equipment, can provide insight into probable source locations. An example is the use of chlorinated solvents in degreasing operations. In 1970 trichloroethylene (TCE) accounted for 82% of all chlorinated solvents used in vapor degreasing; by 1976, its share had declined to 42%.[15] A degreaser is also designed to handle solvents only within a certain boiling range; TCE and PCE have boiling points of 96.8 and 121.4 °C, respectively. Obtaining the manufacturer's operating manual for the degreaser can therefore provide information concerning the inclusion or exclusion of chemicals used by the degreaser. This information coupled with knowledge of when the degreaser commenced operation and its historical location can provide a bracket of where and when a release of a particular chlorinated solvent occurred. In some

[15] Blackford, J., "Trichloroethylene" in *Chemical Economics Handbook*. Stanford Research Institute, Menlo Park, CA 697.301A-697.302Y (1975).

cases, a chlorinated solvent is associated with a specific type of activity or user; 1,1,2,2-trichloroethane, for example, is used almost exclusively in military applications.

Soil contamination by polychlorinated biphenyls (PCBs) is another example of using information about a chemical's use to identify the timing of a release. PCBs are listed on laboratory reports with a numbered designation such as PCB 1254; the 12 refer to the number of carbon atoms while the 54 refers to the number of chlorines. Different carbon and chlorine combinations are manufactured for specific uses during discrete time periods. For example, PCB-1016 was manufactured between 1971 and 1976 and used as an insulator fluid for electric condensers and as an additive in high-pressure lubricants. PCB-1254 was used as a secondary plasticizer in the manufacture of polyvinyl chloride (PVC) and in capacitors; it was produced from 1957 to 1977.[16] The date of manufacture of PCBs can therefore be combined with its particular use to bracket the date on which it was available and to identify the location of equipment at the facility that would use a particular PCB formulation.

A variation of this approach frequently used in dating releases associated with petroleum refineries is to create timelines for various unit processes (i.e., detergent alkylate units, polymerization plants, aromatic isomerization, etc.) that produce unique waste streams that can then be associated with their detection in various disposal or subsurface areas. Similarly, changes in the products distilled at the refinery can provide data in the associated waste streams generated during a particular time. The following table provides an example of this type of analysis.

Table 2. Changes in Refinery Products*

Date	Crude Capacity	Vacuum Distillation	Thermal Operations	Alkylation	Catalytic Reforming
1950	18,000	0	6470	1890	6320
1951	38,000	0	5790	1200	2063
1952	45,000	0	6587	2400	5400
1953	65,000	1710	1200	1910	6500
1954	70,000	2700	500	2700	7000

* barrels of crude oil per calendar day

This type of analysis also can provide estimate quantities of waste generated using the total refinery crude oil throughput and then estimating from American Petroleum Institute (API) estimates the amount of waste generated per barrel of crude oil from the various unit processes.

CHEMICAL FINGERPRINTING

"Chemical fingerprinting" is a term used to describe the ability to distinguish the composition, age and often the origin of a chemical. Chemical fingerprinting is most commonly used in hydrocarbon contamination cases. In its simplest form,

---

[16] Monsanto. *Polychlorinated Biphenyls*. A report on uses, environmental and health effects and disposal. White Paper. pg. 18 (1998).

it identifies the type of hydrocarbon (diesel, gasoline, jet fuels, kerosene, Stoddard solvent, etc.) as a means to identify the source and often the timing of a release. More sophisticated techniques used to identify the age of the hydrocarbon include examination of the composition of fuels as a function of the time of formulation or to identify additives associated with a discrete time period. This approach can also often discriminate whether a chemical release was a single event, a series of events, or a continuous release.

Techniques used to identify the age of a hydrocarbon release include analysis of proprietary additives, the composition of antiknock formulations, trace metals analysis, hydrocarbon profiling, physical characteristics, and degradation models.

Proprietary Additives

Proprietary additives are compounds added to hydrocarbon products for specific purposes. Additives often have discrete time intervals during which they were introduced into a product formulation. The use of additives for hydrocarbon fingerprinting requires a prior knowledge of the additive package and the ability to detect a unique additive that is not masked by other chemicals or obscured by degradation.

Gasoline additives include antiknocks, antioxidants, metal deactivators, corrosion inhibitors, and antiicers, lead scavengers, dyes and oxygenates.[17,18] Examples are shown in Table 3.

The composition of additive packages varies with time. For example, a typical additive package for gasoline formulated in the 1980s was 62% tetraethyl lead, 18% ethylene dibromide and 2% inactive ingredients such as stability improvers, dyes and antioxidants.[19,20]

Diesel fuels also contain additive packages. Diesel often contains quality-enhancing additives such as diesel ignition and stability improvers, corrosion inhibitors and surfactants that can be similarly associated with discrete periods of

---

[17] Younglass, T., Swansinger, J., Danner, D., and M. Greco, Mass spectral characterization of petroleum dyes, tracers and additives. *Analytical Chemistry*, 57: 1894-1902 (1985).

[18] Barker, J., Gillham, R., Lemon, L., Myfield, C., Poulsen, M., and E. Sudicky, Chemical fate and impact of oxygenates in groundwater: solubility of BTEX from gasoline oxygenated compounds (1991).

[19] Kaplan, I., and Y. Galperin, How to recognize a hydrocarbon fuel in the environment and estimate its age of release. In: *Groundwater and Soil Contamination: Technical Preparation and Litigation Management*. Eds. Thomas Bois and Bernard Luther. John Wiley & Sons, Somerset, NJ pg. 145-200 (1996).

[20] Lee, L., Hagwell, M., Delfino, J., and S. Rao, Partitioning of polycyclic aromatic hydrocarbons from diesel fuel into water. *Environmental Science and Technology*. 26:2104-2110 (1992).

Table 3. Proprietary Additives for Gasoline

Type of Additive	Examples
Antiknock	Alkyl leads
Antioxidants	p-phenylenediamine; alkyl substituted phenols
Metal Deactivators	disalicylpropanediamine
Corrosion Inhibitors	Carboxylic acids and diimides
Antiicers	Short chained n-alcohols (freeze point depressants); amines and ethoxylated alcohols with long hydrocarbon chains.
Oxygenates	Methanol, methyl-tertiary butyl ether (MTBE)
Lead Scavengers	Ethylene dibromide

time.[21,22] Different sources of diesel can often be distinguished by analyzing the sulfur content of the diesel; the sulfur content is usually different, depending on the original source of the crude oil. Another approach for distinguishing between different sources of diesel is to perform an analysis of the polynuclear aromatics (PNAs) and a "peak to peak" PNA comparison between samples. PNA analysis in addition to the sulfur analysis can usually distinguish between two different diesel sources, prior to comingling. PNA analysis can assist in defining the relative age or use of motor oil. Used motor oil, for example, will contain more PNAs than a sample of the same oil that has not been used.

Antiknock Additives

Alkyl leads are the most frequently encountered antiknock additives. The first reported use of a lead antiknock additive was in 1923 by the General Motors Development Company in Dayton, Ohio, which used tetraethyl lead. By 1950, most gasoline in the United States was leaded; in 1960, tetramethyl lead was marketed. Consumption of all lead alkyls peaked in 1969.[23] For premium grade gasoline, these concentrations were as much as 2.9 grams per gallon. Subsequent reductions in lead concentrations in gasoline occurred due to regulatory concerns in the late 1970s to 1985. Tetraethyl lead was reportedly the only alkyl lead additive added to leaded fuels after 1980. Only tetraethyl lead is currently used as an additive in leaded gasoline in amounts up to two orders of magnitude less than added in pre-1980. The history of lead additives to gasoline frequently provides a basis for bracketing the age of the gasoline in the soil or groundwater. Figure 3 includes some common additives relative to when they were introduced and/or used in

---

[21] Global Geochemistry Corporation, *Characterizing petroleum contaminants in soil and water and determining source of pollutants*. pg. 37 (1991).

[22] Rhue, R., Mansell, R., Ou, L., Cox, R., Tang, S., and Ouyang, Y., The Fate and Behavior of Lead Alkyls in the Environment: A Review. *Critical Reviews in Environmental Control*. 22(3/4): 169-193 (1992).

[23] Cline, P., Delfino, J., and Rao, S., Partitioning of aromatic constituents into water from gasoline and other complex solvent mixtures. *Environmental Science and Technology,* 25:914-920 (1991).

gasoline.[24]

The most common organic lead alkyl additives are tetraethyl, triethylmethyl, and methyldiethyl tetramethyl lead. Redistribution reactions of equimolar amounts of tetraethyl and tetramethyl leads can also produce trimethyl, trimethylethyl, dimethyldiethyl and methyltriethyl lead.[25] Older gasoline included these lead compounds along with lead scavengers such as ethylene dibromide and 1,2 - dichloroethane; these additives were first introduced in 1928. The concentration of leads in a leaded gasoline was reported as shown in Figure 3 and Table 4.[26]

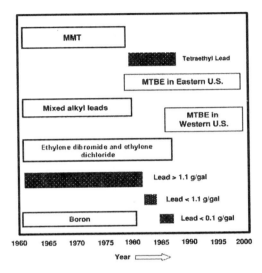

Figure 3. Chronology of Gasoline Additives from 1960 - 1998

Table 4. Additive Concentrations

Leaded Gasoline Additive	Concentration (mg/l)
Tetraethyl lead	600
Tetramethyl lead	5
Dichloroethane	210
Dibromomethane	190

The concentration of organic lead in a sample has been argued as a means to determine when the fuel was released into the subsurface. In 1982, the allowable

[24] University of Wisconsin, National Institute of Hydrocarbon Fingerprinting, College of Engineering and Professional Development, University of Wisconsin at Madison (1995).

[25] Gibbs, L., How gasoline has changed. In: *SAE Technical Paper Series,* Fuels and Lubricants Meeting and Exposition, Philadelphia, Pa. October 18-21 (1993).

[26] Hurst, R., Davis, T. and Chinn, B., The lead fingerprints of gasoline contamination. Environmental Science and Technology. Vol. 30, No. 6., pg. 304-307 (1996).

levels of lead in leaded gasoline was 4.2 grams per gallon. It was changed by the Environmental Protection Agency (EPA) in 1984 to a maximum of 0.1 gram per gallon. This concentration applies to the average quarterly production from a refinery or "pool standard." The pool standard is based on the total grams of lead used by a refinery in a given time period divided by the total amount of gasoline manufactured in that time frame by the refinery. As a result, individual batches of gasoline can contain 4.2 grams per gallon per EPA requirements and 0.8 grams per gallon in California. It has been argued that these guidelines can be used to predict the time frame during which the product was manufactured. A challenge to this argument is that the lead content of an individual sample is not conclusive because the lead content for any given time frame is based on the pool standard. The consequence of this practice is that individual gasoline samples vary from batch to batch and therefore cannot be used to date the year of manufacture.

A recent technique forwarded as a means to age dating is the examination of lead isotope ratios of carbon, hydrogen, sulfur and nitrogen in gasoline impacted soil or water samples. A common isotope used for this purpose is lead. This technique is based on the premise that the use of one particular source of lead with distinctive high isotopic ratios increased progressively from the late 1960s to the late 1980s. High precision lead isotope ratio analysis is used to calibrate these changes as a function of time. It is reported that this technique allows one to establish the time of formulation to within 1 to 5 years. Examples of the degree of resolution for different time periods using this analysis are 1 to 2 years for 1969-1982, 2-3 years for 1982-1990 and 3 to 5 years for 1955-1968.[27] The stable isotope ratio of sulfur can also be used to help identify source relationships between samples contaminated with heavy hydrocarbons.

Other antiknock ingredients used in fuels include iron-based compounds. A well-known compound is iron pentacarbonyl which was marketed in the 1930s. Another is the manganese additive, methyl cyclopentadienyl manganese tricarbonyl (MMT), which was used as an antiknock and lead alkyl supplement in the United States from 1957 until 1978,[28,29] and was later commercialized as a supplement to tetraethyl lead. Although MMT can be age diagnostic, its absence in gasoline does not necessarily indicate a basis for age dating as it was not routinely added by all manufacturers. It is currently an additive in Canadian gasoline. Analytical techniques are not readily available to test for MMT and usually require a specialty laboratory to perform the analyses.

Oxygenates are blended with gasoline for the purpose of increasing the oxygen content and reducing carbon monoxide emissions. Oxygenated compounds used for this purpose include methanol, methyl tertiary butyl ether (MTBE), ethanol and tertiary butyl alcohol, tertiary methyl ether (TAME) and ethyl tertiary butyl ether (ETBE). ARCO began using tertiary butyl alcohol in 1979. MTBE is used to

---

[27] Russell, T., Petrol and diesel additives. *Petroleum Review*, October 1988. The Institute of Petroleum. pp. 35-42 (1988).

[28] Faggan, J., Bailie, J., Desmond, E., Lenane, D., An evaluation of manganese as an antiknock in unleaded gasoline. *SAE Automobile Engineering Meeting*, Detroit, Michigan, October 13-17, pg. 21 (1975).

[29] Walker, J., Colwell, R., and Petrakis, L., Biodegradation rates of components of petroleum. *Canadian Journal of Microbiology*. 22, 1209-1213 (1976).

improve the octane rating and/or improve the tolerance for moisture in gasoline. MTBE has been an additive in gasoline since about 1979; current unleaded gasoline contains as much as 15% by volume. MTBE was introduced into East Coast, Gulf and Midwest gasoline after 1980 and into West Coast gasoline after 1990. MTBE is about 25 time more soluble than benzene and is not retarded by soil as it travels in groundwater. As a result, it is often found at the leading edge of a groundwater plume without the presence of the other BTEX compounds; in these situations, its presence can be used qualitatively as an indicator of the length of the downgradient plume.

The changing formulation of fuels over time also provides opportunities for dating a release. Prior to 1975, diesel was primarily straight chained while post-1975 diesel was thermally cracked. This distinction can be determined analytical with only several milliliters of product, thereby providing a bracket for when the product was available.

Trace Metals

Trace metal analysis can be useful to confirm information about the type of hydrocarbon that is tested. For example, waste oil is more likely to contain lead, zinc, chromium, copper or aluminum from the abrasion of an engine than a fuel. Nickel, vanadium and sulfur are present in low gravity crude oils but are absent or present in minimal quantities in refined products.

Metals can also be additives to a hydrocarbon fuel; the addition of barium and zinc to motor oil is an example. Calcium, phosphorous and zinc are additives common to lube oils but are not dominant in crude oil. While not a trace metal, boron was a common gasoline additive in use from 1956 to 1981 and, if detected with gasoline, may provide an indicator of a pre-1981 formulation. Another example is the addition of borate to gasoline in the 1960s by Atlantic Richfield Company, ARCO.

CHEMICAL PROFILING

The term "chemical profiling" refers to the ability to identify individual chemicals in a sample. This information is then used to estimate the time that the chemical has been in the subsurface. The presence of gaseous hydrocarbons, isobutane, n-butane, iso-pentane and n-pentane in a sample contaminated with gasoline can be used to determine whether a gasoline released into the subsurface is "fresh" or "weathered." Fresh gasoline normally contains n-hexane and n-heptane in higher concentrations than methylcyclohexane (MCH) and n-octane. After the gasoline weathers in the subsurface, the MCH concentration increases relative to n-hexane and n-heptane and carbon seven (C7) normal paraffins. The difficulty with this analysis and testimony is that the terms "fresh" and "weathered" are relative terms that allow a wide range of interpretations by forensic geochemists.

CHEMICAL DEGRADATION MODELS

Hydrocarbons

The degradation of specific petroleum fractions in a fuel has been proposed as a means to age date a hydrocarbon.[30,31] The basis of this approach is reliance on the biodegradation half-life of hydrocarbon compounds in the soil or groundwater. The estimated half-life is the time required for one half of the compound to biodegrade. A summary of the biodegradation rates of selected BTEX and polynuclear aromatic hydrocarbons (PAHs) compounds is summarized.[32,33]

One approach relies on the volatilization of BTEX (benzene, toluene, xylene, and ethylbenzene) compounds in groundwater as a qualitative indicator of the time that the product has been in the subsurface. This volatilization sequence is complicated by the concurrent biodegradation by various bacteria. The sequence of BTEX loss in groundwater begins with benzene because it diffuses most rapidly out of free phase gasoline and partitions into groundwater followed by toluene, ethylbenzene, and xylene. The reverse sequence occurs with BTEX in soils. Toluene, ethylbenzene, and xylenes are preferentially retained by soil relative to benzene; ethylbenzene, and xylenes are also more resistant to degradation than benzene or toluene. Chemists reviewing hydrocarbon chromatograms often observe that orthoxylene is removed first in hydrocarbon contaminated soils followed by ethylbenzene, toluene, meta- and paraxylene, and finally benzene. BTEX degradation at each site is therefore unique due to different biological populations and the original composition of the BTEX compounds in the gasoline.

Calculating ratios between these four compounds has been used in environmental cases as a means to identify the relative age of a hydrocarbon release. In BTEX impacted soils, the concentration ratio of benzene plus toluene to ethylbenzene plus xylene changes from about 0.8 in the original fuel to about 0.4 in five years. For BTEX impacted groundwater, if the ratio between benzene and toluene to ethylbenzene plus xylene is between 1.5 to 6.0 near a suspected source, the release probably occurred within the last 5 years. This ratio decreases exponentially with time because of the preferential transport of benzene and toluene which, in turn, increases the less soluble ethylbenzene and xylene concentrations. The degradation of benzene to toluene with time also results in a reduction of the BTEX ratio. A common technique used to present ratio associated BTEX data includes trilinear and star diagrams. Examples of each techniques are

---

[30] Raymond, R., Hudson, J., and V. Jaminson, Oil degradation in soil. Applied and Environmental Microbiology. 31(4)522-535 (1976).

[31] Kaplan, I., Alimi, M., Galperin, Y., Lee, R., and S. Lu., Pattern of Chemical Changes in Fugitive Hydrocarbon Fuels in the Environment. Society of Petroleum Engineers, SPE 29754, *SPE/EPA Exploration & Production Environmental Conference*, Houston TX, March 27-29 (1995).

[32] Montgomery, J. and L. Welkom, *Groundwater Chemicals Desk Reference*: Lewis Publishers, Chelsea, MI (1990).

[33] Chem-Bank, Hazardous Substances Databank: National Library of Medicine Compact Disk Database (1992).

Table 5. Biodegradation Half-life of Hydrocarbons

Compound	Biodegradation half-life (hours) (a)	
	Soil	Groundwater
Benzene (C_6H_6)	120-384	240-17,280
Toluene ($C_6H_5CH_3$)	96-528	168-672
Ethylbenzene ($C_6H_5C_2H_5$)	72-240	144-5472
o, m, p-xylene ($C_6H_4(CH_3)_2$)	168-672	336-8640
Acenaphthene ($C_{12}H_{10}$)	299-2448	590-48096
Anthracene ($C1_4H_{10}$)	1200-11040	2400-22,080
Benzo(a)pyrene ($C_{20}H_{12}$)	1368-12,720	2,736-25,440
Chrysene ($C_{18}H_{12}$)	8904-24,000	17,808-48,000
Fluoranthene ($C_{10}H_{10}$)	3,360-10,560	6,720-21,120
Fluorene ($C1_3H_{10}$)	768-1440	1536-2880
Naphthalene ($C_{10}H_8$)	398-1152	24-6192
Phenanthrene ($C_{14}H_{10}$)	384-4800	768-9600
Pyrene ($C_{16}H_{10}$)	5,040-45,600	10,080-91,200

(a) Measured at 25 degrees Celsius

shown in Figure 4.[34] For star diagrams, the "rays" of each star are usually scaled so that a single component with a high concentration does not overwhelm the lower concentration components of the fuel.

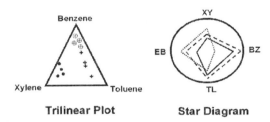

Trilinear Plot   **Star Diagram**

Figure 4. Examples of BTEX Ratio Diagrams

Significant uncertainty exists in using a ratio analysis because of the variation of BTEX compounds in the original gasoline as well as environmental alterations to the product. For example, under anaerobic conditions, toluene may be more rapidly degraded than benzene.

These uncertainties result in a wide range of ratios for identically aged spills, especially in different soils. Knowledge of the range of BTEX in fresh and weathered gasoline illustrates the uncertainties associated with such ratio analyses. Table 6 summarizes BTEX ranges in different grades of dispensed gasoline and ranges of BTEX hydrocarbons in free product, water and soils.[31]

---

[34] Luhrs, R., Pyott, C., Stewart, N., Graphical evaluation of gasoline contaminated water: a powerful new approach. National Groundwater Water Association Focus Conference on Eastern Regional Ground Water Issues. Newton, MA. October 13-15 (1992).

Table 6. Range of BTEX Hydrocarbon Content (mg/ml)* in Gasoline

Gasoline Grade	Benzene	Toluene	Ethyl benzene	Xylene
Leaded Gasoline	6.6-14.8	18.6-64.4	6.2-14	32.1-77.4
Regular Unleaded	5.0-20.0	17.9-44.3	5.8-12.0	27.1-48.6
Unleaded Plus	7.1-17.3	23.9-42.6	7.7-10.0	37.5-50.5
Super Unleaded	6.6-23.0	22.4-81.0	6.6-16.0	33.4-65.8

* To convert to mg/l, multiply by 1000.

In colder climates in the U.S., the composition of gasoline can change up to four times a year to accommodate the Reid Vapor Pressure which is higher in wintertime to provide easy startup and low in summertime to prevent vapor lock.

Table 7. Range of BTEX Hydrocarbons in Environmentally Altered Gasoline

Media	Benzene	Toluene	Ethyl Benzene	Xylene
Free Product (mg/ml)	0.16-24.0	0.39-100	2.1-29	9.1-98
Water (ug/ml)	0.02-30.3	0.002-38.3	0.01-5.8	0.005-29.6
Soil (ug/g)	0.01-10	0.01-77.4	0.02-50.9	01-220

In some instances, there may be a need to discriminate between "natural gasoline" and refined gasoline. Refined gasoline contains olefins that are not found in natural gasoline, as well as additives such as MTBE. Natural gasoline contains polyaromatics (multi-ring aromatic compounds) that are not found in refined gasoline; BTEX to TPH ratios are also lower in natural gasoline than in refined gasoline.

Chlorinated Solvents

The presence of chlorinated solvents and their breakdown products has been proposed as a means of identifying how long a chemical has been in the subsurface. This argument is based on the measured degradation rates between chlorinated solvents, primarily for the parent compounds such as tetrachloroethene (PCE), trichloroethane (TCA) and carbon tetrachloride (PCM). The presence or absence of a particular breakdown product is argued as evidence that the parent compound was present for a particular period of time. For example, the compound 1,1 dichloroethene (1,1 DCE) is a breakdown of both TCA and PCE, while chloroethane is a degradation product of TCA or 1,2-dichloroethane. The presence of 1,1 DCE and chloroethane are therefore evidence that PCE, TCA and possibly 1,2 DCA was present. Another example is the presence of chloroform that can indicate the presence of carbon tetrachloride as its parent compound.

A variation to this dating approach is that if the original concentration of a chlorinated solvent introduced into the subsurface is known along with measured values in the soil or groundwater, knowledge of the half-life for that chemical can provide a basis for estimating the time the chemical was released into the sub-surface. One reported method is to use the ratio of the hydrolysis breakdown component of 1,1 dichloroethylene to 1,1,1 trichloroethane; the approximate age

(T) of 1,1,1 trichloroethane at a particular point can be determined by the following equation:

$$T = \ln([TCA]_o / [TCA]_t) / k \tag{1}$$

where

$[TCA]_o$ = the initial concentration of TCA (assumes 1000 molecules)
$[TCA]_t$ = the TCA concentration at time "t"
k = the pseudo first-order rate constant (0.097 yrs-1)
T = age of the TCA in groundwater

The contaminant migration rate is then determined by dividing the horizontal distance to each well by the age of the 1,1,1 TCA in the well. Proponents of this technique cite the following influences that may result in inaccurate age estimations.[35]

▸ Poor sampling and analytical data
▸ An insufficient number of samples
▸ When the 11 DCE/TCA ratio exceeds 0.50. Given that the ratio curve is exponential, as the ratio approaches 1.0, the error in the age prediction increases. The age estimate in colder climates is worthwhile. Although in warmer climates it is not advisable to use this method when the ratio approaches 1.0.
▸ When the biodegradation is a significant factor in the transformation of TCA to its degradation product 1,1 dichloroethane.
▸ When TCE biodegradation is significant and the cis-1,2 dichloroethane (cis-12 DCE) concentration is approximately two orders of magnitude greater than the 11 DCE concentration.

Several convincing arguments to these types of approaches are available. One is that site-specific information is rarely available that can be compared to laboratory derived degradation rates. Wide ranges of half-life are also reported in the published literature. For example, published half-lives in years for PCE at 10 to 25 °C range from 0.7 to 1.3 times 106 years.[36,37] A more specific half-life for groundwater is between 8,640 and 17,280 hours, which is a calculated value based on estimated aqueous aerobic biodegradation.[38] For surface waters, the half-life of PCE based on aerobic river die-away test data and saltwater grab sample data is between 4,320 and 8,640 hours. For 1,1,1-trichloroethane (TCA), published half-

---

[35] Smith, J. and Eng, L., *Groundwater Sampling. A Chemist's Perspective.* Trillium, Incorporated (1978).
[36] Haag, W., and T. Mill, Effect of subsurface sediment on hydrolysis of haloalkanes and epoxides. *Environmental Science and Technology.* 22:658-663 (1988).
[37] Jeffers, P., Ward, L., Woytowitch, L., and Wolfe, L., Homogeneous hydrolysis rate constants for selected chlorinated methanes, ethanes, ethenes, and propanes. *Environmental Science and Technology.* 23(8):965-969 (1978).
[38] Howard, P., Boethling, R., Jarvis, W., Meylan, W., and Michalenko, E., (Editors) *Handbook of Environmental Degradation Rates,* Lewis Publishers, Inc., Chelsea, Michigan (1991).

lives at 10 to 25 °C range from 1.1 to 12 years.[39,40] Published half-lives for selected chlorinated solvents at 10 to 25 °C are summarized in Table 8.[41,42,43, 44,45]

Table 8. Half-Life of Chlorinated Solvents

Compound	Half-Life (Years)
Dichloromethane	704
Dibromomethane	180
Chloroethane	0.12
1,1 Dichloroethane	61
1,2 Dichloroethane	72
1,1,1-Trichloroethane	(1.1) (1.7) (2.5)
1,1,2 Trichloroethane	(140) (170)
1,2 Dibromomethane	2.5
1,1 Dichloroethylene	1.2×10^8
Trichloroethylene	$(0.9) (1.3 \times 10^6)$
Tetrachloroethylene	$(0.7) (1.3 \times 10^6)$
1,2 Dichloroethylene	2.1×10^{10}

The heterogeneity of the physical and chemical systems at a site introduces tremendous uncertainty into degradation rates. An example is whether site-specific information is available to determine if soils are anaerobic or aerobic; this determination is significant as to whether the biological environment exists in which the chlorinated solvent can be degraded and the rates of degradation. TCA, for example, degrades to 1,1 DCE abiotically while TCE degrades to 1,2 and 1,1 DCE anaerobically. Table 9 summarizes the degradation of TCE in aerobic and anaerobic conditions.

---

[39] Cline, P., and Delfino, J., Transformation kinetics of 1,1,1-trichloroethane to the stable product 1,1-dichloroethene. In: R.A. Larson, ed., *Biohazards of drinking water treatment*. Chelsea, MI: Lewis Publishers, Inc., 47-56 (1989).

[40] Dilling., W., Tefertiller, N. and Kallos, G., Evaporation rates and reactivities of methylene chloride, chloroform, 1,1,1, trichloroethane, trichloroethylene, tetra-chloroethylene, and other chlorinated compounds in dilute aqueous solutions. *Environmental Science and Technology*, 9, 833-838 (1975).

[41] Howard, P. et al., *Handbook of Environmental Degradation Rates*. Lewis Publishers, ISBN 0-87371-358-3.

[42] Mabey, W. and Mill, T., Critical review of hydrolysis of organic compounds in water under environmental conditions. *Phys. Chem. Ref. Data* 7, 383-415 (1989).

[43] Jeffers, P., Ward, L., Woyowitch, M., and Wolfe, N. Homogenous hydrolysis rate constants for selected chlorinated methanes, ethanes, ethenes, and propanes. *Environmental Science and Technology*,. 23, 965-969 (1989).

[44] Vogel, T., and McCarty, P., Abiotic and biotic transformations of 1,1,1-trichloro-ethane under methanogenic conditions. *Environmental Science and Technology*, 21, 1208-1213 (1987).

[45] Vogel, T., and P. McCarty, Abiotic and biotic transformations of 1,1,1-trichloro-ethane under methanogenic conditions. *Environmental Science and Technology*, 21, 1208-1213 (1987).

In *Carroll v. Litton Systems Inc.* the plaintiff's chemodynamics expert used the concept of environmental half-life to determine how much TCE had been in water wells prior to 1986.[46] The lead author of the paper upon which the chemodynamics expert relied to determine his half-life values submitted an affidavit stating that the approach was imprudent and prone to enormous error. The plaintiffs' expert furthermore conceded that the rate of error of his approach could not be reduced to below 1,400%. The court found the testimony unreliable and therefore inadmissible under Federal Rule of Evidence 702.

The presence of solvents in the subsurface can inhibit the microbial degradation that may otherwise occur. For example, the anaerobic degradation of carbon tetrachloride is inhibited at concentrations between 80-250 µg/L; for TCE anaerobic inhibition was observed at concentrations of 150 µg/L. These complications introduce significant uncertainty in the use of degradation rates as an indicator of the timing of a release.[47]

Table 9. Aerobic and Anaerobic Degradation Ratio of TCE

Subsurface Environment	Week	TCE (µg/l)
Anaerobic (without oxygen)	0	540
	4	260
	8	340
	73	54
Aerobic (with oxygen)	0	540
	2	540
	4	600
	14	500

Impurities present in the original product can similarly introduce uncertainty in the reliance of degradation rates for chlorinated solvents as an age dating technique. It is not uncommon for industrial grade PCE to contain 1-3% impurities that can include degradation products (TCE, 1,2- DCE). For technical grade TCE, the purity is around 99.97% with no free chloride and stabilizers, such as tymiol or hydrochloromonomethylether, present at concentrations of about 0-2 and 80-120 ppm, respectively. Degradation can also occur prior to a release into the subsurface. For example, the degradation of a chlorinated solvent within a clarifier or sewer pipe prior to its release into the soil can occur prior to its introduction into the soil where further degradation is inhibited.

CONTAMINANT TRANSPORT MODELING USED TO ESTABLISH THE TIMING OF A RELEASE

A frequently encountered allegation in insurance defense litigation is an expert witness who testifies that a contaminant release occurred at a discrete point in time based on the observed presence of the contaminant in the subsurface. The expert relies on the travel time required for the contaminant to be present at its current

[46] *Carrol v. Litton Systems, Inc.* 47 F.3d 1164 (4th Cir. 1995).

[47] Alexander, M., Biodegradation or organic chemicals. *Environmental Science and Technology*, 18, 106-111 (1985).

location. The foundation for this evidence is often presented in the form of calculations or computer models to substantiate an estimated travel time for a specific contaminant.

When forensically examining such evidence, it is conceptually useful to divide the subsurface into three zones: surface (paved and unpaved), soil and groundwater. Each of these zones contains a unique set of transport equations and governing assumptions that cumulatively determine the time required for a contaminant to travel from the ground surface to groundwater.

Liquid and Vapor Transport through Pavement

The transport of a contaminant such as perchloroethylene (PCE) or trichloroethylene (TCE) through concrete or asphalt is commonly believed to be a rapid process. Expert witnesses cite the fact that PCE and TCE are dense non-aqueous-phase liquids (DNAPL) that are heavier than water; as a result, they "sink" through the pavement and soil prior to entering groundwater. This assumption is true if the pavement is cracked allowing unrestricted flow or if the spill occurs over a permeable wood or oakum lined expansion joint. Absent cracks or expansion joints, however, a number of transport variables are encountered that affect if and when a liquid can permeate a pavement surface such as concrete or asphalt.

Common variables used in calculating the time required for a liquid to infiltrate through a pavement surface include the following:

- ▶ The temporal nature of the release (steady state or transient);
- ▶ The hydraulic conductivity of the asphalt or concrete (gas permeability, saturated hydraulic conductivity and unsaturated hydraulic conductivity);
- ▶ Properties of the liquid (viscosity, vapor pressure);
- ▶ The thickness of the liquid on the pavement surface; and
- ▶ Pavement thickness.

Defining the circumstances of the release is important as it provides a baseline to determine whether the liquid was in contact with the pavement for a sufficient time to allow it to permeate the asphalt/concrete surface. For example, assume that a transport model is proposed for which a contaminant is spilled onto a concrete floor with no cracks or expansion joints. If the model does not account for the evaporation of the liquid and/or assumes that the thickness of the liquid on the surface remains constant, the model results will overestimate the transport time through the pavement.

The saturated hydraulic conductivity of the pavement is one of the most important variables in calculating the transport rate of a fluid through a paved surface. The terms "hydraulic conductivity" and "permeability" are associated with the ability of a porous media to transmit a fluid and are used in describing the ability of a contaminant to move through a paved surface. Permeability and hydraulic conductivity are often used interchangeably; they are not, however, the same. Permeability refers to properties associated with the media through which the fluid is migrating; these properties include the distribution of the grain sizes, the sphericity and roundness of the grains, and the nature of their packing. It does not include fluid properties. The saturated hydraulic conductivity of a material is simply a measurement of the ability of a fluid to be transmitted through the material. The value used for hydraulic conductivity includes terms that account for the density and viscosity of fluid.

Many pavement transport models assume that the pavement is already saturated with liquid prior to the release. If the pavement through which a contaminant is moving is not saturated, the liquid transport may be dominated by unsaturated flow; in these cases, the velocity may be several times slower than the saturated hydraulic conductivity value.

Values for saturated hydraulic conductivity are expressed in dimensions of length per time. Published values for saturated hydraulic conductivity are usually provided for the conductivity of the media to water. If a fluid other than water is released onto the paved surface, a correction to the saturated hydraulic conductivity value for the free phase liquid is required to account for the difference in viscosity and density. For example, the saturated hydraulic conductivity of water through a mature, good quality concrete is about 10-10 centimeter per second. As a result, this value must be corrected for differences in liquid density and viscosity if the liquid is a free phase liquid such as a chlorinated solvent or petroleum fuel; this correction is made by using the definition of hydraulic conductivity as follows:

$$K = kpg/u \tag{2}$$

where

k = intrinsic permeability:

p = fluid density:

g = gravitational constant (980.7 cm/sec2); and

u = fluid viscosity;

and

$$k = (Ku/pg). \tag{3}$$

Fluid density is one of the parameters used in correcting a reported saturated hydraulic conductivity for a non-water liquid. Chlorinated compounds such as PCE, 1.63 g/cm^3 at 20 °C, coal tar at 1.028 g/cm^3 at 7.2 °C and Aroclor 1242, 1.7 g/cm^3 at 25 °C are denser than water (1.0 g/cm^3). Using this information and the saturated hydraulic conductivity value for concrete to water, the corrected saturated hydraulic conductivity of a chlorinated solvent through concrete can be estimated using equation (2).

Fluid density is also important in calculating the height of a free phase liquid needed to enter the capillary fringe or small pore or fracture openings in a fractured clay or bedrock. In the case of PCE at a temperature of 25 °C, the saturated hydraulic conductivity of PCE is 1.6 times that for water (i.e., the PCE moves 1.6 times faster than water through the porous media).

An estimate of the thickness of the spilled contaminant on the pavement surface and the length of time that the liquid is in contact with the pavement are additional variables requiring consideration. For example, if a TCE spill occurred outside on a warm day, liquid evaporation may be rapid, thereby leaving little standing liquid available to produce a force to initiate movement of the liquid into the pavement. Similarly, if the spill occurred within a building with forced air, there will be a rapid exchange of air within the building that also encourages evaporation. If a release occurred into a concrete sump or clarifier, a significant height of the liquid may accumulate which produces a greater hydraulic head available for the liquid to move into the concrete.

Once these factors are considered, an approximation of the ability and time required for a liquid to move through the pavement can be calculated. A simple technique is to use a one-dimensional expression for the vertical transport of the liquid through the pavement using a version of Darcy's equation. This expression defines the downward velocity (v) of the liquid as equal to the downward flux (q) divided by the porosity of the pavement. The downward flux is the saturated hydraulic conductivity multiplied by the vertical gradient. Porosity values for various materials are available in the literature or can be measured directly. This simple expression provides a result expressed in dimensions of length over time; the thickness of the pavement is then divided by this value to estimate the transport time.

As with any transport calculations, there is not a single unique solution; a range of values should be presented along with the assumptions. The final product is an estimate range of velocities and/or times for the transport of the liquid through the pavement.

Vapor Transport

A recent area of inquiry is the transport of vapors such as Freon, TCE, PCE or TCA from a degreaser through pavement and into the underlying soil. Vapor transport or gaseous diffusion is generally more rapid than liquid transport. Considerations in developing a vapor transport model include:

- ▸ Vapor density;
- ▸ Whether the vapor source is constant or transient above the pavement;
- ▸ The vapor pressure of the compound;
- ▸ The Henry's Law constant of the compound;
- ▸ Pavement thickness;
- ▸ The concentration of the vapor above the pavement;
- ▸ The concentration of the vapor within or below the pavement prior to the spill; and
- ▸ The porosity and thickness of the pavement.

The significance of vapor density is that it provides a qualitative basis to determine whether the vapor density, if greater than air, has the possibility of accumulating for a sufficient time period to allow it to permeate a paved surface. If so, then the topography of the paved surface requires examination to determine whether it provides a feature to accumulate the vapor for a sufficient period of time to allow transport through the concrete or asphalt to occur. Vapor degreasers, for example, are often set in a concrete basin to collect any liquid spills from the degreaser. While cement catch basins are effective at mitigating liquid spills, they exacerbate the potential for vapor transport through the concrete. A catch basin can act as an accumulator for the dense chlorinated vapor from the degreaser and minimizes the dilution of the dense vapor with the atmosphere. Soil samples collected under such cement structures often do not detect contaminants while the vapor concentrations are high, often at parts per million in vapor (ppmv) levels.

An example of vapor transport through pavement occurs when chlorinated vapors are detected in soil gas below a pavement with a known vapor source while soil samples tested for these same solvents are not detected. One explanation for this situation is explained by vapor transport through the pavement that then moves into the underlying soil as a vapor cloud. The rate of transport of the vapor cloud within the underlying soil can be approximated by using the effective diffusion coefficient for the compound; for many vapors this value is about 0.1 cm^2/sec. A general approximation is that the soil porosity reduces the gaseous diffusivity by a factor of 10. For many vapors, therefore, the gaseous diffusion coefficient can be approximated at 0.01 cm^2/sec (0.1*0.1 cm^2/sec). An approximation of the distance that a vapor cloud can move through the soil for many volatile compounds can be estimated by the following relationship:

$$\text{Distance} = (2 * 0.01 \text{ cm}^2/\text{sec} * 31,536,000)^{1/2} = 800 \text{ cm} = 25 \text{ ft.} \qquad (4)$$

The significance of these vapor clouds is that over time they can move through the subsurface and can contribute to groundwater contamination.

CONTAMINANT TRANSPORT THROUGH SOIL

If pavement calculations indicate that a liquid has entered the soil, estimated transport times for the contaminant can be calculated for the second zone (soil). Key variables for performing this calculation are:

▸ Saturated hydraulic conductivity values of the soil;
▸ Soil porosity;
▸ Variability of vertical verses lateral hydraulic conductivity;
▸ Presence of lower permeability horizons such as clay;
▸ Fluid density and viscosity; and
▸ Depth to groundwater.

As in the case of contaminant transport through asphalt or concrete, the hydraulic conductivity for fluid characteristics of the contaminant must be adjusted using the relationship described in equations 1 and 2. For example, if the contaminant of interest is diesel, the saturated hydraulic conductivity of the soil to water can be adjusted for the transport of diesel through this same soil by the following relationship:

$$(K_{diesel} - K_{water}) \, (\, [(\text{water} /(\text{diesel}] \, [(\text{diesel} / (\text{water} \,] \,) \qquad (5)$$

Assuming that the viscosity of diesel is 0.042 centipoise (water = 0.1 centipoise) and the density of diesel is 0.84 gram/cm^3 (water = 1.0 gram/cm^3), then equation 4 yields an expression that describes the saturated hydraulic conductivity of diesel through the soil equal to about 0.20 the velocity of water through this same soil. Diesel therefore travels slower than water through this soil; without adjusting for the difference in viscosity and density for diesel, the calculated transport time using the hydraulic conductivity water overestimates the rate of diesel transport. The next step in developing a travel rate for one or more soil horizons for which the adjusted saturated hydraulic conductivity is known is to use a one- dimensional vertical infiltration equation for each unit. The input variables for this calculation include the saturated hydraulic conductivity of the soil, soil porosity, and the hydraulic gradient for each significant soil type. The calculated travel time for each type of soil will vary due to the difference in hydraulic conductivity and soil depth. After separate calculations are performed for each soil layer from below the pavement to the capillary fringe, the travel time for each soil horizon is added to provide a range of transport times for the contaminant.

GROUNDWATER MODELING

Two applications of groundwater models are commonly encountered to estimate the timing of a contaminant release. These are termed confirmation and reverse models. Both variations are alleged to predict the timing and in some cases, location of a contaminant release.

When forensically reviewing a groundwater model, identify whether it incorporates the time required for the contaminant to travel from the ground surface to the groundwater. If the model does not include this component, it can grossly underestimate the date of the release (depending on the depth of the vadose zone and the hydraulic conductivity of the sediments). The time required for the contaminant to move from the ground surface to the water table is a function of both the media through which the contaminant is transported as well as the physical properties of the contaminant. For non-aqueous phase liquids (NAPLs), the saturated hydraulic conductivity values (K) of the porous media through which the fluid is passing must be corrected for the properties of the NAPL, as most saturated hydraulic conductivity values are relative to water.

Confirmation Modeling

The principle of confirmation modeling is to identify a release and to use that point in time to begin the model simulation to fit data observed at some further date. This technique is frequently used in insurance coverage cases to confirm historical testimony about the release of a chemical into the subsurface.[48,49]

A confirmation model is premised on the hypothesis that a release occurred at a specific point in time; as a result, model parameters are adjusted so that model predictions agree with measured water and contaminant levels at some subsequent time. For example, historical information indicating a TCE release in 1968 is modeled to conform to groundwater level and contaminant concentration data measured in 1995.

A successful challenge to confirmation modeling includes the following:

[48] *Hughes Aircaft Company vs. Hartford Accident & Indemnity Company*, Superior Court of the State of California, Los Angeles County. Case No. No. 92-6031-LGB (JR), (1994).

[49] *Hughes Aircraft Company vs. Brian Eustace Beagley, et al.*, Superior Court of the State of California, Los Angeles County, Case No. BC062120 (1995).

- adjust model-input parameters within a reasonable range for those parameters to produce a result consistent with measured values but inconsistent with the alleged released date;
- identify model uncertainties such as the direction, velocity or gradient of the groundwater flow for the time modeled; and
- compare the input parameters of the confirmation model with other site models of testing for consistency.

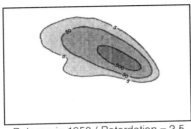

Release in 1950 / Retardation = 2.5

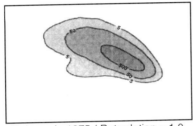

Release in 1975 / Retardation = 1.0

Figure 5. Non-Unique Solution: Date of Release from Groundwater Modeling

There is not a single unique solution in confirmation modeling; as a result, the input variables can be adjusted to conform to a prescribed result. Figure 5 illustrates this situation where the only parameter adjusted in the model was the retardation factor used for the contaminant. Selection of a retardation factor of 2.5 produced a plume that originated in 1950 while selection of a retardation factor of 1.0 produced a contaminant plume beginning in 1975. The plume shapes are identical for the measured plume geometry in 1996 from whence the actual data was obtained and the plume contoured.

The key factor in the examination of confirmation models is to realize that there is no single unique solution to the model; any combination of input variables will result in identical results.

Reverse Modeling

Reverse modeling is a technique in which the direction and velocity of groundwater is used to predict, in reverse, when and where a contaminant entered a groundwater system. This technique is termed "reverse" or "backward extrapolation groundwater modeling."[50,51,52,53] In its simplest application, reverse modeling relies upon the observed length of a contaminant plume and a representative groundwater velocity to estimate the timing of a release. Common assumptions are that the groundwater gradient is constant through time, that soil hydraulic conductivity is constant in a horizontal direction and that a selected retardation coefficient is reasonable. This approach is predominantly used in insurance cases such as *Sterling v. Velsicol Chemical Corporation* to identify the alleged timing of a release or to associate a particular release with the commencement of a soil or groundwater plume (*Carrier Corporation v. Detrex*, 1996).[54,55]

Model Applications

Hydrogeologic Variables

Confirmation and reverse modeling rely on hydrogeologic and contaminant characteristics to mathematically simulate the origin and timing of a release. Hydrogeologic variables include the groundwater gradient, soil porosity, velocity, and horizontal and transverse dispersivity. The reliability of these values is due in part to whether they are measured in the field laboratory or extracted from published measurements.

Of the hydrogeologic parameters, saturated hydraulic conductivity (K) usually has the greatest impact on the modeling results. For example, it is generally recognized that the most representative measurements for determining the hydraulic conductivity of a formation are obtained with a pump test. Hydraulic conductivity values that rely upon slug tests, sieve analysis, and laboratory measurements of soil cores are considered less reliable; results from a slug test, for example, are generally reliable to about one or more orders of magnitude with its accuracy increasing with a less permeable aquifer. Since the gradient of the groundwater table and changes in soil porosity differ significantly with soil texture, a scientifically defensible approach is to use a range of values for the saturated hydraulic conductivity, hydraulic gradient, and soil porosity. This range of variables is then used to develop a corresponding range in the groundwater velocity.

---

[50] Kezsbom, A. and Goldman, A. The boundaries of groundwater modeling under the law: standards for excluding speculative expert testimony. *Environmental Claims Journal*, 4 (1) (Autumn 1991).

[51] Kornfeld, I., 1992. Comment to the boundaries of groundwater modeling under the law: standards for excluding speculative expert testimony. *Tort and Insurance Law Journal*, 28(1), (Fall 1992).

[52] Morrison, R. and Erickson, R., Chapter 7, Groundwater Investigations. In: *Environmental Reports and Remediation Plans: Forensic and Legal Review*. John Wiley Publications, Somerset, NJ. pg. 155 (1995).

[53] Bois, T. and Luther, B., 1996. Groundwater and Soil Contamination: *Technical Preparation and Litigation Management*. Chapt. 7. John Wiley & Sons, Somerset, NJ., pg. 135-144 (1996).

[54] *Sterling v. Velsicol Chemical Corporation*. 855 F.2d 1188, 1199 (6th Cir. 1988).

[55] *Carrier Corporation v. Detrex Corporation*, Superior Court of the State of California, County of Los Angeles, No. C 703625 (1996).

Dispersivity is a hydrogeologic characteristic used in both modeling approaches. Dispersivity is the three-dimensional spreading of a contaminant plume in groundwater and is identified in the three dimensions as longitudinal, transverse, and vertical dispersivity. Dispersivity is dependent on the aquifer characteristics and the geometry of the contaminant source area.

Dispersivity is a fitted parameter that allows considerable latitude in calibrating or adjusting a groundwater model to fit a prescribed result. A value for dispersivity is obtained by fitting mathematical models to plume data or dye tracer tests performed in the field. Values for dispersivity increase with distance from the source, although a relatively stable value (macrodispersivity) should be obtained at some distance from the source.

In confirmation and reverse modeling, dispersivity is used to fit the shape of the plume to the observed plume at one point in time. Longitudinal dispersivity values used with solute transport models are commonly in the range of 90 to 300 feet while horizontal dispersivity values can be as much as 150 feet. There is little physical evidence for using such large numbers except to simulate contaminant concentrations that compare favorably with observed values. In cases where no data exists to estimate dispersivities, EPA recommends multiplying the length of the plume by 0.1 to estimate the horizontal dispersivity.[56,57] Other authors have used probabilistic theory to estimate transverse and vertical dispersivity as 0.33 and 0.056 times the plume length, respectively.[58,59,60]

---

[56] Wilson, J., Enfield, T., Dunlop, W., Cosby, R., Foster D. and Baskin, L. Transport and fate of selected organic pollutants in a sandy soil. *Journal of Environmental Quality*. 10: 501-506 (1981).

[57] Lallemand-Barres, A. and Peaudecerf, P., Recherche de relations entre les valeurs mesurees de la dispersivite macroscopique d'un milieu aquifere, ses autres caracteristiques et les conditions de mesure. Etude bibliographique. *Bull. Bur Rech. Geol. Min (BRGM)*, Ser. 2, Sec. III, No.4, pp. 277-284 (1978).

[58] Salhotra, A., Mineart, P., Hansen, S., and Allison, T., Multimed, the Multimedia Exposure Assessment Model for Evaluating the Land Disposal of Wastes -- Model Theory. EPA 600/R-93/081, May 1993. Pg. 122. (1993).

[59] Gelhar, L., and Axness, C., Stochastic analysis of macro-dispersion in three dimensionally heterogeneous aquifers. Report No. H-8, Hydraulic Research Program. *New Mexico Institute of Mining and Technology*, Soccorro, New Mexico, pg. 140 (1981).

[60] U.S. Environmental Protection Agency, Water Quality Assessment: A screening procedure for toxic and conventional pollutants in surface and ground-water. Parts I and II (revised 1985). EPA/600/6-85-002a (Part I, 609 pp.), EPA/600/6-85/002b (Part II, 444 pp) Environmental Research Laboratory, Athens, GA (1985).

Table 10. Reported Retardation Values for Selected Chlorinated Solvents

Site Location	Chlorinated Solvent	Retardation Coefficient
Palo Alto, California	Chloroform (CHCl3)	2.5-3.8
	Bromoform (CHBr3)	6
	1,1,1 Trichloroethane (C2H3Cl3)	12
	Chlorobenzene (C6H5Cl)	33
R. Aare, Switzerland	Perchloroethylene (CCl2CCl2)	5
Gloucester, Ontario	1,4 Dioxane (C4H8O2)	1.6
	Tetrahydrofuran (C4H8O)	2.2
	1,2 dichlorobenzene (C6H4Cl2)	7.6
	Carbon tetrachloride (Ccl4)	23
	Benzene (C6H6)	8.8
Borden, Ontario	Carbon tetrachloride (CCl4)	1.8-2.5
	Perchloroethylene (CCl2CCl2)	2.7-5.9
	Bromoform (CHBr3)	1.9-2.7
	1,2 dichlorobenzene (C6H4Cl2)	1.2-2.86
Otis Air Force Base, Maine	Trichloroethylene (CHCl:CCl2)	6-9
	Perchloroethylene (CCl2CCl2)	1.0
	Dichlorobenzene (C6H4Cl2)	1.0-1.1
Rocky Mountain Arsenal, Colorado	Trichloroethylene (CHCl:CCl2)	1-2
	1,1,1 Trichloroethane	1-2

Contaminant Properties

Contaminant characteristics used in modeling impact the modeled transport of a contaminant and include variables such as contaminant density and viscosity, retardation and biodegradation. The selected retardation value has the greatest impact on modeling results. The retardation value of a selected chemical in groundwater is a fitted parameter. If groundwater flow is 6 feet per day and a selected retardation coefficient for PCE (perchloroethylene) is 2, PCE is therefore transported at a rate of 3 feet per day. Given that published values for the retardation of PCE in sand and gravel aquifers [61,62] are between 1 (no retardation) and 5, the retardation rate is used to fit the observed detection of PCE at a monitoring well to fit a selected time of release. While retardation values for TCE (trichloroethylene) are reported as less than 10 and usually between 1 and 2.5, these values can similarly be adjusted to correspond to a prescribed time of release of TCE. The following are reported results of observed retardation coefficients for chlorinated solvents in sand and gravel aquifers.[63]

[61] Schwarzenbach, R., Giger, P., Hoehn, W. and Schneider, J., Behavior of organic compounds during infiltration of river water to groundwater. Field Studies. *Environmental Science and Technology*, 17. pg. 472-479 (1983).

[62] Barber, L., Thurman, M., Schroder, M. and LeBlanc, D., Long-term fate of organic micropollutants in sewage contaminated groundwater. *Environmental Science and Technology*. 22, 205-211 (1988).

[63] Mackay, D., Characterization of the distribution and behavior of contaminants in the subsurface. In: *Ground Water and Soil Contamination Remediation: Toward*

In general, predicted retardation coefficients are lower than measured field values.[64,65, 66,67,68,69] Predicted retardation values are generally two to five times lower than measured values.

Arguments for the use of confirmation and reverse groundwater models are that the direction of groundwater flow and velocity at time periods prior to the first measurement are unknown. As a result, the rate of transport of a contaminant as compared to groundwater is unknown with certainty. At sites where the hydraulic gradient changes due to seasonal variations or from nearby surface water bodies or groundwater pumping, the velocity and direction of flow can change dramatically. These factors introduce significant uncertainty and variability in terms of when the contaminant entered groundwater. As parameters such as retardation and dispersivity of the groundwater are usually not measured but rather fitted parameters, the use of these values introduces significant uncertainty.

At best, reverse modeling only provides the time at which a contaminant entered the groundwater at a given location. In cases where groundwater is shallow or the contaminant is introduced into the groundwater via a dry well or cistern, this may be a reasonable assumption. However, in cases where the release occurred at the surface, the time required for the contaminant to flow through the soil prior to entering the groundwater must be considered.

A successful challenge to reverse modeling usually revolves on the representativeness of the hydrogeologic and chemical parameters used in the model. Given that there is no information to verify the accuracy of the modeling results at an earlier point in time, the use of reverse modeling becomes highly speculative.

Compatible Science, Policy, and Public Perception, National Academy Press, Washington, D.C., pg. 70-90 (1990).

[64] Mehran, M., Olsen, R. and Rector, B., Distribution coefficient of trichloroethylene in soil-water systems. *Ground Water*, 25, 275-282 (1987).

[65] Mackay, D., 1990. Characterization of the distribution and behavior of contaminants in the subsurface. In: *Ground Water and Soil Contamination Remediation: Toward Compatible Science, Policy and Public Perception. Report on a Colloquium sponsored by the Water Science and Technology Board*, National Academy Press, Washington, D.C., pp. 70-90 (1990).

[66] Mackay, D., Freyberg, D., Roberts P. and Cherry, J., A natural gradient experiment on solute transport in a sand aquifer. 1. Approach and overview of plume movement. *Water Resources Research*. 22, pg. 2017-2029 (1986).

[67] Ball, W. and Roberts, P., Long term sorption of halogenated organic chemicals by aquifer material. 1 Equilibrium. *Environmental Science and Technology*. 24, pg. 1223-1236 (1991).

[68] Curtis, G., Roberts, P. and Reinhard, M., A natural gradient experiment on solute transport in a sand aquifer. 4. Sorption of organic solutes and its influence on mobility. *Water Resources Research*. 22, 2059-2067 (1986).

[69] Pankow, J. and Cherry, J., *Dense Chlorinated Solvents and other DNAPLs in Groundwater*. Waterloo Press. Guelph, Ontario. pg. 522 (1996).

CONCLUSIONS

Absent direct testimony or other conclusive evidence, various forensic techniques are available to identify the timing and origin of a contaminant release. When used in concert with other evidence, they can provide convincing information concerning the origin and timing of a contaminant release. Techniques such as reverse groundwater modeling or the use of BTEX ratios as indicators of the origin and date of a release should be scrutinized to determine whether they are scientifically defensible.

11 Using Epidemiology to Explain Disease Causation to Judges and Juries

Linda S. Erdreich

CONTENTS

INTRODUCTION

This chapter describes erroneous beliefs and assumptions many people hold that can affect their interpretation of epidemiologic and other scientific data. In legal cases about environmental causes of disease (toxic torts), the epidemiologist can provide effective background information to counter these common beliefs and the underlying assumptions. Therefore, the information provided by an epidemiologist can be helpful, regardless of whether or not epidemiologic data are available for the chemical or physical agent in a specific toxic tort case.

Epidemiology is the basic science of public health, and relies on rigorous objective procedures and statistical analysis as does any other science. Epidemiologic information is difficult to convey to the layperson for reasons that go beyond its technical complexity and reliance on probability and statistics. People hold intrinsic beliefs about diseases and their causes, which in many cases are mistaken, but these ideas are nevertheless brought to the courtroom and affect communications with judges and juries.

The probable origin of these beliefs is the way people interpret the information that they receive, or seek out from the mass media. Because the results of epidemiologic research are intrinsically linked to health, governmental and health organizations provide advisory messages to the general public, for example descriptions of dietary strategies and healthy behaviors to prevent cancer and heart disease. This information is widely available; it is offered in physicians' offices and in magazines. In addition, articles appear in the news media regarding epidemiologic studies and suspected environmental causes of disease, and the numbers of articles about toxic agents is far out of proportion to their influence on actual mortality.[1] Given the way people respond to the availability of information, it is not surprising that people may exaggerate links between disease and chemicals or physical agents, and minimize the role of genetics and diet. The communications process is further complicated by the language of epidemiology, which uses ordinary terms in highly specific ways.

BELIEFS AND ASSUMPTIONS ABOUT CAUSES OF DISEASE

Judges and juries, as members of the general public, hear about putative causes of disease in many ways, from the dietary messages of the American Heart Association and the American Cancer Society, articles in health, women's, and news magazines, and television and newspaper headlines. These media sources also report results of individual studies and describe the public's fears regarding environmental exposures and disease, such as hazardous waste sites, chemical spills, electromagnetic fields from power lines, or reported high cancer rates in specific places. Regardless of the topic, the following beliefs appear to underlie the public's concerns:

▸ The causes of cancer are well known.
▸ Environmental pollutants are the cause of most cancers and other adverse health conditions.
▸ Scientific studies, particularly a study in people, can prove the safety of a specific chemical or product.
▸ A single study in people can prove cause and effect.

These beliefs are faulty, and lead to further faulty reasoning regarding causes of disease, such as the following:

▸ *If the causes of cancer are known, then we can identify the cause in any individual case.*
▸ *If environmental pollutants are a major cause of cancer, someone who has cancer can identify an exposure from the environment that must be the cause.*
▸ *If a cluster of cancers appears in my neighborhood or community, it most likely was caused by something in our environment.*
▸ *Smoking causes cancer, so if the plaintiff smoked, it must be the cause of his disease?+*
▸ *If science can prove safety, one study is all we need to do.*

Regardless of the scientific merits of the argument regarding the putative cause in a specific legal action, these beliefs impact the jury's reasoning, often in ways incompatible with an unbiased assessment of the scientific information. Underneath most of this faulty reasoning or false beliefs is a misinterpretation of epidemiologic data, consequently an epidemiologist can provide testimony that will be instrumental in modifying these beliefs.

---

[1] Frost, K., Frank, E. and Maibach, E., Relative risk in the news media: a quantification of misrepresentation. *American Journal of Public Health* 87:842-844 (1997).

Origins of beliefs about environmental causes of disease

The habit of looking to the environment for a cause grows out of familiarity with known risk factors of environmental origin such as asbestos, years of public concern regarding disposal of toxic wastes, numerous laboratory studies of chemical carcinogenicity in animals, and epidemiologic studies of worker populations. However, the epidemiological definition and use of the phrase "environmental" risk factors includes smoking and alcohol consumption, individual dietary factors, and other voluntary behaviors. Public health messages about 'environmental risk factors' include anything that is not genetic or intrinsic to the individual, thus adding to public confusion.

While many environmental and genetic factors that cause cancer or raise an individual's risk of cancer are documented, the causes of most cancers are unknown. Cancer is not one disease, but many, and just as different medical approaches are used to treat different types of cancer, different factors affect the risk for different cancer types. In addition, in any given individual, it is unlikely that a cancer arose from a single factor or cause. A reasonable inference from epidemiologic and medical data is that nearly every type of cancer has several contributing causes. A notable exception is mesothelioma, a rare type of cancer singularly linked to asbestos.[2]

The inability of the layperson to recognize that each cancer is a specific disease with its own collection of causal or risk factors, albeit incomplete, is a source of faulty belief and illogical conclusions. Each of the commonly known risk factors such as smoking cigarettes, drinking alcohol, and a high fat diet, applies to specific types of cancers, but not to all types of cancer. The faulty belief is often reflected in statements such as "I do not smoke or drink, and I eat a low fat diet, therefore something in the environment caused my cancer." This belief is incorrect because it is based on the premise that the cancer type in question is explained by smoking, drinking, diet, and "the environment," and only these factors, none of which is true. More realistically, known contributing factors, or "risk factors" for specific cancers explain at best only a small portion of the incidence of that cancer in the population, Breast cancer is a prime example: Contributing factors are known to increase an individual's risk for breast cancer, but these risk factors do not explain all cases of breast cancer, nor do they predict with accuracy who will get the disease.[3, 4]

People who believe that chemicals or other agents in the environment are the cause of cancer are willing to attribute a person's cancer to any environmental source - smokestacks, power lines, chemical industries. A compelling illustration is the public's response to a report of elevations in cancer rates, including breast cancer, in the Upper Cape region of Cape Cod, Massachusetts. The general public immediately pressed for an evaluation of suspected environmental hazards, despite

[2] Greenwald, P., Kramer, B.S. and Weed, D.L., Eds. *Cancer Prevention and Control*. New York: Marcel Dekker, Inc. (1995).

[3] Helzlsouer, K.J. "Early detection and prevention of breast cancer," in *Cancer Prevention and Control*, edited by P. Greenwald, B.S. Kramer, and D.L. Weed. New York: Marcel Dekker, Inc., 1995.

[4] Kelsey, J.L., Ed. *Epidemiologic Reviews: Breast Cancer*. 15 (1993).

the very limited evidence to suggest that these environmental contaminants might increase breast cancer risk, particularly at the low levels that exist in the environment. Their concerns focused on pollution of groundwater and air from various industrial sources, pesticide exposure from agricultural activities, electromagnetic fields from power lines, and chemical and electromagnetic fields from a military base. In Long Island, a reported elevation in regional breast cancer rates evoked a similar response; residents demanded studies of environmental exposures, although environmental exposures other than ionizing radiation have not been established as risk factors for breast cancer.[5]

Beliefs regarding evidence for causality

Among the preconceived opinions that members of the jury may bring to the courtroom, is the belief that a specific product or exposure is harmful. To be more convincing in counteracting those beliefs, it helps to understand the reasoning behind them. Far too often, beliefs about harm develop from anecdotal data, that is, an isolated case, or a group of cases perceived to be a cluster. Anecdotal data is intuitively appealing, but from a scientific perspective, it is highly flawed. Such data are convincing because in order to view it in proper perspective, one must comprehend probabilities and the role of chance, and many people do not.

Two recent examples of persuasive anecdotal data pertain to exposure to physical agents, not chemicals. The first example is a law suit linking use of a cellular telephone to cancer, *Reynard v. NEC Corporation*.[6] Various news media reported that a law suit had been filed on behalf of a woman who had been diagnosed with a brain tumor several months after she began using a cellular phone. Many people believed that this story was evidence the cell phone had caused the cancer, based on the faulty reasoning that what follows an exposure or event was caused by the event, or *post hoc ergo propter hoc*. Those who reason numerically and think about probabilities recognize that cell phones were widely used in the population, and brain tumors, although rare, are not unheard of; about 11,000 deaths from brain cancer occur in the U.S. each year.[7] Without additional data, this anecdote, a single case report, provides no evidence on the question of whether the use of the phone was the likely cause of her disease, or whether the two occurred together by chance.

The second example is the question whether the traffic radar devices that law enforcement personnel use can cause them to develop cancer. The question arose after a police officer gathered reports from several states of cancer among police officers who had used these traffic radar devices. More dramatically, the police officers rested the device in their laps when they were not monitoring traffic, and

---

[5] Kulldorf, M., Feuer, E.J., Miller, B.A. and Freedman, L.S. Breast cancer clusters in the northeast United States: A Geographic Analysis. *American Journal of Epidemiology* 146(2):161-170 (1997).

[6] *Reynard v NEC Corp., 887* F.Supp. 1500, 42 Fed. R. Evid. Serv. 729 (M.D. Fla. 1995).

[7] Ries, L.A.G., Hankey, B.F., Miller, B.A., Hartman, A.M., Edwards, B.K., *Cancer Statistics Review 1973-1988*. National Cancer Institute. NIH Pub. No. 91-2789 (1991).

were concerned about testicular cancer, and other cancers that first appeared in the groin or leg area. (To scientists who study the subject, the radio frequency exposure from the traffic radar devices was considered to be extremely low.)

The limitation in linking this collection of cases, or cluster, to a single cause is that there was no accessible information regarding the actual rate of cancer in police officers in general, or in those that used the radar devices. The relevant question is whether or not these cases represent a real increase over the normal background rate, and whether the increase can be related to a common, documented exposure. The method for compiling the relevant information is found in epidemiology. Epidemiology provides a systematic way to examine the rates of diseases in particular populations, to document changes over time, and to make comparison among groups that have different characteristics. Epidemiologic studies can be designed to compare disease occurrence rates between people who were, and were not, exposed to a specific chemical, medical treatment, diet, or product.

Illustration: Explaining Epidemiology in the Courtroom

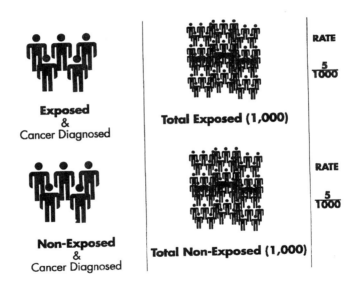

Figure 1. Four diagrams used to demonstrate that a case report or anecdotal data (upper left) provide incomplete information. The top two diagrams illustrate the perspective gained by considering the source population (upper right) and illustrate the derivation of a rate. The two bottom diagrams demonstrate the importance of comparing rates to determine whether exposure increases the risk of disease.

When *Bendure v. Kustom Signals,*[8] a lawsuit filed by police officers, came to trial in 1993, the defense was aware of the anecdotal data about cancers in police

---

[8] *Bendure vs Kustom Signals Inc.* No. C-91-1173 (N.D.Cal. 1993).

officers who had used radar devices. As the epidemiology expert, my task was to help the jury understand why the anecdotal information was insufficient. The goal was to help them understand that, to make decisions about cause, it is essential to compare the frequency of cancer that occurred among police officers who used these radar devices, to the frequency of cancer that occurred in other police officers or in other men who do not use that radar. This is basically a definition of rates, and an explanation of epidemiologic studies, but these terms were not presented until after the visual explanation.

Figure 1 shows the simple diagrams that were used sequentially to explain the difference between anecdotes and rates to the jury. First, part A of the figure was displayed as a visual summary of what was known; the case reports that included the plaintiff and several other police officers. Then, to demonstrate that anecdotal data are incomplete, and therefore flawed, the diagrams of part A and B of the figure were presented together to show that the case reports provide no information on the number of police officers who used the device but did not have cancer. Once the frequency of cancer in "exposed" persons is presented, it is logical to ask whether this frequency, or rate, is any higher than the rate in those who do not use these devices. The frequencies in the diagram are hypothetical; the diagram is designed to show that the anecdotal case reports offer incomplete information, and therefore cannot provide evidence regarding cause and effect. The epidemiologic term for these frequencies is "incidence rate," and the figure describes an epidemiologic study, but these technical terms were not presented until the diagrams were explained.

After this diagram was explained, one would normally present epidemiologic data on exposures to the chemical or product in question. No epidemiologic data are available on these specific traffic radar devices, which emit radio frequency energy, although at very low levels. However, an epidemiologic study of cancer rates in people who worked in a radar research laboratory was relevant. The testimony explained the need for an appropriate comparison population, to emphasize the importance of control groups, and to reinforce the idea that cancer occurs in non-exposed populations. Other witnesses provided information from laboratory studies of the effects of exposing animals to radio frequency energy at various levels of intensity.

INTERPRETING EPIDEMIOLOGIC STUDIES

Associations reported in epidemiologic studies have the same instant appeal as anecdotes. If exposure increases the rate, or risk, relative to the unexposed, then the two are said to be associated. "Association" is the relationship of two variables that tend to occur together more often than chance would explain. It often appears that if they tend to occur together, then one is the cause of the other. An association reported in epidemiologic studies provides better data than an anecdote of a few cases of disease, and is intuitively more convincing.

Distinguishing statistical associations from causation

The literal meaning of an association in an epidemiologic study is that in this study, people with the disease were more likely to have had this exposure, or that exposed people are more likely to get the disease. Epidemiologic studies are more compelling for resolving questions about people than laboratory studies of cells in flask, or studies of mice and rats exposed to high doses. Despite the control over exposure, diet, genetics and environment in well-designed laboratory studies, the implications of the results for human health are often unclear. However, despite this intuitive appeal and the real value of studies of people in their normal environment, one must recognize the limitations of epidemiologic studies.

Because epidemiologic studies are observational studies, not experimental exposures, they have sources of error that reduce the validity of the results. Epidemiologic studies have limited means of control over other, unmeasured, exposures that can affect disease and thus confound the results for the exposure of interest. Studies of human populations include people who have different genetic backgrounds, a variety of different diets, and a range of behaviors that can affect health. Often there are a limited number of people that qualify for the study, and not all of those are available or will participate, thus introducing a source of error. Each study must be examined to assess the extent to which each of these limitations, potential distortions of the results, applies. These limitations reduce the reliability of a study, and it is not unusual for associations from a study to fall short of proving cause and effect .

One way of clarifying these limitations of epidemiology studies to judges and juries is to provide illustrations of realistic associations that are not a direct result of cause and effect, to support the basic concept that other factors must be considered. For example, a statistical correlation between airport noise and mortality rate should not be taken to indicate the fatal effects of such noise levels.[9] Further analysis showed that differences in age and socioeconomic status in the airport area were more likely explanations for the link.[10]

Just as a single epidemiology study reporting a positive association may be a compelling argument for causality to those who are unfamiliar with uncertainties in science, the public also widely assumes that a single study in humans is the best route to demonstrate safety. This is evidenced by the routine requests for epidemiology studies to be performed around a given water source or hazardous waste site, or novel technology. In a court of law, those presenting evidence may single out a study or a few studies that favor their position, whereas the scientific method requires consideration of all of the relevant data to support inferences about causality. These inferences are what science can provide to address the concerns phrased as "proving that it is safe." Criteria for assessing causation from epidemiologic studies and other scientific data as noted below, universally point out the value of evaluating all of the relevant studies.

---

[9] Meecham, W.C. and N. Shaw, Effects of jet noise on mortality rates. *British Journal of Audiology* 13:77 (1979).

[10] Frerichs, R.R., B.L. Beeman, and A.H. Coulson. Los Angeles airport noise and mortality–Faulty analysis and public policy. *American Journal of Public Health* 70:357 (1980).

A somewhat different problem occurs when "negative" epidemiology studies exist. The term "negative" is often used to describe a study that did not report a positive association between the study variables, usually a disease and a suspected causative agent. When these results arise from a study of weak study or insufficient sample size, the value of the information is weak, a fact that can lead to misuse of these studies in the courtroom. The lower the level of exposure, and the smaller the size of the study, the less likely that any risk, if it exists, would be detected. Many people are unfamiliar with statistics and probabilities and therefore are not likely to recognize that there is a limit to the amount of risk that can be detected by a scientific study, particularly an epidemiologic study. This is only one of the reasons why a single study cannot prove safety, or universal absence of an effect. The single study provides evidence in proportion to its quality and to the background of related data, but these concepts involve complex issues of science and probability.

Guidance for assessing causation from epidemiologic studies and other scientific data

Scientists assess research data cautiously in recognition of the uncertainties of scientific studies and of epidemiologic studies in particular. Most people view science as intrinsically accurate, so the need for regarding scientific evidence with

Table 1. Hill's Criteria: Association or Causation?[11]

Strength of Association	Strong Associations Are More Convincing
Consistency	Repeated observation in different places, circumstances and times.
Specificity	An association limited to a particular type of disease is convincing.
Temporality	The exposure must precede disease
Coherence	A cause-and-effect association should not conflict with knowledge about the history and biology of the disease.
Biological Gradient	An observed dose-response relationship strengthens the evidence.
Plausibility	It is helpful if the causation is biologically plausible.
Experimental	If taking preventative steps (removing the exposure) works, it can support the causation hypothesis.
Analogy	—

[11] This Table summarizes the considerations described by A. B. Hill in a lecture "The environment and disease association or causation?" (Ref. 14). The first five criteria were used in the U.S. Surgeon General's report *Smoking and Health* to evaluate the evidence for a causal association between smoking and its effects on health (Ref. 15).

caution is not readily recognized. For making decisions about the meaning of diverse scientific studies to human health, scientists methodically assess the evidence from data from many studies of different designs. To help convince non-scientists of the importance of this activity, the expert witness should explain the role of standard guidance for evaluating and interpreting evidence to assess causality. Foster and Huber[12] discuss logical thought processes and methods that scientists have developed to assess the merit and validity of scientific data, and include excerpts of such guidance in their book. Several of these discussions are written for non-scientific audiences.[13]

Guidance for interpreting evidence is found in the criteria for causality used in epidemiology.[14] These general principles, summarized in Tabel 1, are known as the Hill Criteria, after the medical statistician who first published them, or the Surgeon General's criteria because of their use to evaluate data regarding smoking and health.[15,16] These criteria have been the subject of much philosophical discussion, e.g., Susser, and Rothman, but they have served public health scientists for decades, and can serve to inform judges and juries of the process used to ensure objectivity and accuracy in assessing scientific data. They have been, and continue to be, used as guidance for inferring causation in regulatory and legal decisions.

THE TECHNICAL LANGUAGE OF EPIDEMIOLOGY

One of the usual roles of the epidemiologist in the courtroom is to evaluate studies related to the agent or product that is the subject of the case. This generally requires explaining the goals, methods, strengths and limitations of epidemiology. The results of epidemiologic studies are expressed in terms specific to the discipline, such as relative risk, mortality ratio, odds ratio, and confidence interval, that are clearly technical and require explanation. Other terminology, equally quantitative and technical, is conveyed in terms that have a meaning in ordinary conversation, such as risk, bias, chance, incidence, and association.

The differences between the common and the technical interpretation of these terms can become a barrier to communication. For example, the term *bias* in epidemiology refers to a systematic error in study design or measurement that can

---

[12] Foster, K.R. and P.W. Huber. *Judging Science: Scientific Knowledge and the Federal Courts.* Cambridge, MA: The MIT Press (1997).

[13] Sagan, C. *The demon-haunted world.* New York: Ballantine Books (1996)

[14] Lilienfeld, D.E. and P.D. Stolley. *Foundations of Epidemiology.* Ed. A.M. Lilienfeld. 3rd ed. New York: Oxford University Press (1994).

[15] U.S. Department of Health, Education, and Welfare, Public Health Service. *Smoking and health: report of the advisory committee to the surgeon general of the public health service.* Princeton, New Jersey: D. Van Norstrand Co., Inc., 1964.

[16] Hill, A.B. "The environment and disease: association or causation?" in *President's Address, Proceedings of the Royal Society of London, Meeting January, 1965.* Reprinted in *Evolution of Epidemiologic Ideas*, edited by Sander Greenland. Chestnut Hill, Massachusetts: Epidemiology Resources Inc., 1987. pp 295-300.

affect results, and does not indicate prejudice or favoritism. To most people, the term *risk* is synonymous with danger or harm, but in epidemiology, a risk factor is an exposure or condition that increased the likelihood of disease in a population, perhaps only a minuscule amount, or in a single study. In addition, the term is used regardless of the weight of the evidence.

The concepts of measurement and uncertainty, of error and of chance are fundamental to science. An underlying root of the problem of communicating science is what John Paulos call "innumeracy" – an inability to deal comfortably with the fundamental notions of number and chance.[17,18] This problem is particularly acute in epidemiology, which routinely measures rates, estimates risks as probabilities, and includes quantitative estimates of uncertainty in its results. For example, incidence is a rate of disease, such as the number of new cases that occur in the state's population each year. It is reported for a designated population (denominator), over a specific time period and in a defined geographic area. In contrast, people may observe several cases of disease in a familiar environment, view these as abnormal 'incidents,' and without comparison to background rates, consider the observations as a disease cluster indicative of a harmful exposure.

The inability to understand the concept of probability means that what is intuitively persuasive may be wrong. This leads to the blind acceptance of the associations reported in epidemiologic studies, discussed above. Intuition also underlies the common notion that what follows an event was caused by the event (*post hoc ergo propter hoc*). Psychologists have explored these problems and present them deftly[19] as "How we know that isn't so: the fallibility of human reason in everyday life." Scientists, experts, and lawyers can make the same intuitive mistakes, or they can assume that members of the jury will make these errors and present evidence that will be misleading. For example, it is intuitively persuasive but not quite accurate to interpret epidemiologic estimates of a relative risk, a risk increase relative to background, as actual risk increases, e.g. to present a relative risk or odds ratio of 1:8 in a single study as proof of an 80 percent increase in risk, regardless of the statistical reliability of the estimate, level of exposure in question, or information from other studies. It is also misleading to highlight individual cases of disease in a common environment or occupation as a cluster, or as unusual events that must have an environmental cause.

CONCEPTS TO COMMUNICATE

Regardless of whether specific epidemiology studies are important evidence in a toxic tort case, epidemiology is a rich source of information that can be used to address faulty assumptions regarding causes of disease and the interpretation of scientific data. The epidemiologist can provide information to explain the concepts listed below with or without using the plaintiff's disease as an example.

---

[17] Susser, M. Judgement and causal inference: criteria in epidemiology studies; historical paper. *American Journal of Epidemiology* 141:701-715 (1995).

[18] Paulos, J. A. *Innumeracy: Mathematical Illiteracy and its Consequences.* New York: Vintage Random House (1990).

[19] Gilovich, T. *How we know what isn't so: the fallibility of human reason in everyday life.* New York: The Free Press, 1991.

▸ Many factors contribute to the development of most chronic diseases.

▸ The causes of most cancers and birth defects are largely unknown.

▸ Each type of cancer is a specific disease, and the known causes, such as they are, differ for each disease

▸ The known causes of cancer are predominantly life style and genetic factors; environmental chemicals and physical agents are not necessarily a contributing cause to every type of cancer.

▸ An association or correlation or single study alone is usually insufficient to prove cause and effect, or safety. Decisions about causes of disease, or about safety, are not made from isolated scientific studies, but from considering and judging all relevant data and applying scientific reasoning.

If judges or juries believe that the causes of cancer are fairly well known, and that environmental pollutants are a major cause of cancer, they may be less likely to evaluate the evidence necessary for the specific case at hand. This evidence includes information regarding the known causes of the disease, the contribution of this specific exposure to disease, and the timing and dose that could increase the risk for the specific disease in the case. Without information about the specificity of causes of disease, the jury can be easily swayed by arguments that smoking or some other single risk factor is fully responsible for a disease, regardless of the evidence. The criteria for inferring causality used in epidemiology can be used to support the importance of considering all of the scientific evidence, not just isolated epidemiologic studies, associations, case studies, or anecdotal information in making decisions about human health.

12 Medical and Scientific Evidence of Causation: Guidelines for Evaluating Medical Opinion Evidence

*Susan R. Poulter**

CONTENTS

INTRODUCTION

Recent decisions of the United States Supreme Court have stimulated an abundance of analysis and guidance on the standards for evaluating scientific evidence. This guidance[1] has attempted to familiarize judges and lawyers with the methods and basic theories of many scientific disciplines, from genetics and DNA

* Copyright 1998, Susan R. Poulter. This chapter was presented at the Annual Symposium on Specialized Knowledge, sponsored by the Institute for Advanced Legal Studies, University of Denver College of Law, April 30, 1998. It is adapted from the author's presentation, *Diagnosing Faulty Medical Testimony in Toxic Injury Litigation: Science or Law?*, presented at *Explaining Science to Judges and Juries*, a symposium sponsored by the Division of Chemistry and the Law, American Chemical Society, Las Vegas, Nevada, Sept. 10, 1997. The author gratefully acknowledges the College of Law Research Fund for support.

[1] *See, e.g.,* Federal Judicial Center, *Reference Manual on Scientific Evidence* (1994); David Faigman, et al., *Modern Scientific Evidence* (1997).

fingerprinting, to toxicology, statistics and other diverse fields.

Medical testimony has largely escaped this attention, a fact that is surprising because medicine is often the subject of expert testimony. Medical testimony is important and frequent not only in medical malpractice cases, where expert testimony is usually required on the standard of care, but in many other kinds of personal injury cases where medical testimony is needed to establish the causes and extent of injury. Even more surprising, however, is the controversy over whether medical testimony should be subject to the standards applicable to scientific evidence at all.

This chapter suggests standards for evaluating medical expert testimony, and will also suggest criteria for determining when medical opinion should be subjected to "scientific" standards, and when it need not be.

THE EVIDENTIARY FRAMEWORK

The principles governing the admissibility of scientific evidence were laid out by the United States Supreme Court in *Daubert v. Merrell Dow Pharmaceuticals, Inc.*,[2] a case that construes Rule 702 of the Federal Rules of Evidence, which governs expert testimony. In *Daubert*, the Court stated that the trial court is to function as the "gatekeeper" to determine whether expert testimony is based on "scientific knowledge" and fits the issues in the case. In order to determine whether opinion is grounded in the theories and methods of science, the court can consider, among other things, whether the methods or theories on which the expert relies are testable and have been tested; whether the methods are the subject of standards for their application; whether they have been subjected to peer review; publication and general acceptance; and the known or expected rate of error.[3] Many courts have taken this gatekeeping role to heart, and *Daubert* pretrial hearings to resolve controversies over expert testimony have become commonplace.

A strong gatekeeping role under *Daubert* was recently reaffirmed by the Supreme Court in *General Electric Company vs. Joiner*,[4] in which the Court held that appellate courts reviewing trial court admissibility decisions must apply a deferential standard of review. The *Joiner* Court rejected the "particularly stringent review" the Eleventh Circuit had applied to the trial court's exclusion of plaintiff's medical evidence.

A number of state courts have now followed *Daubert*,[5] although some that do not still avert to the general acceptance standard of *Frye vs. United States*, the predominant federal standard before *Daubert*. But it is probably safe to say that *Daubert* has stimulated more critical scrutiny of expert scientific testimony in many jurisdictions, however the jurisdiction characterizes its standard.

The role of the trial judge is not limited to deciding admissibility questions,

---

[2] 113 S. Ct. 2786 (1993).

[3] *Id.* at 2796-97.

[4] 118 S. Ct. 512 (1997).

[5] *But see State v. Crosby*, 927 P.2d 638 (Ut 1996)(retaining its own similar standard); *Lindsey v. People*, 892 P.2d 281 (Colo. 1995)(adhering to the *Frye* general acceptance standard).

however. The judge will often be called upon to decide whether the plaintiff has enough evidence to go to the jury, that is, whether the plaintiff's evidence is sufficient to make out a prima facie case. If the court concludes that the plaintiff's evidence is insufficient, the court will grant a summary judgment for the defendant and the plaintiff is out of court.[6] Sufficiency is not really an evidentiary ruling; it is measured against the substantive elements of the tort and burdens of persuasion - what is the plaintiff required to prove and to what degree of certainty? But it is inextricably linked to the court's evidentiary rulings, since those rulings determine what evidence is available to meet the plaintiff's burden.

THE ROLE OF CAUSATION IN TOXIC INJURY CASES[7]

In most jurisdictions, tort law requires that claimants prove a causal relationship between their injuries and the wrongful behavior of the defendant, and that they establish that causal relationship by a "preponderance of the evidence."[8] That standard of proof has been expressed in essentially quantitative terms as requiring that the plaintiff produce evidence that causation is more probable than not.[9]

Toxic injury cases are notorious for the difficulties of linking the disease to a toxic exposure. There are a few recognized signature diseases, where the disease is highly, if not uniquely, associated with a toxic agent.[10] For these conditions, the existence of the disease, with even sketchy evidence of exposure, is strong evidence of a causal relationship.

Most toxic injury cases, however, involve latent diseases, such as cancer or birth defects, that exist in the background population and often have other known causes or risk factors.[11] These diseases exhibit no clinically identifiable markers to distinguish cases caused by a toxic exposure from those caused by other known or even unidentified background causes. Thus, in many toxic injury claims, the medical causation issue, sometimes called the specific or individual causation issue, if it can be made out at all, is established through inferences drawn from other kinds of evidence - the plaintiff's diagnosis, evidence that the toxic exposure is capable of causing the disease in question (termed general causation), and evidence that the plaintiff was exposed to the agent.[12]

The application of the more probable than not standard of proof in these situations, requires the juror or trial court to find at least a 50% likelihood that the

---

[6] See, e.g., Joiner, 118 S. Ct. at 515.

[7] See generally Susan R. Poulter, Science and Toxic Torts: Is There A Rational Solution to the Problem of Causation?, 7 High Tech. L.J. 189 (1992).

[8] See id.

[9] Id. See also DeLuca v. Merrell Dow Pharmaceuticals, Inc., 911 F. 2d 941, 958-59 (3d Cir. 1990) (doubling of background risk required to prove causation statistically). See generally David H. Kaye, Statistical Significance and the Burden of Persuasion, Law Probs. 13 (Autumn 1983).

[10] See Poulter, supra note 7, at 229.

[11] Poulter, S.R., Reference Guide on Toxicology: Fitting Science to Law, 36 Jurimetrics J. 169, 177-78 (1996).

[12] See Poulter, supra note 7, at 216-17.

toxic exposure caused the plaintiff's condition.[13]   Thus, the task of the expert witnesses is to evaluate the relative likelihoods that the toxic exposure, other known causes, or unknown background risks caused the plaintiff's disease. The role of medical witnesses in this process depends on the kind of evidence that the court is willing to accept as meeting minimal requirements of proof.

PARADIGMS OF CAUSAL PROOF

There are two contrasting paradigms of proof in toxic tort cases that represent the minimum and the maximum of what courts have required as sufficient proof of causation.

Proof with Statistical Evidence

Many courts would deem a plaintiff's case sufficient if based on perhaps a number of epidemiologic studies indicating an increase in disease due to the toxic exposure, together with evidence that the plaintiff is suffering from the disease associated with the exposure and was in fact exposed at a level consistent with doses in the epidemiologic study. An example is lung cancer among cigarette smokers - smoking is known to cause at least a 10-fold increase over background in rates of lung cancer.[14] Thus, among smokers, nine out of ten cases, or 90% of cases, can be attributed to smoking.[15] The expert (as well as the jury) is thus permitted to infer that the smoker-plaintiff's lung cancer was caused by smoking.

In this kind of example, medical testimony is certainly relevant to the diagnosis of lung cancer, and to the prognosis, which may be relevant to damages. Medical testimony may be relevant to exposure, if the plaintiff has confided his or her smoking habits to the physician. Further, a physician is probably in as good a position as a toxicologist or epidemiologist to state the well-known fact that among smokers, over 90% of lung cancer is attributable to smoking cigarettes, and to draw the inference that the plaintiff's case was more likely than not caused by smoking.[16]

---

[13] *See, e.g., Daubert v. Merrell Dow Pharmaceuticals, Inc.*, 43 F. 3d 1311 (9th Cir. 1995), *cert. denied*, 116 S. Ct. 189 (1995). Not all courts adhere rigorously to this standard, however.

[14] E. Cuyler Hammond and Daniel Horn, Smoking and Death Rates-Report on Forty-four Months of Follow-up on 187,783 Men. I. Total Mortality, 166 *J. Amer. Med. Ass'n* 1159 (March 8, 1958). The relative risk, the ratio of lung cancer rates in the exposed to unexposed populations, varies with degree of exposure.

[15] The attributable fraction is the fraction of cases among the exposed that is attributed to the exposure under study. Attributable fraction = (relative risk - 1)/relative risk. In the case of smoking, the attributable fraction of lung cancer is calculated as (10 - 1)/10, or 90%.

[16] Smokers' lack of success in recovering for smoking-related injuries from tobacco companies is not due to difficulties in proving causation, but to juries' acceptance of the argument that smokers assumed the known risks of smoking, which include lung cancer.

Clinical Evidence

At the opposite end of the spectrum of proof are cases where there is no epidemiologic evidence supporting a link between disease and toxic agent.[17] In these cases, the testimony on general causation often rests on toxicological evidence of various kinds, evidence often characterized by a high degree of uncertainty.[18] A medical witness may then purport to link that evidence to the plaintiff by eliminating other causes, stating that he or she relied on standard laboratory tests, examination of the patient and medical history;[19] sometimes this line of reasoning is explicitly labeled as "differential diagnosis."[20] It is this kind of medical opinion testimony that raises concerns under *Daubert*; the remainder of this paper will suggest the problems such evidence can present and criteria for testing the reliability of such testimony.

"Differential Diagnosis," A Mischaracterization of Legal Fact-Finding

The first line of justification for medical opinion testimony on cause is that it constitutes a "standard medical technique." Certainly, diagnosis is at the heart of medical practice and is a skill that medical training, not to mention texts and professional articles, instills in students and practitioners. Thus, the mention of diagnosis generally and "differential diagnosis" particularly is likely to hit a responsive chord in judges and juries. Indeed, general acceptance and "the existence and maintenance of standards" are factors that *Daubert* specifically lists as indicators of reliability.

In many purported applications of "differential diagnosis" in toxic tort cases, however, the use of the term is a misnomer. Medical dictionaries define differential diagnosis as the process of identifying the patient's disease or condition by comparing symptoms.[21] Differential diagnosis of causation differs in subtle but important ways - it focuses on identifying causes of disease, not diseases or

---

[17] Epidemiologic evidence may be absent altogether, or it may be negative, as in the Bendectin cases. *See,* e.g., Joseph Sanders, From Science to Evidence, 46 *Stanford L. Rev.* 1, 22-24 (1993)(analyzing the evidence presented in Bendectin litigation and jury responses to it).

[18] *See* Poulter, *supra* note 11, at 175-76 (discussing Federal Judicial Center's Reference Guide on Toxicology).

[19] *Ferebee v. Chevron Chemical Co.*, 736 F.2d 1529 (D.C. Cir. 1984), represents a case resting almost entirely on clinical findings; neither epidemiologic nor toxicologic evidence was apparently offered.

[20] See discussion of *In re Paoli RR Yard PCB Litigation,* *infra* at notes 27-28 and accompanying text.

[21] Differential diagnosis is defined as "the determination of which of two or more diseases with similar symptoms is the one from which the patient is suffering, by a systematic comparison and contrasting of the clinical findings." *Stedman's Medical Dictionary* (25th ed. 1990).

conditions.[22] Toxic tort differential diagnosis may not focus on symptoms or any measurable clinical indicator; for most cancers and birth defects, for example, there are no clinical indicators that distinguish among causes. Further, in many if not most cases, ascertaining the cause of a patient's cancer or birth defect is not relevant to any therapeutic purpose.[23] Rather it is the legal system that seeks an answer to the question of cause.

Traditional Applications of Differential Diagnosis

Consider, by way of contrast, a more traditional case of a patient who goes to the doctor with a sore throat. The physician may consider a bacterial or viral infection, or an allergic reaction as possible diagnoses. He or she will examine the patient's throat - the appearance may be relevant to determining the nature of the illness. A throat culture may be in order. Through examination, medical history (has the patient had allergies before?), and clinical tests, the physician will determine the most likely cause and prescribe treatment accordingly.[24]

In other cases, the causes may not be so circumscribed. For back pain, for example, the possible causes may include muscle strain, a ruptured disc, a pinched nerve, or perhaps other conditions. The initial diagnosis may be quite indeterminate and uncertain. Nonetheless, the physician will probably choose what seems the most likely diagnosis and begin a process of treatment by trial and error, reconsidering and ordering new tests if the initial diagnosis and treatment prove unfruitful. No one would object to the physician's contingent diagnosis and treatment in accordance with that diagnosis where the patient is suffering; certainly, no criticism of that process is intended herein. The underlying assumption is that it is preferable to do something rather than nothing, at least when the treatment is not particularly hazardous, debilitating or costly. Further, the efficacy of treatment

---

[22] In *Mancuso v. Consol. Edison Co. of New York, Inc.*, 967 F. Supp. 1437 (S.D.N.Y. 1997), the court defined differential diagnosis as follows:

> This method of considering all of the relevant potential causes of a plaintiff's symptoms and eliminating alternative causes based upon physical examination, clinical tests, and a thorough case history is called a "differential diagnosis."

Id. at 1446 (citing *Federal Judicial Center, Reference Manual on Scientific Evidence* 214 (1994)). The plaintiff's disease, on the other hand, will usually be determined and uncontroversial, although that has not been true in the breast implant litigation, where plaintiffs often claim atypical autoimmune disease, a condition without an accepted constellation of symptoms and clinical findings. *See Hall v. Baxter Healthcare Corp.*, 947 F. Supp. 1387 (D. Ore. 1996).

[23] This is not to say that physicians are uninterested in causes of disease or cancer. Such information is useful in counseling patients about their risks of disease or of bearing a child with a birth defect, and in determining whether diagnostic screening procedures are appropriate. *See infra* note 42 and accompanying text.

[24] Clearly, these examples are rather simple ones, as medical diagnosis may often be more complex, and will not necessarily proceed in a straight line. *See generally* Jerome P. Kassirer and Richard I.Kopelman, *Learning Clinical Reasoning* 2-46 (1991).

is dependent on an accurate diagnosis of the condition; thus, the patient's response to treatment provides validation of the diagnosis.

Toxic Injury Differential Diagnosis

The toxic tort case looks different, however. The patient might come to the office with a complaint, which turns out, unhappily, to be brain cancer. The pathology report will identify the specific type of tumor, but the malignancy will likely be one for which there is no identified cause. Alternatively, there may be known risk factors associated with an increase in disease rate, but many, if not most, cases remain unexplained. A "differential diagnosis" of cause in such a case would purport to establish the cause by ruling out the known risk factors for the cancer, assuming they were not present in the plaintiff.[25] Nothing can be determined clinically about the cause of this patient's disease,[26] however, and doing so would not affect the course of treatment.

The concern with terminology is not simply a semantic quibble. If the underlying logic were sound, the adaptation of a medical term to legal applications would not raise an eyebrow. Courts, however, sometimes rely on physicians' characterization of their testimony as "the standard techniques of differential diagnosis," and often give the testimony only cursory review.[27] Courts may accept a characterization of differential diagnosis as "generally accepted," thus almost automatically deciding in favor of admissibility under the applicable evidentiary standards.[28] The logical underpinnings of differential diagnosis can be made explicit, and their validity examined under scientific criteria.

---

[25] *See,* e.g., *Rubanick v. Witco Chemical Corp.,* 593 A.2d 733 (N.J. 1991)(colon cancer claimed to result from PCB exposure).

[26] For some cancers, testing to determine whether the patient has a genetic predisposition to the disease in question may indicate whether heredity, rather than some other factor, is likely responsible for the plaintiff's disease. Such a diagnosis may be useful for further counseling of the patient and the patient's family, but is still unlikely to influence the choice of treatment modalities.

[27] In *Joiner v. General Electric Co.,* 78 F.3d 524 (11th Car. 1996), *rev'd,* 118 S. Ct. 512 (1997), the witness described his methods as "the basis of diagnosis for hundreds of years." *Id.* at 532. In *In re Paoli RR Yard PCB Litigation,* 35 F.3d 717 (3d Cir. 1995), *cert. denied,* 513 U.S. 1190 (1995), the court makes frequent references to "the standard techniques of differential diagnosis." *Id.* at 733. In *Joiner,* the technique of differential diagnosis was also applied to the diagnosis of Joiner's cancer as a small cell carcinoma, a conventional use of the method. *See Joiner v. General Electric,* 864 F. Supp. 1310, 1313 (N.D. Ga. 1994), *rev'd and remanded,* 78 F.3d 524 (11th Cir. 1996).

[28] The *Paoli* court noted that the fact the differential diagnosis is "generally accepted" favored admissibility under the Federal Rules of Evidence, citing *Daubert vs. Merrell Dow Pharmaceuticals.* 35 F.3d at 758. In *Joiner,* the court accepted the plaintiffs' witnesses characterizations of their methods as "traditional medical assessment techniques" that were "generally accepted" in the medical profession. 78 F.3d at 531.

Misapplied Techniques

An assertion that a witness has performed differential diagnosis is frequently accompanied by the assertion that he or she relied on the standard methods of physical examination, laboratory tests, and medical history. These methods are notnecessarily probative of the causal question. It seems obvious that the attorney challenging the testimony should inquire as to what these techniques would show, requesting references to medical literature, where appropriate. Where these methods have not been validated for the purpose of establishing cause, testimony that purports to rely on them should be rejected as lacking the fit *Daubert* requires.

Logical Errors

The validity of toxic injury differential diagnosis rests on two unstated, and usually untested, assumptions. First, such reasoning treats toxic exposure and the other risks as alternatives. In other words, it assumes that the disease was caused by the toxic exposure *or* some other cause, such as the other identified risk factors.

Second, it assumes that most causes of the disease in question are known; otherwise, the elimination of other risk factors would not significantly increase the likelihood that the toxic exposure was the cause of the plaintiff's disease. A critical evaluation of medical testimony on cause requires that the reasoning be made explicit and evaluated as a matter of logic. It should then be possible to ascertain whether the factual basis for differentiating among causes is present, or whether critical pieces of evidence are missing. Individual causation evidence must, in the end, present a roughly quantitative picture of the fractions of disease attributable to the toxic exposure, the other known causes, and unidentified background causes.[29]

Ruling in the Toxic Cause

In the typical toxic injury case, the absence of epidemiologic evidence is problematic on two counts. First, toxicological evidence available in most cases must be considered highly uncertain. Risk assessments, for which much of the toxicological evidence available today is produced, routinely employ many gap-filling assumptions, a number of which are selected to err on the side of overesti-mating risk.[30] Thus, quantitative risk assessments are understood to represent upper bounds, rather than the most likely level, of risk. The confidence intervals of such predictions are wide when mechanistic uncertainty is taken into account, and the

---

[29]   It may be useful to think of the total population of cases (in the exposed population) as a pie, with slices of the pie representing the fractions attributable to the toxic exposure, other known causes, and unidentified background causes. This model is deceptively simple, however, and works only where the causes actually operate as alternatives. When the causes are synergistic, part of the pie is attributable to the combined effects of the causes that act synergistically. For those cases, it is conceptually incorrect to posit the cause of the disease as one cause or the other. *See* Poulter, *supra* note 7, at 233-35 & nn 209-215.

[30] Poulter, *supra* note 11, at 176-78.

fraction of disease attributable to the toxic exposure is very sensitive to variations in the quantitative risk estimate.[31] As a result, risk assessment toxicology, including animal bioassays, provide little assurance that the toxic exposure represents a realistic possibility that can be identified through a process of eliminating other known causes.[32]

Ruling Out Other Causes

A related and more serious objection arises when this line of testimony ignores the existence and magnitude of background causes and their contribution to the population of cases. Where the toxicological evidence is uncertain, epidemiologic evidence is needed to estimate the fraction of cases attributable to background causes.[33] Without such evidence, there is no basis for an opinion that the plaintiff's condition is more likely the result of the toxic exposure than of unidentified background causes. "Differential diagnosis" cannot eliminate causes that are unidentified, since there is no way to know whether the plaintiff is subject to them or not. Pointed questions to the witness about the percentage of cases attributable to other risk factors and to unidentified background risks will identify gaps in the factual basis necessary to make a differential diagnosis of causation.

In *General Electric Company vs. Joiner*,[34] a case that the Supreme Court decided in late 1997, the plaintiff was diagnosed with lung cancer at the age of 37, after having been employed in baking out mineral oil residues from electrical transformers contaminated with some amount of PCBs.[35] Despite the fact that Joiner had also smoked for eight years, had been raised by smokers, and had two close relatives who had died of lung cancer, the plaintiffs' witnesses opined that exposure to polychlorinated biphenyls and their pyrolysis products, tetrachlorodibenzodioxin (TCDD) and polychlorinated dibenzofurans (PCDFs), promoted Joiner's lung cancer, relying primarily on animal studies.

The level of Joiner's occupational exposure was very uncertain and his family and personal history suggest other likely causes for his early lung cancer. His witnesses did not claim to have eliminated other causes, but rather to have determined that the exposure to PCBs and PCDFs promoted or activated a cancer

---

[31] For example, consider a risk assessment that predicts a doubling of background risk of a cancer that occurs at a background rate of $1/1000$. If the risk estimate, which is calculated as the expected number of additional cases, is too high by a factor of 10, the fraction of cases attributable to the toxic risk drops from 50% $[(2 - 1)/1]$ to 9 % $[(1.1 - 1)/1.1]$. *See supra* note 15.

[32] In *Nat'l Bank of Commerce v. Dow Chemical Co.*, 965 F. Supp. 1490 (D. Ark. 1996), the court rejected the plaintiff's causation opinion based on differential diagnosis as inadmissible, holding that the expected causes must be "ruled in" before some can be ruled out through differential diagnosis. *Id.* at 1520. *See also* Hall v. Baxter Healthcare Corp., 947 F. Supp. 1387, 1413 (D. Ore. 1996)(requiring proof of general causation as predicate to differential diagnosis).

[33] *See* Poulter, *supra* note 11, at 177-79.

[34] 78 F.3d 524 (11th Cir. 1996), *rev'd*, 118 S. Ct. 512 (1997).

[35] *Id.* at 528.

initiated through those other causes. The evidence here seems insufficient to "rule in" the PCB and PCDF exposures as causes, and it is difficult to see how standard medical diagnostic techniques could have elucidated anything further that was useful in the analysis.[36]

An obvious case of the role of unexplained background causes is found in *In re Paoli Railroad Yard PCB Litigation*,[37] where the plaintiffs attributed a variety of otherwise commonplace ailments to PCB exposure.[38] The plaintiffs' medical witness claimed to have performed differential diagnoses, eliminating alternative causes. Yet it is clear that unidentified background causes are significant for most of these conditions, and unknown causes cannot be ruled out. The court held that the witness could testify as to causation for plaintiffs she had examined, while upholding the exclusion as to plaintiffs she had not examined.[39]

Synergistic Causation

A third set of problems concerns cases where multiple causes act in a synergistic fashion.[40] Differential diagnosis assumes that the identified causes or risk factors operative as alternatives, not in combination. The assumption that risk factors, including the toxic exposure, represent alternative causes is true only if the various risks are additive. Additivity is only one of several ways in which risk factors for the same disease may relate. The combined effects may be the same, greater (i.e., synergistic), or less than the sum of the effects as measured separately. Synergistic risks, such as the combined effects of smoking and asbestos on lung cancer, should not be treated as alternatives. Where risks are synergistic, a significant fraction of the cases may result from the combined effects of two risk factors, and their contribution to those cases cannot be disaggregated.[41]

In most cases, it probably makes sense to assume that causes do not act

---

[36] The trial court found Joiner's experts inadmissible, a decision upheld by the United States Supreme Court. *See supra* note 34.

[37] 35 F.3d 717 (3d Cir. 1995), *cert. denied*, 513 U.S. 1190 (1995)

[38] The plaintiffs complained of cancer, joint pain, hypertension, cardiovascular disease, elevated cholesterol, and liver disease, among other things, and in addition to fear of future disease. In re *Paoli RR Yard PCB Litigation*, 706 F. Supp. 358, 361 (E.D. Pa. 1988), *rev'd and remanded*, 916 F.2d 829 (3d Cir. 1990), *cert. denied*, 113 S. Ct. 1584 (1991). Exposure was also disputed, with plaintiffs' adipose tissues exhibiting essentially background levels of PCBs (contested).

[39] 35 F.3d at 755-71.

[40] *See* Poulter, *supra* note 7, at 234.

[41] In these cases, the causal attribution "pie" might have segments for background risk, for each of the two risks factors alone, and a segment representing cases caused by the combined effects of both risks. Perhaps surprisingly, the presence or absence of other risk factors that are multiplicative or synergistic does not increase or decrease the fraction of disease attributable to the toxic exposure. Thus, when the causes are synergistic, as with smoking and asbestos and lung cancer, it is incorrect to pose the question as one of whether the disease was caused by one factor or another. *See id.*

synergistically, absent evidence to the contrary, and if the logic of eliminating other causes is otherwise sound, to admit the opinion. But in cases such as asbestos and smoking, where causes are known to act synergistically, differential diagnosis is not a sound technique for distinguishing between them.

REASONS FOR UNSOUND MEDICAL TESTIMONY

If it Looks Like a Duck . . .

There are several reasons why witnesses offer and courts admit unsound medical testimony on causation. First, as noted previously, the subject matter of causation testimony is sufficiently close to what is commonly understood as medical practice that both experts and judges may not recognize the subtle but important differences in the legal and medical enterprises. There is no scientific or medical discipline that has developed widely applicable methods for identifying the causes of particular cases of latent disease or birth defects.[42] Thus, courts and the parties take the closest thing - medical testimony by a physician. Risk factors for disease, whether smoking, dietary habits, or chemical or radiation exposure, are relevant to medical counseling. It probably does not seem like too great a stretch to apply that same knowledge retrospectively and opine *post hoc* on the cause of a patient's disease. As discussed earlier, even the terminology is borrowed, seemingly giving the imprimatur of the medical profession to the expert's undertaking.

Ambiguous Legal Standards

Some confusion about the nature of the testimony sought may be engendered by the ambiguity of the legal standards applicable to causal proof. Although the general standard of proof is "more probable than not," some courts speak in terms of "reasonable medical certainty" or "reasonable medical probability."[43] Because physicians are accustomed to working under a lot of uncertainty in any event, "reasonable medical certainty" may seem to accommodate a great deal of uncertainty, and might be taken to suggest that the physician should identify the

---

[42] Environmental toxicologists are rarely called upon to identify the cause of a particular individual's disease. Rather they are concerned with identification of substances that cause increased risk of disease in an exposed population. They may have occasion to investigate clusters of disease, but even those are identified as concentrations of multiple cases in excess of background rates. Nor are epidemiologists likely to focus on establishing the causes of individual cases, at least outside of the legal system. There is, however, a developing field of environmental medicine. *See Environmental Medicine* (Stuart M. Brooks, et al., eds. 1995).

[43] *See Kannankeril v. Terminix International, Inc.*, 128 F.3d 802 (3d Cir. 1997); *Richardson v. Richardson-Merrell, Inc.*, 857 F.2d 823, 830 (D.C. Cir. 1988), *cert. denied*, 493 U.S. 882 (1989). *See also* Margaret Berger, *Evidentiary Framework*, in Federal Judicial Center, Reference Manual on Scientific Evidence, 208-211 (1994).

most likely cause among known causes of the plaintiff's condition,[44] rather than whether the toxic exposure is "more likely than not" the cause. The distinction between "more probable than not" and "most likely cause" is subtle, but it can be significant where there are significant levels of background disease of unidentified cause.

What's Good for the Goose . . . .

Unsound medical testimony may get less scrutiny than it deserves because it is expedient at different times for both plaintiffs and defendants to claim that clinical testimony on causation is appropriate or even required. For example, in the *Paoli* decision discussed previously, it was the defendants who claimed that the plaintiffs' physician-witness should have performed differential diagnosis, despite the limited value that such an undertaking would have in the causation analysis.[45]

In general, defendants tend to claim that a differential diagnosis should have been done when it was not done, especially when the plaintiff is relying on inference from epidemiology or toxicology, and when there are other plausible causes that the plaintiff cannot rule out.[46] Differential diagnosis arguments have a point when the plaintiff is subject to other known risk factors that have not been accounted for, but having invoked the need for differential diagnosis under the mantle of "standard" medical techniques, defendants are hard pressed to distinguish the cases where plaintiffs take the same mantle upon themselves, properly or improperly.

Plaintiffs, on the other hand, tend to rely on differential diagnosis when the other known risk factors are absent. In *Landrigan vs. Celotex Corporation*,[47] the plaintiff attributed his colon cancer to asbestos exposure. Landrigan's expert testified that he did not drink excessively or eat a high fat diet, both known risk factors for colon cancer.[48] On that basis, the expert opined that it was more likely than not that Landrigan's colon cancer was attributable to asbestos exposure, even though the epidemiologic studies indicated at most a 50% increase in disease rate with asbestos exposure.[49]

A more problematic attempted use of differential diagnosis was presented in *Daubert vs. Merrell Dow Pharmaceuticals, Inc.*,[50] one of the cases in which the plaintiffs attributed birth defects to the antinausea drug Bendectin. The plaintiffs'

---

[44] *See Hall v. Baxter Healthcare*, 947 F. Supp. 1387 (D. Ore. 1996).

[45] 35 F.3d at 752.

[46] *See, e.g., Mancuso v. Consol. Edison Co. of New York, Inc.*, 967 F. Supp. 1437 (E.D.N.Y. 1997)(defendant insisting plaintiffs' witnesses required to use differential diagnosis where injuries, including learning disability, were claimed to result from PCB exposure).

[47] 605 A.2d 1079 (N.J. 1992).

[48] *Id.* at 1086-89.

[49] *Id.* at 1086. *See also Rubanick v. Witco Chemical Corp.*, 593 A.2d 733 (N.J. 1991).

[50] 43 F.3d 1311 (9th Cir. 1995), *cert. denied*, 116 S. Ct. 189 (1995). This opinion is the remand decision after the 1993 Supreme Court decision.

medical causation witness attempted to rule out other causes of the birth defects, thereby to make out their claim that Bendectin caused the victim's limb abnormalities.[51] The Ninth Circuit, however, recognized that the witness had no basis for ruling out what may well be a large cohort of unidentified background causes.[52]

It's Not Science, It's An Art

Legal standards that seem to reference medical norms fuel yet another variation on the argument that medical testimony should be taken at face value - clinical medicine is not science, or at least is not "hard science," and it therefore should not be subjected to rigorous scientific standards of validation.[53] There is an incongruity, however, in asserting that evidence that cannot meet scientific standards is probative on scientific issues.

At its core, the causation issue in a toxic tort case invokes the application of scientific principles. Our very attempt to answer the questions of whether a substance causes disease and whether it caused a particular instance of a disease assumes that causation occurs through the operation of generally applicable physical, chemical, and biological processes.[54] Because the operation of these processes is not directly observable, it may not be possible to elucidate them with a high degree of certainty, but claims about the nature and operation of those processes are essentially scientific claims, and they can and should be subjected to scrutiny according to scientific criteria.

There is much truth to the assertion that medical diagnosis involves a large measure of experience-based medical intuition.[55] In medicine, it is frequently preferable to do something rather than nothing, even where the choices must be made under uncertainty. That does not mean, however, that the selection among choices is unscientific, and even a cursory examination of the process of clinical reasoning makes it readily apparent that it is scientific in that it involves observation, hypothesis generation and testing of those hypotheses.[56] The degree of uncertainty remaining is important in relation to the objective of the exercise, and

---

[51] *Id.* at 1319.

[52] The case contains no discussion of proffered testimony on the fraction of cases attributable to other known risk factors or unidentified background causes.

[53] In *Moore v. Ashland Chemical, Inc.*, No. 95-20492, 1997 WL 644054 (5th Cir. Oct. 20, 1997), the court held that clinical medical testimony on the cause of the plaintiff's reactive airway disease was subject to scrutiny under the "knowledge, principles and methodology of clinical medicine," not the factors of *Daubert v. Merrell Dow Pharmaceuticals, Inc.*, which the court characterized as applicable only to "hard science" or "Newtonian" science.

[54] Indeed, *Daubert's* criterion of whether a theory or method is "testable" appears to be a more colloquial expression of the notion of "falsifiability," philosopher of science Karl Popper's touchstone for what constitutes a scientific statement. *See* Sean O'Connor, The Supreme Court's Philosophy of Science: Will the Real Karl Popper Please Stand Up?, 35 *Jurimetrics J.* 263 (1995).

[55] *See* Kassirer & Kopelman, *supra* note 24.

[56] *Id.*

it is the differences in objectives that are important in evaluating medical testimony in toxic injury cases. Unfortunately, the more probable than not standard of proof sometimes requires more than science can deliver.

CONCLUSION

Medical testimony on toxic injury causation is an exercise in drawing inferences from toxicology, epidemiology, and medical diagnosis. Courts are often diverted from scrutinizing the underlying reasoning by the resemblance of the subject matter to familiar medical practice, by the labeling of testimony as a standard medical technique, and by claims that medical science is not "hard science." This lack of scrutiny does not serve the legal system well because the validity of the expert's opinion is dependent on the availability of the information necessary to establish cause by a process of elimination. Testimony that invokes scientific principles should be evaluated according to scientific standards. It is those standards, rather than labels, that permit courts to distinguish between sound reasoning and speculation.

13 Explaining Toxic Chemical Risk in The Courtroom – Authority, Storytelling, and Science

Wayne Roth-Nelson

CONTENTS

INTRODUCTION

There are several approaches taken by expert witnesses who testify on toxic chemical exposure, whether examining causation where there is disease already present or instead there is some risk of future illness.

0-8493-1197-7/98/$0.00+$.50
© 1999 by CRC Press LLC

> ▸ They can just assert their reputation and authority as a way to vindicate their opinion;
> ▸ They can tell a persuasive story that appeals to intuition and imagination; or
> ▸ They can argue the scientific evidence using data and rational analysis.

Ideas presented here on capturing the minds of judge and jury using one or another approach pertain to civil or criminal cases where a toxic injury is claimed or being prosecuted. But there is little relevance to *regulatory* cases under judicial review. The scientific theory and argument that sustains government regulation of toxic chemicals is so intermixed with policy choices that it has special problems beyond this discussion.

The syndicated newspaper columnist, John Leo, recently commented on *Amistad*,[1] the cinematic courtroom drama of Steven Spielberg's about a mutiny of Africans aboard a slave ship. Former president John Quincy Adams, in strategizing how to win in court on their behalf, vows that whoever "tells the best story" will win. But Leo observes that an emphasis on narratives and storytelling in the courtroom over facts and argument really is a phenomenon of the 1990s, and would have made no sense at all to the "flinty, no-nonsense Adams." Indeed, toxic injury litigation in the 1990s often seeks to sway the jury with a good story as opposed to a dry explanation of scientific evidence. Jury researcher Dorothy Kagehiro suspects that most jurors are more attuned to narrative persuasion than to numbers.[2] Researcher Jane Goodman learned from interviews of judges, lawyers, expert witnesses, and jurors that anecdotal evidence is believed more persuasive than expert data or statistics.[3]

EXPERTS' USE OF STORYTELLING

Jury analyst Ann Burnett Pettus found that, while jurors do consider evidence presented in the trial, they do not view it in the same way as do those in the legal field.[4] Apart from legal definitions of proper or improper evidence, jurors view evidence as a form of *story or narrative*. The unclear, nonsensical story of an expert witness can appear "trumped-up" and will be deemed ineffective as evidence. Jurors, according to Pettus, are so eager to discover a complete story that makes sense, they will search for the "truth" from any illuminating storyline or even their own experience that seems relevant. They will go beyond the formal boundaries of legal evidence because the picture of what really happened is so rarely clear-cut. One legal scholar has noted how litigants, unable to counter a seemingly well-informed story offered by the opposition, are highly disadvantaged.

[1] See, e.g., editorial page of *Daily Camera* (Boulder, Colorado), Monday, January 5, 9 (1998).

[2] Kagehiro, Dorothy K., Defining the standard of proof in jury instructions. *Psychological Science* 1(3):194-200, 198 (1990).

[3] Goodman, Jane. 1992. Jurors' comprehension and assessment of probabilistic evidence. *American Journal of Trial Advocacy* 16:361-389, at 367.

[4] Pettus, Ann Burnett, The verdict is in: A study of jury decision making factors, moment of personal decision, and jury deliberations—From the jurors' point of view. *Communications Quarterly* 38(1):83-97, 92 (1990).

Even worse, he concluded, was expressing some ignorance or uncertainty which, although accurate, often is less persuasive than a plausible theory, even a false one![5]

EXPERTS' ASSERTIONS OR EXPERTS' DATA?

The Third Circuit, in *United States v. Downing,* observed how a jury faced with interpreting scientific evidence often is unreasonably persuaded by the "aura of infallibility" in which such evidence may be cloaked.[6] This problem can be accentuated where the court is *not* presented with the scientific data on which the expert relies. Instead, it must accept the expert's unsupported assertions as to the accuracy of his or her conclusions, without really explaining the science at all. But, depending on the make-up of the jury, many jurors want to be trusted with the supporting scientific data and theory. The weaknesses of an elitist approach—asserting scientific credibility by according distinction and prestige to certain scientists—have compelled juries faced with competing "truths" to independently judge the credibility and veracity of expert witnesses. The jury is aided in demystifying scientific elitism by the adversarial approach of experts in the courtroom.[7]

DIFFERENCES IN THREE APPROACHES

Many expert witnesses routinely infer their opinions on toxic causation or risk from clinical observations and logical reasoning, backed-up by their personal credentials and credibility. Opinion testimony takes the authoritarian and sometimes elitist position: "This is so because I say it's so, and with my expertise, I know best." Scientific theorizing, data analysis, and rational argument are highly analytical, often depending on models of mathematical logic and probability to explain science and to simulate the probability (odds) favoring causation or risk. After all, probability is the very language of science. Calculating the chances of toxic causation or risk from a plaintiff's chemical exposure takes the position: "This is so because, look here, the research data prove it." But storytelling uses words and pictures that rely on anecdote, analogy or metaphor to make causation or risk convincing. Storytelling often poses absolutes: What is True or False? What is Good or Evil? Storytelling is highly intuitional, depending on simple notions of right or wrong, and takes the position: "This is so because, listen up, it just makes common sense."

---

[5] Sanders, Joseph, Jury deliberation in a complex case: *Havner v. Merrell Dow Pharmaceuticals. The Justice System Journal* 16(2):45-67, 60 (1993).

[6] Eggen, Jean Macchiaroli,.. Toxic torts, causation, and scientific evidence after *Daubert. University of Pittsburgh Law Review* 55:865-955, at 938-39 (1990).

[7] Kantrowitz, Arthur, Elitism vs. checks and balances in communicating scientific information to the public. *RISK—Issues in Health and Safety* 4:101-111, 104 (1993).

ISSUES WITH AUTHORITARIAN OPINION

Withholding the factual basis for expert assertions can offend the intelligence of some jurors, depending on their own susceptibility to authority figures. Toxic tort legal scholar Allan Kanner suggests that a "populist" tends not to defer to an expert's judgments, while someone raised in a more hierarchical setting, an immigrant perhaps, or a member of a strict religious group, tends to take experts more seriously and is more likely to be deferential.[8] Also, some *classes* of experts, particularly those presenting so-called "hard" science, such as chemists and physicians, may be regarded as more trustworthy and convincing than psychologists and appraisers, for instance.[9] Where there is a "battle of experts," particularly if both sides hold similar credentials and utilize the same data but reach opposing opinions, the jurors may just ignore or even discount the value of *all* the probabilistic or other scientific evidence.[10] Finally, in the absence of objective evidence or when confronted with bewildering scientific evidence in support of an expert opinion, a jury may fixate on the expert's personality or demeanor. For instance, jurors have characterized one or another expert as "believable" or as "rambling and redundant," or they believed an expert "called all the right shots" or "did everything but answer the question." The appearance of sincerity or moral certainty may replace hard facts.

ISSUES WITH PROBABILISTIC DATA

According to psychologist Jane Goodman, a juror's prior mathematical experience has been found a useful and significant predictor of his or her responses to the crucial scientific evidence.

> Jurors may minimize the importance of non-empirical evidence in comparison with the more logical mathematical evidence that appears irrefutable and less impeachable.[11]

However, "not all scholars share the view that jurors will become mesmerized by probabilistic evidence." Other studies have shown that, in everyday situations, jurors will systematically err when interpreting probabilistic evidence, that "statistics are less persuasive than are people, and that anecdotal evidence is more persuasive than expert data." There are other issues with probability and the scientific method:

- Probability models may present too many variables and uncertainties, which can undermine a jury's trust;
- Math or computer models can require blind trust in so-called "Black Boxes," whose inner workings are opaque to all but the narrow specialist;

---

[8]   Kanner, Allan, Environmental and toxic tort trials. The Michie Company; Charlottesville, VA. 566 pp., 89 (1991).

[9]   *Supra* Note 3, at 386.

[10]   *Supra* Note 6, at 940.

[11]   *Supra* Note 3, at 367.

▸   Probability models can conflict with common-sense reasoning, and when they are too simplified, can lead to "Junk Science"; and

▸   It can be highly disconcerting to realize that either plaintiff or defense theories are *possible* to some degree; it is just that one or the other is more *probable*.

ISSUES WITH STORYTELLING

Sometimes stories can communicate more powerfully than probability statistics, and beliefs can persuade better than probability theories. Probability models are closer to scientific truth, while stories can be more convincing, even if scientifically incorrect. Science often seeks 90 or 95 percent certainty, but civil juries need only 51 percent certainty to infer toxic causation or risk. Storytelling can appear to reach the legal standard of more probable than not (at least 51%), but stories that conflict with the scientific findings frequently may offer even less certainty than that, and mislead both judge and jury. Storytelling promotes a reliance on extralegal evidence, such as "hunches" about what really happened. Inferences of causation or risk inherently are tied to evidence that is statistical in nature. This is particularly the case with results of laboratory experiments with animals by toxicologists or of human population studies by epidemiologists that associate toxic exposure with disease. Allan Kanner comments on the relative merits of "precise" scientific evidence and admittedly imprecise non-quantitative proof:

> Some have suggested that the seemingly precise nature of statistical proof will cause jurors to weigh it more heavily than equally probative but admittedly unscientific, non-statistical proof. It is not, however, universally accepted that statistics are either precise or more persuasive than vivid anecdotal reports ... Scientific evidence standing alone will distract the juror from equally relevant unscientific evidence, unless that unscientific proof is vivid and salient anecdotal evidence.[12]

ILLUSTRATIVE PROBLEM FOR A JURY

A Sample Toxic Tort Trial

An actual case tried in a federal district court is used here to illustrate the challenge of communicating toxic causation and risk in the courtroom.[13] The jury in this case was faced with deciding if the plaintiff's reported illness, more likely than not, was caused by inhalation exposure to toxic hydrocarbon vapors (Plaintiff Theory), or it *was not* (Defense Theory). Neither side tried to reach the jury strictly by asserting authoritarian opinions backed-up only by expert credentials and sheer believability. Instead, the trial testimony pitted a narrative approach, bolstered by inventive scientific theories, against an explanation of scientific data and

---

[12] *Supra* Note 8, at 80.

[13] Author served as expert witness on issues of toxic chemical exposure, dose, dose-response, disease causation, and cancer risk.

mainstream probability theory. Opposing theories of causation use the Storytelling and Common Sense approach on the plaintiff's side and Scientific Probability Analysis on the side of the defense. The opposing theories are identified here as the "SmokeStream Story" versus the "VaporFog Model," respectively.

The SmokeStream Story.

This story relies on a theory that disease symptoms reported after breathing hydrocarbon smoke streaming from a nearby industrial plant exhaust stack are actually cause and effect, and causation is inferred. The SmokeStream Story rests on a novel assumption: a stream of fumes jetting from the exhaust stack traveled intact to contact the plaintiff at *full strength*. In other words, the plaintiff's exposure hundreds of feet away from exhaust-stack fumes was just about as concentrated and toxic as if the plaintiff directly breathed the stack emissions. The storyline of SmokeStream may be synopsized as follows:

A dark jet of poisonous hydrocarbon smoke containing cancer-causing chemicals streamed from the exhaust stack of a nearby plant. It drifted across the plaintiff's property and into open windows. At night it surrounded the house in a dense cloud. The plaintiff was exposed day and night over most of a year to breathing the same high concentration of fumes shooting from the exhaust stack. The result was highly toxic doses to lungs and skin. Severe respiratory and other systemic illness were the direct result of exposure; an indirect result is a high risk of cancer in the future.

Storytelling With Pictures.

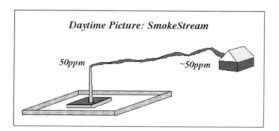

Figure 1. In the daytime illustration of the SmokeStream Story, one sees the "dark jet poisonous hydrocarbon smoke."

The storytelling approach often relies on simple pictures as well as narrative to assist the judge and jury, Figures 1 and 2. In the daytime picture of Smoke-Stream, Figure 1, one sees the "dark jet of poisonous hydrocarbon smoke" drifting into open windows, and there is no apparent loss in the density and toxicity of the smoke plume (~50 ppm or parts per million). This depiction ignores the basic science: a much lower concentration would occur hundreds of feet downwind because extreme mixing, dilution, and dispersion in clean air results from hot, high-velocity exhaust and wind transport; aerosol condensation would produce early fallout close to the plant. Also ignored is the low frequency of actual exposure; the plaintiff's house was directly exposed downwind from the plant only 11 percent of the time, mostly in daytime. In the nighttime picture, Figure 2, one sees the "house surrounded in a dense cloud."

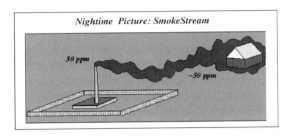

Figure 2. In the nighttime illustration of the SmokeStream Story, one sees the "house surrounded in a dense cloud."

However, in actuality, the house is sited on high terrain overlooking ravines that would collect heavier-than-air hydrocarbons dissolved in condensed water vapor in the form of ground fog. This would happen only when there was *no* wind, or 24 percent of the time, mostly at night.

The VaporFog Model

The probability approach relied on a theory that reported disease symptoms were unrelated to breathing tiny droplets of hydrocarbons dissolved and diluted in water vapor (aerosol) that discharged from the plant stack and condensed as fog. The VaporFog Model rests on a different assumption: exposure of the plaintiff hundreds of feet away from exhaust-stack emissions was at a harmless concentration because aerosol fog travels highly mixed, diluted and dispersed in clean air. In place of anecdotal narrative, the exposure model, an EPA peer-reviewed computer model of point-source, airborne contaminant dispersion, employs both deterministic and probabilistic inputs:

- Deterministic input variables—type of terrain; exhaust stack height and diameter; gas exit velocity, temperature and emission rate;
- Probabilistic input variables—wind-speed and direction; air temperature; atmospheric stability, based on daytime wind speed and solar radiation, and on nighttime wind speed and cloud cover.

The model calculates a probabilistic output: air concentration of hydrocarbon vapors at variable distances downwind, or at concentric distances with no wind. The common sense basis for each model variable can be explained to a judge and jury. Emphasis on scientific peer review and model validation is important in securing their trust in what for them may be a mysterious "Black Box."

Probability Modeling and Graphics

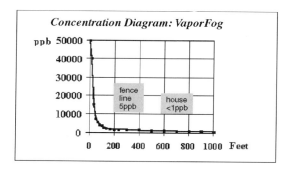

Figure 3. In a graphic rendition of the VaporFog Model, the exposure
concentration diminishes with distance from the source

The probability modeling approach relies heavily on data, often depicted in
charts or diagrams to assist the judge and jury (Figures 3 and 4). An exposure concentration "curve" (Figure 3) shows how the average concentration (ppb or parts
per billion) diminishes very rapidly with distance away (feet) from the emissions
source. The shape of the abrupt curve at 100 feet away from the source results from
rapid mixing due to the heat, velocity and condensation of vapor emissions. Then
aerosol fallout reduces the vapor concentration to only several ppb at the fence line
of the plant or at the edge of the plaintiff's property, even with a worst-case
exposure.

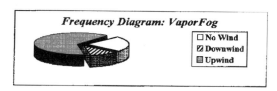

Figure 4. In another graphic rendition of the VaporFog Model
the exposure frequency varies with the wind direction.

An exposure frequency "pie chart" (Figure 4) shows how exposure conditions
vary with wind direction. The worst condition occurs when the plaintiff's property
lies directly downwind from the vapor plume, which occurred only 11 percent of
the time. There is limited exposure when there is no wind; the vapor emissions
disperse in every direction, thereby becoming very attenuated. There is no exposure
when the property lies upwind (or crosswind) from the plant exhaust stack during
65 percent of the time.

SmokeStream Versus VaporFog: Exposure Concentration.

A comparison is made of exposure concentrations indicated by the Smoke-
Stream Story and the VaporFog Model for just one toxic hydrocarbon found in the

Table 1. Comparative benzene exposure concentrations indicated by the SmokeStream Story and the VaporFog Model.

Worst-Case Exposure		
Story or Model Variables	*SmokeStream Story*	*VaporFog Data*
How CONCENTRATED Was Inhalation Exposure?		
At Emmision Source?	*Stack Emmisions*	*<1 PPB (Breathing Zone)*
At Plant Fence Line?	*Stack Emmisions*	*10 PPB (Mixing Dispersion)*
At Plaintiff's Property Line?	*Stack Emmisions*	*5 PPB (As above)*

plant emissions (Table 1). Concentration values are for a *worst-case* exposure to benzene, a known carcinogen. How will a judge or jury respond to VaporFog levels of benzene no greater than 5 ppb in the breathing zone at the plaintiff's property line, or near that level inside the dwelling (assuming open windows)? By comparison, the Smoke- Stream story asserts a breathable level as concentrated as in the emissions plume *at the stack* (~50,000 ppb or 50 ppm). How about the storyline assertion that the plume concentration of benzene was essentially unvarying from emission source to plaintiff's property? How does that square with a computer model simulation of less than 1 ppb (benzene) in the ground-level breathing zone right below the elevated stack (emission source), or 10 ppb at the plant fence line after mixing, dilution and dispersion? Were these conflicting expert opinions equally credible?

SmokeScreen Versus VaporFog: Exposure Duration and Frequency

Table 2. Comparative benzene exposure periods and frequencies indicated by the SmokeStream Story and the VaporFog Model.

Worst-Case Exposure		
Story or Model Variables	*SmokeStream Story*	*VaporFog Data*
How FREQUENT Was Inhalation Exposure?		
Consecutive Days?	*About Nine Months*	*50 Days (No Emission Controls)*
Hours Out of 24?	*Usually Day and Night*	*15 Hours (Downwind/ No Wind)*

A comparison was made of the worst-case exposure periods and frequencies between the SmokeStream Story and the VaporFog Model (Table 2). How will a judge or jury respond to VaporFog data that specify an exposure duration of 50 consecutive days (period when there were no emission controls at the plant), as compared to the SmokeStream storyline that claimed about nine continuous months and made no distinction regarding the installation of emission controls? How about the storyline assertion that inhalation exposure occurred usually all day and night, as compared to the calculated exposure frequency of an average 15 hours out of 24 when there was either no wind or the plaintiff's dwelling was downwind? Were the plant records concerning emission controls and the meteorological records concerning wind direction and velocity more credible to judge and jury than the plaintiff expert's assertions?

SmokeScreen Versus VaporFog: Internal Dose

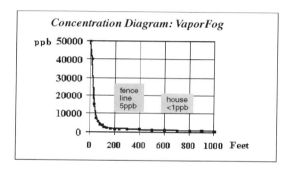

Figure 3. In a graphic rendition of the VaporFog Model,
the exposure concentration diminishes with distance from
the source of the emission.

The well-worn adage in toxicology that "the dose is the poison" often is ignored in the courtroom, particularly where a trace concentration or tiny dose of a potential toxicant could prove *de minimus* or harmless. A comparison of the worst-case, dose-response parameters between the SmokeStream Story and the VaporFog Model is found in Tables 3 and 4.

Table 3. Delivered and absorbed benzene inhalation doses indicated by the VaporFog Model and the SmokeStream Story.

Worst-Case Exposure		
Story or Model Variables	*SmokeStream Story*	*VaporFog Data*
What DOSE Was Received from Inhalation ?		
Delivered Dose?	*Ignored*	*0.50µg/kg/day*
Absorbed Dose?	*Ignored*	*0.25µg/kg/day*

In Table 3, the *delivered* dose (0.50 ug/kg/day or micrograms per kilogram of body weight per day) is the quantity inhaled; the internal or *absorbed* dose (0.25 ug/kg/day) is the quantity actually assimilated in tissues of the respiratory system, that is, excluding what is exhaled. How will a judge or jury respond to VaporFog probability calculations of delivered and absorbed doses, as compared to the SmokeStream storyline that just ignores the dose

SmokeScreen Versus VaporFog: Dose-Response

In Table 4, the dose-response is the probable benzene cancer risk, an *added* numerical chance (odds) of cancer, as well as the estimated non-cancer risk as a percent of the No Observable Adverse Effects Level (NOAEL), which is expressed as a Hazard Quotient (HQ). The dose-response, if large enough, can provide an inference of causation where there is a disease already diagnosed, or predict the risk of future illness where there is not. How will a judge or jury respond to Vapor-Fog probability calculations of dose-response as compared to no quantification of health risk by plaintiffs, depending instead on powerful words and narrative to suggest undeniable causation or risk? Is the model calculation of 5 in 100,000 odds of added cancer risk (or total risk of 25,005 in 100,000), as well as a Hazard Quotient of 0.25 (25% of NOAEL), more credible to judge and jury than plaintiff's anecdotal testimony on risk?

Worst-Case Exposure		
Story or Model Variables	SmokeStream Story	VaporFog Data
What DOSE-RESPONSE Was Expected ?		
Added Cancer Risk?	Unquantified	Added Odds 5 in 100,000 (Total 25,005 in 100,000)
Added Non-Cancer Risk?	Unquantified	HQ= 0.25 (< NOAEL)

Table 4. Benzene cancer and noncancer dose-response (risks) indicated by the VaporFog Model and the SmokeStream Story.

Outcome of the Illustrative Case

The judge in this case admitted the quantitative, probabilistic evidence offered by the defense, as well as the novel theory of "non-attenuation," that is, no diminution of emission levels with vapor transport, as presented by plaintiffs. Although the jury was *not* persuaded that causation was a reasonable scientific certainty or more probable than not, the outcome easily might have been reversed. A number of factors unrelated to the merits of the evidence favored the plaintiff's strategy, that of stressing the maximum potential toxicity of the chemical vapors, and dramatizing the worst possible health consequences. For example, the jurors were "home-grown" and probably looked upon the plaintiff as one of "them." Jurors averaged a ninth-grade education, probably indicating limited interests in math and science, and might be expected to be skeptical of a "Black Box" computer model. The defendants had "deep pockets" so the jury might be expected to give some benefit of doubt to poor plaintiffs since defendants could afford to pay. However, a jury factor possibly weighing against the plaintiffs was seating a juror who managed a gasoline station and might appreciate that benzene or other hydrocarbon vapors would smell much more concentrated right at the pump, then rapidly diminish in odor with distance away from the pump. Other factors possibly influencing the outcome were the comparative personality attributes and communication styles of the expert witnesses.

USING SCIENCE TO REACH VERDICTS

Placing Science on Trial.

A jury should *not* have to place science itself on trial by having to decide scientific "truth" by a majority vote, thereby reaching a wrong-headed verdict.[14] For example, while examining how lay persons perceive chemical risks, researchers tested this statement concerning the general principle in toxicology that the "dose is the poison:"

> It's not how much of the chemical you are exposed to that should worry you, but whether or not you are exposed to it at all.[15]

Non-college-educated respondents, presumably less exposed to science, agreed (45%) more than those with a college education (27%), and women agreed more (48%) than men (28%). Peter Huber, a notorious critic of "junk" science in the courtroom, offers further discouragement:

> Ninety-seven percent of prospective jurors will know that hot air rises. But 40 percent will believe that lucky numbers have a scientific basis.[16]

The court ought not to allow the jury to "reinvent" science by validating untested theories or discarding mainstream scientific methods. The trial court can use its power to hold pre-trial hearings to determine beforehand whether the named experts will testify on personal theories or hunches, or whether they will opine on a well-developed, supportable thesis found acceptable in the scientific community.

Seeking Scientific Certainty

Legal standards of "proof" are not the same as scientific standards with which experts are familiar. Scientists most often expect 90 or 95 percent confidence in testing a cause-and-effect hypothesis. Judges have interpreted "preponderance of the evidence," used in most civil cases, as indicating a probability of little more

---

[14] LeBlanc, III, Sam A., Scientific truth in toxic tort litigation. *For the Defense* [April]:2-10, 3, 10 (1993).

[15] Kraus, N., Malmfors, T. and Slovic, P., Intuitive toxicology: Expert and lay judgments of chemical risks. *Risk Analysis* 12(2):215-232, at 222 (1992).

[16] Huber, P., Junk science and the jury. *The University of Chicago Legal Forum* [Annual]:273-301, at 273 (1990).

than half, [17] so civil juries must deal with great uncertainty in toxic injury litigation. Any inadequacies in jury deliberation are masked by the fact that a verdict for either party can appear to be reasonable.[18] Juries may dislike a 51-percent threshold of "truth" because it suggests a permissible risk of penalizing an innocent defendant or rewarding an undeserving plaintiff. In the words of U.S. Court of Appeals Judge Hugh Bownes, ". . . the scales of justice have to tip only ever so slightly [49 to 51%] in favor of the plaintiff for [him or] her to prevail."[19] However, studies show mock jurors misinterpreted "preponderance" as indicating a probability almost indistinguishable from "reasonable doubt," the standard used in criminal trials and interpreted by judges to be about 90 percent or greater.[20]

Inferring Specific Causation

Jurors may have difficulty understanding that probabilistic evidence only establishes a statistical association as circumstantial proof of causation in a *population*.[21] Such evidence provides only a partial inference of specific, individual level causation. Whether a plaintiff can prove facts from which an inference of general, population level causation could be made, relies on factors such as the strength of a statistical association between chemical exposure level or dose and the disease in question. Whether there exists clear biological plausibility of a causal link and consistency among various research studies are important as well. But the inference of *individual* causation hinges on whether a plaintiff can prove facts to support an adequate degree of *external validity*—that the key characteristics of the research populations, including their exposure and dose levels, their ages and balance of gender and race, their genetic features, and their history of disease, among other factors, are similar enough to those of the plaintiff to infer individual level causation. The inferential gap from statistics about groups to conclusions about individuals is an evidentiary problem. However, the use of *subgroup* statistics to select out research subjects closely similar to the plaintiff can improve inferential reliability.[22] This approach is capable of meeting legal standards of "more probable than not" or "reasonable scientific certainty." Nevertheless, juries most often make little distinction between general and specific causation.[23]

---

[17] Green, M. D. Expert witnesses and sufficiency of evidence in toxic substances litigation: The legacy of *Agent Orange* and Bendectin litigation. *Northwestern University Law Review* 86:643-699, at 697 (1992).

[18] *Supra* Note 5, at 46.

[19] Bownes, The Hon. H.H., Should trial by jury be eliminated in complex cases? *RISK—Issues in Health and Safety* 1:75-81, at 76 (1990).

[20] *Supra* Note 2, at 195, 198.

[21] *Supra* Note 6, at 262.

[22] Walker, V.R., Direct inference, probability, and a conceptual gulf in risk communication. *Risk Analysis* 15(5):603-609, 608 (1995).

[23] *Supra* Note 5, at 63.

Communicating Low-Level Risks

Any *quantified* toxic chemical risk at all, or even a weak statistical link between types of exposure and disease, can be *perceived* by a jury to suggest causation or significant risk. Except possibly for prescription drugs, the public generally tends to view chemicals as either safe or dangerous, and they appear to equate even small exposures to toxic or carcinogenic chemicals with almost certain harm. Thirty percent of lay respondents in a survey did not agree that a 1 in 10,000,000 added lifetime risk of cancer from exposure to a chemical was too small to worry about.[24] Lay persons do not process small probabilities easily, and fail to distinguish adequately between probabilities of 1 in 1,000, 1 in 10,000, and 1 in 100,000.[25] Although a low-level risk such as 1 in 1,000,000 may be perceived as real, individuals may not actually alter their behavior or choices unless faced with a "high-end" risk, one that is way above the average—a worst-case scenario.[26] Risk levels presented in the courtroom should be placed in perspective by comparing an individual plaintiff's risk with both the high-end and average risks of others similarly exposed to the same toxicant. At the same time, any special *susceptibility* of the plaintiff should be demonstrated, such as exposure *in utero* or infancy, pregnancy, advanced age, or with a complicating illness.

EXPLAINING TOXIC RISK: THE BASICS

In the toxic tort case without a presently diagnosable injury or illness, but there is a risk of that happening in the future, the problem is one of inferring *personal* risk, as opposed to inferences of population risk. Depending on the available exposure data for the plaintiff and dose-response data available from relevant research populations, the objective is to *quantify* individual exposure, dose, and expected dose-response. Data deficiencies may force a qualitative or semi-quantitative approach.

Many plaintiff cases that feature a presently diagnosable injury or illness do not go beyond mere *succession* to demonstrate causation, just because one event succeeded another. For example, let's say that a plaintiff observed a neighbor's field being sprayed with pesticide and, thereafter, the plaintiff became ill, so it was inferred that the pesticide actually caused the illness. Such an inference of causation is weak because it ignores any proof, even circumstantial, of actual personal exposure, a personal dose, or comparison of an expected with an observed personal dose-response. Moreover, there may be no consideration of an alternative cause of illness or even multiple causes that may or may not include the pesticide exposure.

---

[24] *Supra* Note 15, at 225.

[25] *Supra* Note 3, at 375.

[26] Johnson, B. B., Slovic, P., Presenting uncertainty in health risk assessment: Initial studies of its effects on risk perception and trust. *Risk Analysis* 15(4):485-494, 486 (1995).

First Principle: Look at Personal Exposure

Here are some key questions to raise and to answer in the courtroom:

▸ Was the suspect chemical actually *detected* in air, water, soil, food, drugs or consumer products to which the plaintiff was exposed?
▸ Was the plaintiff actually exposed via ingestion, inhalation, dermal absorption or radiation, and at what likely level or concentration?
▸ How frequent and prolonged was the plaintiff's likely exposure—was it acute, subacute, subchronic, or chronic?

Many plaintiff or defense arguments fail to quantify or even approximate a level of exposure. In the example of the alleged pesticide exposure, the plaintiff may have smelled the odor of a pesticide outdoors off and on daily, an airborne spray may have been visible, and the suspect pesticide may have fit into a highly toxic class of chemicals. Yet a case for exposure failed to provide estimates of an airborne source concentration, dilution, dispersion, drift, and fallout (deposition). Also missing was a breathing-zone concentration (ppb) or exposure time (hours per day, days per week, total weeks). In the absence of documented exposure, including actual measurements, a qualified health risk scientist often can reconstruct a reasonable and likely exposure scenario from documented studies of similar exposure. While lacking in precision and reliability, such surrogate studies nevertheless may meet the more-probable-than-not legal standard for causation in a civil lawsuit.

Second Principle: Look at Personal Dose

Key factors to communicate to judge and jury should include:

▸ How much and how fast the suspect chemical probably was delivered to the plaintiff by swallowing, breathing, skin contact, or direct radiation?
▸ How much and how fast the delivered dose probably was absorbed systemically or by certain target organs?

Many plaintiff or defense arguments fail to quantify or even approximate an amount of dose. In the pesticide exposure example, the plaintiff may have breathed a highly toxic pesticide whenever spray was visible or an odor was detectable. Yet a case for exposure failed to provide estimates of an airborne dose by quantifying the breathing rate (cubic meters per hour or m^3/hr), a delivered lung dose (mg/kg/day), an absorbed lung dose (% delivered dose), or an odor threshold (ppb). Again, in the absence of any measured dose, a dose reconstruction that is reasonable and likely sometimes can be provided by a health risk specialist from surrogate studies.

Third Principle: Look at the Relevant Dose-Response

Answers to key questions to raise in the courtroom should include:

▸   What was the plaintiff's dose compared to a *reference dose* for adverse
    response or risk among relevant research subjects?
▸   What probability statistics show similar doses to subjects like the plaintiff that
    are similar to adverse responses like the plaintiff's?
▸   Are the relevant research results *consistent* and biologically *plausible?*

Many cases fail to evaluate dose-response. In the pesticide example, the argument may have been made that the plaintiff's inhalation of toxic pesticide explains
his or her illness that followed and has appeared in other exposed subjects. What
is missing is any reference doses or risks and associated probability statistics
among research subjects with comparable exposures and manifestations of illness.
Obviously, a lack of directly relevant epidemiological or toxicological studies that
provide reference doses or statistical associations between exposure and disease at
levels of exposure and with results directly relevant to the plaintiff and the suspect
chemical will be an impediment. Sometimes surrogate data are useful that derive
from other chemicals or other diseases in the same "family."

Fourth Principle: Look at Alternative or Multiple Causation

Judges and juries should be informed about the plaintiff's lifestyle and medical
history:

▸   Were there alternative toxic exposures involving environment, diet, smoking,
    drugs, soaps, cosmetics, or other products, or were there disease organisms or
    even genetic factors that could explain the plaintiff's condition?
▸   Is it possible that the plaintiff's condition involves *multiple causation,*
    implicating not only the suspect chemical but other toxic agents, chemicals or
    pathogens or genes, working in combination or interactively, or resulting in
    uncommon susceptibility.

Some additive or interactive toxic effects can even be quantified, and many
cases may overlook lifestyle choices. In the example of pesticide exposure, the
plaintiff may have been a smoker or asthmatic with respiratory symptoms observed
and recorded before the neighbor's field was sprayed. Afterward, they may have
appeared to worsen, so the pesticide was presumed to trigger the reported illness.
But there is a disregard for the possibility that a lifestyle choice could have
predisposed the plaintiff to illness or interacted with pesticide dose effects. Besides
the voluntary risks of smoking or dietary choices, for instance, there are involuntary
risks of genetic inheritance or exposure to communicable diseases that can increase
susceptibility to toxic exposures. Although this area of scientific research is still
rudimentary, some combinations of toxic chemicals with dietary, smoking and drug
habits or even with certain disease infections or genetic factors can influence the
case for causation.

CONCLUSIONS

The optimum use of probability analysis as evidence of toxic causation or risk calls for judiciously weighing clinical observations and medical opinion along with quantified probability estimates. Probabilistic evidence can neutralize subjective or unsubstantiated claims about exposure conditions and associated health risks. It can reduce unnecessary reliance on experts' professional intuitions and help substantiate medical judgments regarding causation. Inferences of personal causation or risk drawn from uncertain quantitative evidence carry as much relevance and reliability as intuitive clinical judgments, expert assertions, and anecdotal evidence. It is better to balance opinion testimony of experts with quantitative, probabilistic evidence than to rely just on one or the other. Each is needed to cross-check the truth of toxic causation and risk. Telling a good story using common sense can be highly persuasive although common sense can be flat wrong. Using stories ungrounded in objective evidence can sometimes lead to jury nullification.

14 Science in the Patent Infringement Decision-Making Process: Problems and Proposed Reforms

Michael D. Kaminski

CONTENTS

INTRODUCTION

The legal profession generally has been under a veritable siege in the past few years. Although criticism of the civil justice process has proceeded along many fronts, perhaps nowhere is it more telling than in the area of scientific evidence. Not only are judges and juries ill equipped to render competent decisions on the increasingly complex scientific issues before them, abuses of scientific evidence and the employment of so-called "junk science" or "funny science" are frequent. Such events do nothing to foster confidence in the legal system.

Anecdotal examples of the inability of certain judges and juries to apply common sense to scientifically inaccurate legal theories advanced to them make both the headlines and the monologues of late-night talk show hosts from time to time.[1] Although these anecdotal examples are not as widespread as the general population imagines, it is enough to make us question whether an alternative decision-making scheme for legal issues involving science would be more appropriate.

Several reforms have been previously proposed to arrest these developments. Most recently – and most importantly – the Supreme Court's 1993 *Daubert*[2]

---

[1] Two favorite examples include a civil action involving the loss of psychic abilities as a result of a car accident and, in another action, the desire to switch genders as a result of a car accident. Both are discussed below.

[2] *Daubert v. Merrill Pharmaceutical Inc.*, 509 U.S. 579, 113 S.Ct. 2786 (1993).

decision was intended to stem this tide by conferring on trial judges "gatekeeper" responsibility for the admissibility of scientific evidence.

In the patent infringement arena, however, the *Daubert* decision has done little to improve the situation. On the other hand, the "junk science" problem was never as pronounced in patent cases as in other areas of law. Scientific evidence in patent cases is typically more subtly problematic than being "junk science." In patent infringement cases, each side's technical expert witnesses' testimony seems based on good scientific principles. Yet their respective interpretations of what operative facts control the eventual outcome – be it infringement or validity - are typically diametrically opposed. These interpretations provide the trier of fact with two extreme scientific positions to choose from without the benefit of a *Daubert* ruling to guide their choice, because neither position is excludable as "junk science." This situation is explained in more detail below.

Prior to considering these issues, however, a general description of the basic legal actors – the judge, jury, and expert witnesses – will be provided.

LEGAL DECISION-MAKING "ACTORS" – JUDGES, JURIES, AND EXPERT WITNESSES

As with legal proceedings involving more mundane and perhaps more comprehensible evidence, patent trials involving scientific issues may be conducted with or without a jury. When a jury is present, it makes factual determinations, while the judge is confined to holdings of law. In the absence of a jury, the judge fulfills both aspects of the decision making in the so-called "bench trial." In the early 1970s, patent trials were presented to juries only about 5% of the time. These days, the situation has become an almost turnaround, now with over 75% of patent trials presented to juries.

Why this turnaround? The biggest perception of the reason is that patent lawyers recognize that jurors generally favor upholding patents. They favor patents because they are not technically equipped to understand the underlying technical facts and therefore favor the "status quo," by upholding the patent which, after all, has been officially "sanctioned" by the U.S. Patent and Trademark Office. The statutorily-mandated "presumption of validity" accorded patents reinforce the juror's belief.

To exaggerate to prove a point, who are judges and who are jurors? Judges are very intelligent. However, they are almost always lawyers who did not graduate from university with a technical degree. Rather, they have almost always graduated with some sort of liberal arts degree. At most, they took an incidental science course or two as freshmen or sophomores. Jurors are people who typically have not gone to college. Each group's lack of technical expertise just aggravates its inability to understand the inherent technical issues in patent infringement cases.

Of course, the Seventh Amendment of the United States Constitution governs whether a judge may impanel a jury for trial or hear the case herself. For all practical purposes, the Seventh Amendment's broad jury trial guarantee attaches to almost all cases involving complex scientific issues. If either party requests a jury, the court must accede to its demand, albeit sometimes grudgingly.[3] If no party requests a jury, the trial is heard only by the judge.

The Supreme Court had provided one potential exception to the Seventh Amendment in its *Ross v. Bernhard*[4] decision, although this exception never expanded beyond judicial debate. In that decision, the Court held that a jury trial could be denied in any particular lawsuit where, among other factors, the complexities of that suit would exceed the practical abilities and limitations of a jury. In other words, the argument may be made that certain scientific issues in a case may be too complex to be understood by a jury, and therefore, a jury should not be impaneled even if it was requested. While this argument would seem to encompass many cases involving scientific evidence, at least one reported attempt to invoke *Ross v. Bernhard* in patent litigation failed,[5] and a jury ultimately heard the issues. More recent decisions by lower courts since then unanimously have approved of jury trials in scientifically intricate patent suits.[6]

To persuade the judge or jury to reach a desired result, parties to the patent suit always bring technical expert witnesses to testify. By advising the lay judge and jurors about topics beyond these decision makers' near or total lack of scientific experience, these technical expert witnesses supposedly give objective testimony based on scientific evidence. Revised pre-trial procedures now expand and streamline the ability of opposing parties to discover the views and planned testimony of expert witnesses.[7] For example, reports from such experts as to the subject matter of their expected testimony are typical. The rules do not, however, carefully screen the qualifications of the experts brought to trial.[8]

TWO CRISES OF THE CIVIL JUSTICE SYSTEM

Although our civil justice system, including juries, has had remarkable longevity,[9] it has not been particularly amenable to the increasing complexity of scientific issues set before it. Two problem areas are immediately apparent: (a)

---

[3] See e.g. *American Hoist & Derrick Co. v. Iowa & Sons, Inc.*, 725 F.2d 1356 (Fed.Cir.), cert. denied, 469 U.S. 821 (1984).

[4] *Ross v. Bernhard,* 396 U.S. 531 (1970).

[5] See *Tights, Inc., v. Stanley*, 441 F.2d 336, 340-344 (4th Cir.) cert denied 404 U.S. 852 (1971).

[6] *See* e.g. *Structural Rubber Products Co, v. Parker Rubber Co.*, 749 F.2d 707, 718-722 (Fed.Cir. 1984).

[7] See Fed.R.Civ.P 26(b)(4).

[8] Fed.R.Evidence 702 requires only that the witness qualify as an expert by "knowledge skill, experience, training, or education."

[9] The jury system was firmly entrenched in English common law by the thirteenth century. William Holdsworth, *A History of English Law,* 1, 316 (3d ed. 1922).

scientifically illiterate judges and juries, and (b) the parade of so-called "junk science" or some lesser degree of it that has increasingly marched through American courtrooms.

Scientifically Illiterate Judges and Juries

Given the general lack of scientific literacy in American society, it should not be surprising that most judges and jurors have no technical training. Because the Seventh Amendment mandates a jury panel that is a cross-section of the community in which the court is located, juries with no technical training whatsoever typically result.

This lack of scientific understanding becomes particularly acute in patent litigation, which frequently involves cutting edge technologies that may be unfamiliar even to the "average" scientist or engineer. Expert witnesses often must present their testimony in extremely basic terms in an attempt to describe complex devices and processes to lay judges and jurors. They frequently resort to analogies to simplify the concepts. For example, a computer system may be compared to a kitchen in which the hardware is the stove and the software is the recipe. DNA sequences can be compared to a dance step. That these lay judges and lay juries will then decide the fate of extremely valuable, high-technology commercial applications frequently astounds foreign observers of the American court system.

Complex scientific evidence is not confined to patent litigation. Product liability cases typically involve engineering questions. And even seemingly straightforward personal injury litigation often involves medical and actuarial testimony. Environmental litigation concerning the cause, liability for and clean-up of toxic pollution regularly involves chemists and civil engineers. Pathologists, toxicologists, and ballistics experts often testify in homicide trials, and litigants frequently place experts such as psychiatrists, forensic chemists and even fire marshals on the stand in arson cases.[10]

Evidence of how scientific illiteracy affects juror decisions can sometimes be painfully obvious. In one recent patent infringement case in which the author was involved, post-trial interviews of the jurors who decided the case indicated that a juror's sentiments were substantially aligned with her educational level. Five jurors with no more than a high school education voted for the plaintiff/patent owner, with some of them wanting to assess damages at over $100 million. In contrast, four jurors with college training voted for the defendant/alleged infringer. The result of the initial trial was a hung jury.

Unfortunately, the capabilities of the judges in bench trials involving scientific issues may not be much better. Although judges have more control over the

---

[10] John W. Wesley, Note, Scientific Evidence and the Question of Judicial Capacity, *Wm. & Mary L. Rev.* 25, 675, 679-680 (1984).

proceedings than jurors,[11] the vast majority of judges (and their law clerks) have college degrees in the liberal arts, with minimal scientific training. One judge, David Bazelon, former Chief Judge of the Washington, D.C. Federal Court of Appeals, was surprisingly candid in his realization that "substantive review of mathematical and scientific evidence by technically illiterate judges is dangerously unreliable . . . ."[12] In another opinion, he confessed that "I recognize that I do not know enough about dynamometer extrapolations, deterioration factor adjustments, and the like to decide whether or not the government's approach to these matters was statistically valid."[13]

Accompanying the lack of scientific background are the biases that enter the decision making of both judges and jurors. Particularly in jury trials, experienced counsel relate that hometown parties are given the benefit of the doubt when compared with out-of-town litigants. In some patent cases, attorneys may demand a jury trial if their client faced difficult obstacles or made a personal sacrifice in the invention process, or if their client is an individual or small partnership facing a large corporation. The reason for this is that factors such as the reputations of the litigating parties, as well as the personality and appearance of witnesses, rather than scientific credibility, loom large before judges and juries.[14] Further, patent attorneys know that, all else being equal, American juries are known worldwide for their staunch support of the patent system. Perhaps impressed by the blue ribbon and gold seal that the Patent Office attaches to the front of each issued U.S. patent, juries frequently decide the action in the patent owner's favor. Several prominent attorneys have noted that they always request a jury when they represent the plaintiff in a patent infringement suit, for this reason.[15]

The Rise of "Junk Science" or Some Lesser Variation of It

Given the complex scientific settings in a variety of patent infringement lawsuits, parties typically employ expert witnesses for several reasons. First, judges generally have little experience with legal matters involving technology. Most judges have much more experience with criminal cases (like drug trafficking

---

[11] Unlike jurors, judges may consult outside sources for background information and call their own expert witnesses. FRE 201, 706. However, these consultations are only infrequently done and are fraught with their own problems.

[12] *Ethyl Corporation v. Environmental Protection Agency*, 541 F.2d 1, 67 (D.C. Cir.) *cert. denied* 426 U.S. 941 (1976) (Bazelon C.J. concurring).

[13] *International Harvester Co. v. Ruckelshaus*, 478 F.2d 615, 651 (D.C. Cir. 1973) (Bazelon, C.J. concurring).

[14] See V. Bryan Medlock, *Jury Trials of Patent Cases*, in IX Selected Legal Papers of 4th American Intellectual Property Law Association 175, 183-84 (July 1991).

[15] See Anthony Baldo, Juries Love the Patent Holder, *Forbes*, June 17, 1985, at 147.

cases), tax cases, and business litigation. The legal doctrines required in legal matters involving underlying technology facts are viewed as unfathomable areas, difficult to understand and apply. Second, most courts are so overburdened with heavy criminal and civil dockets that judges simply do not have time to study and comprehend a large number of relevant technical documents. Scientific expert witnesses are relied upon to select from and summarize the universe of relevant technical documents and to present explanations cogent to the decision making process.

As previously noted, however, current court procedures allow almost anyone to testify as a "scientific expert."[16] The result has been nothing less than an enormous amount of scientific fraud being practiced on the legal system. A party seeking to prove "damages" under some sort of scientific theory can almost always find someone willing to support that theory, no matter how scientifically baseless that position may be.

Some examples of scientific fraud are of "tabloid" caliber. In one case, a scientific expert convinced a jury that a CAT scan led to the plaintiff's loss of psychic powers. The result was a one million dollar damage award![17] Other "scientific" experts have advocated connections between automobile accidents and breast cancer, environmental pollutants and AIDS, and so on. In one of the more unusual jury verdicts, a Detroit jury awarded $1.5 million to a man who claimed that a car accident caused his subsequent desire for a sex change operation. A psychiatrist's expert testimony supported the plaintiff's claim. Examples such as these indicate that the aura of "science" prompts lay persons to abandon common sense and accept the conclusions of the "Junk Scientists."

The *Daubert* Decision

The Supreme Court stepped into the fray in *Daubert v. Merrill Dow Pharmaceuticals Inc.*, 509 U.S. 579, 113 S.Ct. 2786 (1993). In its decision, the Court changed a 70-year precedent on what standards apply to the admissibility of scientific evidence.

Briefly, the facts of that case were that two parents (the party *Daubert*) brought suit against Merrill Dow in a California state court, alleging that their son was born with limb reduction defects, which were allegedly caused by his mother's ingestion of the pharmaceutical Bendectin. Bendectin was a prescription anti-nausea drug for the treatment of nausea and vomiting associated with pregnancy. The case was eventually transferred to federal court.

Defendant Merrill Dow moved for summary judgment on the grounds that plaintiff could not produce any facts demonstrating a genuine issue of Merrill

---

[16] In fact, it is possible to call a toll free "1-800" telephone number to find "experts" on such exotic topics as alien abduction and AIDS resulting from chemical exposure. Both types have testified in court.

[17] See Peter Huber, *Galileo's Revenge: Junk Science in the Courtroom*, 3-4 (1991).

Dow's liability. It requested the federal court to determine the sufficiency and admissibility of plaintiff's scientific evidence.

To support its motion, Merrill Dow's expert reviewed all of the scientific literature on Bendectin. This entailed over 30 epidemiology studies on 130,000 newborn infants. None of these studies concluded that Bendectin caused birth defects. In opposition, plaintiffs offered the affidavits of eight experts, all concluding that Bendectin caused birth defects. They based their opinions on in vitro studies, in vivo animal studies, pharmacological/chemical structure analysis, and a re-analysis of epidemiology studies. The experts could not have been more diametrically opposed.

The federal court granted Merrill Dow's motion for summary judgment on the ground that plaintiffs lacked sufficient admissible evidence. The court held the plaintiff's evidence inadmissible because it did not "have general acceptance in the field in which it belongs."[18]   The standard the Court applied -- the "general acceptance" standard -- was first used in the judicial decision of *Frye v. U.S.*[19] dealing with admissibility of evidence derived from the polygraph machine; that standard was unanimously applied since then by the courts. The federal court of appeals affirmed the district court's decision. Next stop the Supreme Court.

The Supreme Court, in a unanimous decision, opined that the *Frye* "general acceptance" test was superseded by the adoption of the Federal Rules of Evidence, particularly Rule 702. Rule 702 provides that the standard for admitting expert scientific testimony in a federal trial is that it is admissible if the trial judge believes that it will assist the trier of fact. The *Frye* test was at odds with the rule's liberal thrust of admitting evidence at trial.

Despite displacing the *Frye* test, the Court noted that it did not mean that the rules themselves placed no limits on the admissibility of purportedly scientific evidence, nor is the trial judge precluded from screening such evidence. The Supreme Court reaffirmed the "gatekeeper" role of the trial judge -- it is the trial judge's responsibility to ensure the relevance of expert testimony and the reliability of the methodology upon which the expert relies.

The opinion provides four factors that the trial judge may use when making a preliminary assessment of the methodology underlying scientific expert testimony, although the Court said it was not a definitive checklist or test:

(1) Whether a scientific theory or principle can be and has been tested;
(2) Whether the theory or technique has been subjected to peer review and publication;
(3) The court should consider the known or potential rate of error; and
(4) Whether the theory or technique has gained "general acceptance" in the scientific community.

---

[18] *Daubert v. Merrill Dow Pharmaceuticals, Inc.*, 727 F.Supp. 570, 572 (S.D. Cal. 1989)

[19] *Frye v. U.S.*, 293 F. 1013 (D.D.C. 1923).

After the decision, the post-*Daubert* law has been developing at a rapid pace. Moreover, the early indications are that the *Daubert* decision may be turning the tide of junk science. Indeed, in one survey, nearly two-thirds of cases applying this new standard have excluded certain expert testimony!

Unfortunately, the *Daubert* "gatekeeper" decision applies only to actions pending in federal court. Most states still follow the *Frye* standard, so in state court actions, the *Daubert* decision has had little effect.

"JUNK SCIENCES" IN PATENT INFRINGEMENT TRIALS

Even before *Daubert*, "junk science" was not very widespread in patent infringement trials. Infrequently is scientific evidence used at a patent trial that does not have at least some threshold level of scientific credibility. Very infrequently is the issue raised of a technical expert's theories being totally out of the mainstream. The problem of "junk science" has never really plagued patent infringement trials, unlike other areas of law.

There are several possible reasons for that. First, patent infringement suits already involve established technology. At the very heart of a patent suit is at least one patent. Patents are awarded to new innovations that pass the statutorily-mandated standards of patentability, which is relatively difficult to do. Under those standards, "wacky" or incredible inventors are supposedly weeded-out. Perpetual motor machines, or herbal cures for AIDS or cancer are automatically rejected as unpatentable. If presented to the Patent Office, most "junk science" theories would presumably not pass muster and accordingly not be involved in subsequent patent litigation; because of patents themselves are not themselves "junk science" and they do not in turn spawn junk science theories.

Second, patent attorneys are almost all technically trained themselves. To practice before the Patent Office, in fact, some sort of technical training is required. Maybe there is some "scientific conscience" that people attain with scientific training. The author is of the opinion that most patent attorneys would feel genuinely bad pushing "junk science" technology.

A third reason, perhaps, is the relatively higher quality of technical experts in patent cases. They are usually not so-called "hired guns" who "expert" on an almost full-time basis, traveling the country from case to case. Rather, they are individuals with mostly reputable credentials - mostly professors or retired corporate scientists. With good credentials come some modicum of credibility. Personally the best expert the author searches for is one who is not afraid to tell him what is technically wrong with potential arguments, so that they can be made correct.

Because of these reasons, patent infringement has not been plagued by junk science.

What is most common, however, is a more subtle situation, one that is inherently less susceptible to change and perhaps unlikely to be changed by statute or legal precedent.

Specifically, in patent infringement cases, almost always the phenomenon of "dueling experts" occurs. Early technical experts has an interpretation of how the specific technological field would interpret the situation. Typically, these interpretations are dramatically opposed to each other. These interpretations give the trier of fact two completely different positions, and one of them needs to be adopted and the other rejected. These positions get past any *Daubert* problem, because each expert's position is generally not "junk science." Instead, each expert's "opinion" of the existing technical facts is within his own subjective belief, which is not (and probably can not) be excluded a priori by some kind of *Daubert* standard.

The issues in a patent suite that involves technical evidence are infringement/noninfringement, validity/invalidity, and enforceability/unenforceability. Obviously, each side has a different belief as to what the outcome should be on each issue, and their respective experts espouse their view.

Many of the questions technical experts testify to relate to how "one of ordinary skill in the relevant technical field" would consider an issue. In this way, the technical expert acts as a veritable representative for the rest of the scientists in the field. For example, an issue may be how a certain term is defined in the art to determine which way the infringement questions should be decided. Or, whether a patent is "enabled" whether the patent sufficiently teaches one of ordinary skill in the art how to make and how to use the invention – is another issue. Another issue is whether an invention was already in the possession in the field as an obvious extension of already existing prior art (i.e., obviousness).

The question remains: how can credible experts disagree so dramatically on issues that essentially amount to "what is the state of the art"? The answer is probably not one of "junk science," because it does not involve theories that are not widely accepted. In fact, each technical expert testimony seems to be based on credible bases. Also, the *Daubert* decision does not help very much. The answer to the question has not been debated much.

Maybe the answer has the same punch in as the following joke: "A company needed to hire a statistician. The boss interviewed the first applicant and asked him, what is 2 plus 2? The applicant said 4 and he was not hired. The second applicant was asked the same question and, when he answered 4, was likewise rejected. The third applicant, to the same question, answered, I'm a statistician. I can justify any answer you want. She was hired." Maybe most other fields are like statistics, where various positions can be justified.

The challenge to the technically untrained patent decision-maker is that it has to choose one of the positions. In this way, the challenge is not unlike the one faced by the decision-maker in a "junk science" context.

EARLIER PROPOSED REFORMS

These problems of scant scientific training of decision-makers already had prompted several proposed reforms. None of these reforms ever made any impact on the American judicial system, despite their good intentions. None are currently being pursued in earnest. None of these reforms involve raising the technical expertise of judges or juries.

One proposed solution was simply to impanel jurors who are particularly knowledgeable about the issues to be tried in a case. These so-called "blue ribbon" jurors theoretically would be better able to understand complex scientific evidence.[20] Critics of this proposal, however, felt that the "blue ribbon" approach introduces several undesirable complexities to the jury system.

First, knowledgeable jurors could well bring their own biases into the courtroom. To the contrary, the American jury system asks jurors to determine the facts not on preconceptions, but from the evidence presented at trial and only on that evidence. Jurors who advocate a particular approach may improperly disregard evidence based on conflicting theories, and violate this maxim of impartiality.[21]

Second, at least in criminal cases, a special jury may well violate the criminal defendant's constitutional rights. The Sixth Amendment guarantees criminal defendants the right to an impartial jury of their peers. Not only are scientists perhaps not among the peers of most criminal defendants, they may well have a predisposed professional bias concerning technically disputed subject matter.[22] The use of DNA evidence, as in the O.J. Simpson trials, comes to mind.

Finally, many observers feel that these special juries are unworkable. Referring to "blue ribbon" jurors, Professor Richard Marcus commented that: "[a]ssuming these paragons exist, how are we going to get them to spend three months on a jury rather than doing their valuable work?"[23] At this time, "blue ribbon" juries remain more theoretical than practical.

A more ambitious proposal, widely debated in the 1970's, suggested the creation of an entirely new, specialized Science Court.[24] Eminent scientists would serve as the court's judges; magistrates, chosen from a pool of scientists in "adjacent" disciplines would assist the judges. Through complex, quasi-judicial procedures, the court would adjudicate technologically complex issues.[25]

Although proponents of the Science Court argued that it would be a more precise and accurate forum for scientific disputes, numerous critics rejected the proposal. Some thought that distinctions between scientific, factual issues, which

---

[20] See generally Baker, *In Defense of the Blue Ribbon Jury,* 35 Iowa L.Rev. 409 (1950).

[21] See Wesley, *supra,* Note 10, at 481-82.

[22] See *id.* at 683.

[23] Quote of the Week, Legal Times, Oct. 17, 1983, at 6.

[24] See Kantrowitz, Proposal for An Institution for Scientific Judgment, 153 *Science,* 763 (1967).

[25] See Task Force of the Presidential Advisory Group on Anticipated Advances in Science and Technology, The Science Court Experiment: An Interim Report, 193 Science. 653 (1976).

the Science Court could adjudicate, and social policy, which the court could not, were hollow.[26] Others thought that courts would eventually decide these issues anyway, with a Science Court as simply the first stop in a series of trials and appeals.[27] Also, the structure of the Science Court does not solve the perceived bias problem also possessed by the "blue ribbon" jury. So far, the Science Court remains relegated to law review articles and scientific journal editorials.

Other proposals concerned policing the expert witnesses who provide scientific witnesses. The most recent of these expert-based reform efforts were products of the former Bush Administration, and were expounded by former Vice President Dan Quayle. These reforms would have first required "[a] party . . . to prove that its expert's opinion is based on an established theory that reflects a community of opinion. . . . The . . . recommendations would allow testimony based on respected minority or majority theories while excluding fringe theories."[28] This initial showing should eliminate testimony that "is far afield from mainstream professional practice or current scientific knowledge."[29]

Second, the proposed reforms would have prohibited contingency fees for expert witnesses. Such fees award compensation to the expert for her services only if the party for whom the expert testified wins the case and are set as a percentage of the monetary damages that the party ultimately recovers. Observers consider such fee arrangements to provide perverse incentives to expert witnesses, turning them into "mercenaries or advocates" rather than "impartial and objective evaluators."[30] Finally, these reforms would have required "courts . . . to determine that proposed expert witnesses are legitimate experts in their field before they are permitted to testify."[31] Not only should this determination free trials from unqualified experts, litigants will have less incentive to retain such individuals in the first instance.

CONCLUSION

The problems of ill-informed legal fact finders and junk science have lingered in our courts for decades. Clearly, some sort of reform is in order but it is not yet clear whether the Supreme Court's *Daubert* decision will provide that reform.

---

[26] Casper, Technology, Policy and Democracy: Is the Proposed Science Court What we need?, 194 *Science,* 29 (1976).

[27] See Matheny & Williams, Scientific Disputes and Adversary Procedures in Policy Making: An Evaluation of the Science Court, 3 *Law & Policy Q.* 341, 347 (1981).

[28] Dan Quayle, United States Court of Appeals for the Federal Circuit Tenth Anniversary Commemorative Issue: Civil Justice Reform, 41 *Am. U.L. Rev.* 559, 566 (1992).

[29] *Id.*

[30] *Id.*

[31] *Id.*, at 567

Scientific and technological developments have let to ever increasing use of scientific evidence in the courtroom, but there has not been a concomitant rise in the ability of legal decision makers to comprehend it. The legal system must fill this gap because scientific evidence is simply too valuable to be brushed aside. Properly employed, it has the power to reduce uncertainty and to greatly increase the likelihood of "correct" legal decisions.

One final comment is in order: although judges and juries often are woefully scientifically illiterate, by and large they do try to make decisions fairly and with reasonably careful consideration of the evidence. The problem is not getting judges and juries to seriously consider scientific issues, the problem is giving judges and juries the correct scientific information to think about.

AUTHOR INDEX

SUBJECT INDEX

CASE INDEX